Travel and Tourism

for BTEC National Award, Certificate & Diploma

BOOK TWO
2nd edition

Ray Youell

t and t
publishing
.co.uk

Published by Travel and Tourism Publishing Limited.

www.tandtpublishing.co.uk
info@tandtpublishing.co.uk

First published 2008

British Library Cataloguing in Publication Data is available from the British Library on request.
ISBN 978 0 9550190 3 6

Copyright notice

Designed and typeset by Sulwyn at Gomer Press
Cover design image courtesy of Ocean Village
Printed in the UK by Gomer Press, Llandysul

Table of Contents

Note: Unit numbers exactly follow the Edexcel specifications

Acknowledgements

I am grateful for the help and support of many individuals and organisations in completing this book. Sulwyn and the team at Gomer Press handled the typescript very professionally. But, as ever, the biggest thanks go to Sue, Megan and Owen.

The publishers extend thanks to the following for granting permission to reproduce images throughout this book:

Air Berlin
Arabella Stewart
Association of Train Operating Companies
Best Western Hotels
Birmingham International Airport
Brecon Beacons National Park
British Museum
Brittany Ferries
Canvas Holidays
Cardiff Tourism
Cosmos
Cunard
Delta Airlines
Dartmoor Tourist Association
Dragoman Overland Travel
Eden Project
English Heritage
Exodus Travel
First Choice Holidays
flybe
Gatwick Express
Glasgow Airport/BAA
Headwater Holidays
High & Wild Adventure Travel
Himalayan Kingdoms
Inghams Travel
InterContinental Hotels Group
Ironbridge Gorge Museum
Island Cruises
Jorvik Viking Centre, York

Keycamp Holidays
Kuoni Travel
Legoland Windsor
London & Continental Railways
Longleat
M6 Toll
MORI
National Space Centre
Neilson Holidays
Ocean Village
Outward Bound Trust
P & O Cruises
Ray Youell
Royal Caribbean International
Science Museum
Ski Club of Great Britain
Ski Verbier
Stagecoach
St David's Hotel and Spa, Cardiff
Sustrans
Swissport International Ltd.
Thomas Cook
Transport for London
Travel Trade Gazette
Travmedia
TUI UK/Thomson Holidays
Virgin Atlantic Airways
Virgin Group
Visit Cardiff
Warwick Castle

Introduction

Exactly matched to the 2007 BTEC National Travel and Tourism specifications, this second edition of our popular textbook provides comprehensive coverage of 8 specialist units for the qualification, relevant to the Award, Certificate and Diploma. The units build on the 12 core and specialist units found in the companion textbook, Travel and Tourism for BTEC National Award, Certificate and Diploma Book 1 2nd edition (ISBN 978 0 9550190 2 9), providing everything needed to complete the National Diploma.

How to use this book

Each unit includes:

1. **An introductory page** – giving details of the content and assessment for the unit;
2. **Clearly-labelled sections** – exactly covering the specification content for the unit;
3. **Activities** – based on the assessment criteria to help you learn more;
4. **Focus on industry** – short practical examples of how the travel and tourism industry carries out the key topics in the unit;
5. **Weblinks** – internet links to organisations and topics in the unit;
6. **Case studies** – longer examples of organisations and topics included in the unit, with questions and activities to expand your knowledge;
7. **Unit summary** – concise overview of key topics covered in the unit;
8. **Test questions at the end** – to build your knowledge of what's been covered in the unit (answers to these questions can be found on the Tutor's CD-ROM that accompanies this textbook – ISBN 978 0 9550190 5 0) ;
9. **Sample assignment** – covering all the grading criteria for the unit.

About tandtONLine

Everybody who buys this book can register for free access to tandtONLine, a unique web resource for travel and tourism students and staff. It gives you a host of extra features that are regularly updated by academic staff and industry experts, including:

- The latest news from the travel and tourism industry;
- Key statistics on UK, European and global tourism;
- Glossary of common terms and key definitions;
- Hot links to all the websites featured in the textbook;
- Extra staff teaching resources linked to textbooks, including blank maps, forms and assignments.

Register by going to www.tandtonline.co.uk and completing the online registration form using the unique book code found on the inside back cover of this book.

I hope you find this book a useful companion for your BTEC course and wish you well in your studies.

Ray Youell
Aberystwyth
March 2008

UNIT 10
Investigating the Cruise Sector

INTRODUCTION TO THE UNIT

Cruising is one of the fastest-growing sectors of the travel and tourism industry, offering a wide variety of job opportunities to people from all backgrounds who want to see the world while they work. Cruising has a very glamorous image and has long been considered an expensive way to travel and explore destinations. However, the cruise sector is changing rapidly – new companies have entered the market and offer cruises at package holiday prices. Also, cruising is no longer just for the rich and famous! People from all walks of life go on cruises, tempted by the lower prices and the informality offered by some of the new cruise companies.

In this unit you will learn about the development of cruising and the structure of the cruising industry. The unit also examines different types of cruises, ships and the facilities they offer to meet specific customer needs. You will also have the opportunity to investigate the major cruise areas of the world and investigate the impacts that cruising can have on tourist destinations. Finally, you will look in detail at the many employment opportunities offered by the cruise sector, both on board ship and ashore, and consider the advantages and disadvantages of taking a job in cruising.

WHAT YOU WILL STUDY

When you have completed this unit you should:

1. **Understand the development and structure of the cruise sector;**
2. **Know different types of cruises, ships and the facilities they offer;**
3. **Be able to select cruises to meet specific customer needs;**
4. **Know the impacts of cruising on the main cruise areas of the world;**
5. **Know the employment opportunities within the cruise sector.**

You will be guided through the main topics in this unit with the help of the latest developments, statistics, industry examples and case studies. You should also check out the weblinks throughout the unit for extra information on particular organisations or topic areas and use the activities throughout the unit to help you learn more.

ASSESSMENT FOR THIS UNIT

This unit is internally assessed, meaning that you will be given an assignment (or series of assignments) to complete by your tutor(s) to show that you have fully understood the content of the unit. A grading scale of pass, merit or distinction is used when staff mark your assignment(s), with higher grades awarded to students who show greater depth in analysis, evaluation and justification in their assignments. An assignment for this unit, which covers all the grading criteria, can be found on page 35. Don't forget to visit www.tandtONLine.co.uk for all the latest industry news, developments, statistics and hot links to websites in this unit to help you with your assignments.

Icebreaker

This unit examines many aspects of the cruise industry – one of the most vibrant sectors of worldwide travel and tourism. Working by yourself, or in small groups under the direction of your tutor, see how you get on with the following tasks to help you make a start on this unit:

- Make a list of five different companies that offer cruises;
- Name three popular cruise areas of the world;
- Name three UK ports that cruise ships use to start and/or finish cruises;
- Make a list of the reasons why you think cruising has grown in popularity in recent years;
- Think about the sort of impacts (good and bad) that cruising can have on an island destination in the Caribbean;
- Name three specific on-board jobs that cruise companies offer;
- Make a list of the different types of people attracted to cruising and the facilities that each looks for when booking a cruise holiday.

When you've finished, show your answers to your tutor and compare your answers with what other students in your class have written.

SECTION 1 Understand the development and structure of the cruise sector

The cruise sector of the travel and tourism industry is currently going through a period of rapid growth and change. In the past, cruising was seen as the preserve of the elderly, rich and famous. Today the number of cruise passengers is growing steadily and the sector has introduced products aimed at a wide range of customers, including families, young people and groups. Prices for some cruise products have fallen as the major tour operators have entered the market. For the first time, more than one million British people took a cruise of one sort or another in 2003, according to figures from the Passenger Shipping Association (PSA), the trade body representing passenger shipping interests in the UK (see case study on page 11). In 2006, this figure rose to 1.2 million – double the number of people who took a cruise just a decade ago. Before looking in more detail at the structure of the present-day cruising industry, we begin this section with an overview of the development of cruising.

Cruising is growing in popularity

Development of the cruise sector

Although several theories have been put forward to explain the origins of the concept of cruising, the most widely-accepted story concerns a fantasy article in the Shetland Journal in 1835, in which Arthur Anderson proposed the idea of sailing for pleasure as a passenger on an ocean-going vessel. He suggested trips between Scotland and Iceland in the summer and as far as the Mediterranean in the winter. Two years later his dream moved closer to reality when he co-founded the Peninsular and Oriental Steam Navigation Company, later shortened to P & O.

The early days of cruising

Long-distance international travel by sea dates back to the mid-19th century, when Cunard Line's RMS Britannia (RMS stands for Royal Mail Ship) became the first ship to take passengers on regularly-scheduled, transatlantic crossings aboard the vessel Britannia. This came about because of the need to introduce a dependable mail service between Britain and America, which prompted Queen Victoria's government to invite interested parties to bid for the contract. Samuel Cunard of Halifax, Nova Scotia in Canada was the successful bidder and his contract to deliver the mail across the Atlantic from Britain to North America was signed on 4th May 1839. Cunard was a highly successful and enterprising Canadian businessman and one of a group of 12 individuals who directed the affairs of Nova Scotia. In order to carry out the transatlantic contract successfully, he worked with the engineer Robert Napier and three other businessmen who provided financial backing for the project. These five men founded the British and North American Royal Mail Steam Packet Company, later to become known as the Cunard Line.

In the 1880s, the Orient Line and North of Scotland Company, both later to be taken over by P & O, pioneered modern-style cruises and in 1904 P & O offered its first cruise holiday programme, arranged by Thomas Cook. The tour used the liner Rome, renaming her Vectis in her new role as a 'cruising yacht'.

Cruising in the 20th century

The first half of the 20th century was the heyday for large cruise liners, which were built to serve the increasing numbers of passengers travelling between Europe and North America. The largest passenger steamship of the time, the Titanic, was launched in 1912, but tragically sank on its maiden voyage on the night of 14th April, with the loss of nearly 1,500 lives. The sinking of the Titanic led to safety and communications improvements on board passenger ships to reduce the likelihood of such an event ever happening again. By the end of the 1930s, Cunard operated transatlantic crossings every 10 weeks. Bigger and better ships were introduced and they competed to make the fastest crossing of the Atlantic. Many raced for the 'Blue Riband' trophy awarded to the ship making the fastest transatlantic crossing, most notably the Queen Mary and Queen Elizabeth, launched in 1934 and 1938 respectively. Other important ships of the time included the Mauretania, the Aquitania and the Windsor Castle. Cruising in these ships was a luxurious experience, only available to the rich and famous.

By the 1930s, cruise-orientated amenities and facilities began to feature more prominently in passenger ship design. American ocean liners introduced air conditioning, a majority of cabins with private facilities and some with private verandas. Grace Line's Santa liners even had retractable roofs over their dining rooms to allow passengers to dine under the tropical stars.

The majority of ships in cruise service after World War Two (1939-1945) were liners whose sources of income gradually began to diminish. The number of people emigrating began to decrease (emigrants were an important market for many ship companies). Also, the development of the jet engine and long-haul passenger aircraft, such as the Boeing 707 in 1958, led to a dramatic reduction in the number of passengers using cruise ships from the mid-20th onwards. The decline began in the late 1950s and resulted in ships like the Queen Elizabeth becoming redundant. By the 1970s, the advent of the Boeing 747 'jumbo jet' really saw the end of the golden period of transatlantic cruise liners. With no regular mail contracts for the shipping companies after 1945, cruising became even more important to the shipping industry. P & O's last ship built for scheduled voyages, the Canberra, was launched in 1961, but in little more than a decade jet aircraft had taken many of the company's regular passengers and freight was transferred onto purpose-built cargo ships.

In the late 20th century the true ocean liners declined and diminished in number, being succeeded by cruise liners such as the Oriana, Aurora, Royal Princess, Voyager of the Seas, Monarch of the Seas and many others. Between 1964 and 1972, four companies that came to be known as the 'big four' were founded – Carnival Cruises, Royal Caribbean Cruise Line, Princess Cruises and the Norwegian Caribbean Line.

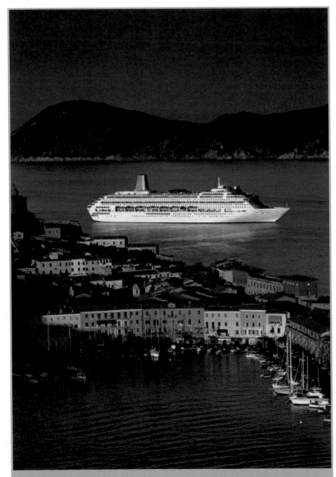

P & O Cruises launched the Oriana in 1995

21st century cruising

The cruise boom of the 1980s continued into the 21st century despite a brief blip in the early 1990s when fewer cruise ships were built due to concern about a possible slowdown in the cruise sector. Today, bigger and brasher cruise ships are being built to service a growing demand from travellers. Despite there being considerable integration and standardisation in the sector, with just three big players – Carnival, Royal Caribbean International and Star/Norwegian Cruise Line – plus other independent operators, there is still a great deal of variety in terms of ships and the products they offer their passengers, whether it be mass-market, small-ship, luxury, family-orientated, adventure or luxury cruising. The cruise ships of the early 21st century tend to be floating hotels or resorts and destinations in their own right.

In 2000, P & O Cruises introduced the Aurora as the UK's second superliner to follow the Oriana. In the same year a notable development took place in the cruising world, with the introduction of the world's first timeshare residential cruise ship called The World, which is the first step at turning the cruise ship into a floating city. In 2004, Cunard launched the Queen Mary 2, the first transatlantic liner to be built for a generation and a year later P & O Cruises introduced the Arcadia. Based on the Vista class ships of the Holland America Line, Arcadia shows how cruise ships have become more standardised in terms of design, but can still show their individualism by brand and company heritage. The world's biggest cruise ship, and flagship of Royal Caribbean International, the Freedom of the Seas, was launched in 2006, boasting the world's first on-board surfing pool, a skating rink and a rock-climbing wall! The vessel can accommodate 4,375 passengers at a time and is used for Caribbean cruises.

Activity 10.1

Design and make an illustrated wall chart or display that explains the key milestones in the development of cruising.

This activity is designed to provide evidence for P1.

The Queen Victoria was launched in 2007 (courtesy of Cunard)

Changing consumer demands and needs in cruising

The changing demands and expectations of passengers are a constant challenge for cruise operators, which must offer new products and services to a wide variety of customers, in order to remain competitive. This has resulted in a number of recent trends in the cruise sector, including:

- Growth in the market;
- Changing popularity of cruise areas;
- Changes in customer demographics;
- More informal cruising;
- Growth in ex-UK cruises;
- Demand for ultra-luxury cruising.

Growth in the cruise market

Between 2004 and 2005, worldwide cruise passenger numbers grew by 7.5 per cent to reach 14.4 million, according to figures published in the *Annual Cruise*

Review. This level of growth was particularly impressive as only four new ships were added to the fleet during the year, compared with an average of ten per year over the previous 15 years. It is forecast that passenger numbers will reach 20 million worldwide by 2012. Cruising is most popular among North Americans – their cruise numbers showed a 9 per cent increase from 8.9 million in 2004 to 9.7 million in 2005.

The UK cruise market, including river and ocean cruises, grew to more than 1.2 million in 2006, making Britons the second largest nationality taking cruise holidays.

Changing popularity of cruise areas

Data from the *Annual Cruise Review* indicates that the Mediterranean remained the most popular cruise destination with the British in 2006, followed by the Caribbean, the Atlantic Isles and UK/Western Europe. Destinations showing the biggest rise in demand between 2004 and 2005 with British cruise passengers were Greenland / Iceland / the Arctic /Alaska (+ 139 per cent), the Far East / Australia (+ 114 per cent) and West Coast USA / Hawaii / Panama Canal (+ 42 per cent).

Changes in customer demographics

Although the UK population is ageing, with an increasing proportion of over-50s compared to under-30s, the average age of cruise passengers continues to fall. This is partly due to the increased numbers of families with children now going on cruises. It is also a reflection of the younger people being attracted to cruising by the new, informal and activity-orientated brands, such as Ocean Village, Island Cruises and easyCruise, all of which are planning to expand their operations in the short-term. All of these factors combine to paint a picture of a changing profile of customers that are attracted to cruising. In short, cruise passengers are:

- Younger than in the past;
- Interested in activities while on board ship and on shore;
- Looking for short cruises as well as extended journeys;
- Interested in travelling with families and friends;
- Looking for adventure.

Cruise companies are increasingly 'segmenting the market', i.e. developing cruise products and services to meet the needs of individual segments of the market, for example families, singles and younger passengers.

More informal cruising

A success story in recent years has been the introduction of more informal cruises, led by companies like Ocean Village, Island Cruises and easyCruise. These fashionable cruises are aimed at younger, and particularly first-time, cruisers. Formality is at a minimum, with no formal dress code, no fixed meal times or seating places, lots of activities on board and ashore, plus coffee shops and alternative entertainment.

FOCUS ON INDUSTRY

Ocean Village

Ocean Village has introduced a second ship – Ocean Village Two – following the successful performance of the informal cruise operator since it was launched in 2003. The 1,690 passenger Regal Princess was transferred from its sister company Princess Cruises to begin Caribbean fly/cruise itineraries in the winter of 2006-2007, moving to the Mediterranean in May 2007 for summer sailings. The original Ocean Village ship, which is marketed as 'the cruise for people who don't do cruises', has to date taken more than 150,000 bookings, 60 per cent of which are from first-time cruise passengers. Facilities on board both ships include two pools, eight bars, four restaurants, a theatre, cinema, spa and nightclub.

Weblink

Check out this website for more information on Ocean Village.
www.oceanvillageholidays.co.uk

Activity 10.2

Carry out some research on easyCruise and compile an information sheet containing relevant information on the company and its products, e.g. ships, destinations visited, on-board facilities, prices, target markets, etc.

This activity is designed to provide evidence for P2.

Growth in ex-UK cruises

More people than ever are choosing to start their cruise holiday from a UK port, thereby saving the time and inconvenience of travelling abroad to a departure port. Between 2004 and 2005, the number of passengers starting their cruises from a UK port rose by 28 per cent, from 316,000 to 403,000, while the market for fly/cruise fell by 6 per cent to 669,000 passengers over the same time period. The number of UK ports attracting cruise ships increased again in 2005 to a record 44, thereby spreading the economic benefits of the cruise industry even further. Popular UK cruise ports include Southampton, Belfast, Newcastle and Liverpool.

Demand for ultra-luxury cruising

The growth in the popularity of mass-market cruising, aimed at a wide variety of passengers travelling on a budget, has led some wealthy customers to seek out small, exclusive cruises that offer exceptional personal service and attention to detail. To meet this demand, nine of the world's top cruising operators have joined forces to offer a variety of experiences, as the next industry example explains.

FOCUS ON INDUSTRY

Ultra-luxury cruising

Nine of the Passenger Shipping Association's ultra-luxury cruise line members have come together to form a new alliance, the Exclusive Collection. The alliance is aimed at attracting discerning holidaymakers seeking a sophisticated, bespoke holiday experience, but who may currently not consider a holiday afloat. Members of the Exclusive Collection are Crystal Cruises, Hebridean International Cruises, Peter Deilmann Cruises, Orion Expedition Cruises, Regent Seven Seas Cruises, Seabourn Cruise Line, Siversea Cruises, SeaDream Yacht Club and Windstar Cruises. All nine cruise lines offer a crew to passenger ratio of at least one to two, thereby ensuring personal service and attention to detail at all times.

Weblink
Check out this website for more information on the Exclusive Collection.
www.exclusive-collection.co.uk

Structure of the cruise sector

Cruising is a global industry, not just in terms of the worldwide destinations visited, but also from an ownership perspective, with just three companies dominating world cruising – Carnival, Royal

Caribbean International and Star/Norwegian Cruise Line. In the following sections of this unit we will examine the range of cruise operators in more detail and explore how cruising links with other sectors of the travel and tourism industry.

Cruise operators

There are many well-established cruise operators across the world, with three companies dominating the sector and accounting for over 80 per cent of all cruise bookings worldwide (see Figure 10.1).

Carnival Corporation and plc (48%)

Royal Caribbean International (25%)

Star Cruises (10%)

Others (17%)

Source: Adapted from Cruise Industry News data

Figure 10.1 – Share of the world cruise market

As Figure 10.1 demonstrates, Carnival is by far the biggest cruise company in the world, followed by Royal Caribbean International (RCI) and Star Cruises. Together, these three operators control approximately 83 per cent of the global cruise market, according to data in the Cruise Industry News Annual Report, leaving a variety of smaller, independent cruise companies to make up the rest. There is a detailed case study on Carnival on page 8.

Founded in 1969, RCI has a fleet of 29 ships, branded as Royal Caribbean and Celebrity Cruises. Royal Caribbean has nine ships and appeals particularly to families and middle-market customers with its combination of value for money and quality. Since May 2005, RCI's Legend of the Seas has been based in Southampton operating an ex-UK cruise schedule for British passengers. Celebrity Cruises operates at the top end of the mainstream, large cruise ship lines. Renowned for good service, high quality catering and on-board facilities, Celebrity has a fleet of ten ships, most carrying around 2,000 to 3,000 passengers each.

FOCUS ON INDUSTRY

Island Cruises

This two-ship cruise line – Island Escape and Island Star – was launched in 2002 as a joint venture between RCI and First Choice. With flexible dining and familiar 'brands' on board, like Costa Coffee, Oddbins wines and Holmes Place gyms, Island was aimed firmly at younger passengers who may have been put off by the formal, 'stuffy' image of traditional cruise lines. For the 2004-2005 season, the company changed its approach to attract more first-time cruisers and families, operating Mediterranean cruises during the summer and cruises from Brazil in the winter.

Weblink
Check out this website for more information on Island Cruises.
www.islandcruises.com

Star Cruises was founded in 1995 and is already the world's third largest cruise operator. It tapped into the cruise potential of the Asia Pacific region and has since acquired Norwegian Cruise Line (NCL) and Orient Lines. Star currently has seven ships operating in the Asia Pacific region. The NCL group operates a fleet of 16 ships in service or due to be delivered.

Case Study

Carnival Corporation and plc

Introduction

Carnival Corporation and plc (public limited company) is the world's biggest cruise operator, accounting for nearly half of all cruises booked in the world. Many of the best-known names in the cruising sector are wholly or partly-owned by Carnival, including Cunard, Princess Cruises and Ocean Village. In 2003, Carnival Corporation and P & O Princess Cruises plc formally merged, the latter now adopting the Carnival name. Carnival's mission is:

'To deliver exceptional vacation experiences through the world's best-known cruise brands that cater to a variety of different lifestyles and budgets, all at an outstanding value unrivalled on land or at sea'.

With its headquarters in Miami, Florida, Carnival has more than 650,000 employees worldwide and operates a fleet of 81 ships, with a further 15 new ships scheduled for delivery between March 2007 and spring 2010. With 144,000 berths and almost 55,000 crew members, there are roughly 175,000 people at sea with Carnival at any given time. The company also owns two tour businesses that complement its cruise operations – Holland America Tours, and Princess Tours in Alaska and the Canadian Yukon. Carnival's combined holiday companies cater for around 5.4 million customers every year.

Carnival brands

Carnival has 10 distinct cruising brands aimed at particular market segments, made up of the leading cruise operators in North America, Europe and Australia:

1. **Carnival Cruise Lines (www.carnival.com)** – reputed to be the most profitable cruise line in the world, this brand operates 20 'fun ships', aimed primarily at the North American market. Destinations include the Bahamas, Canada, the Mexican Riviera and Alaska, with most cruises ranging from 3 to 7 days;

2. **Holland America Line (www.hollandamerica.com)** – a 12-strong fleet of five-star, premium ships sailing from 15 North American home ports, including Baltimore and Boston;

3. **Princess Cruises (www.princesscruises.com)** – there are 11 ships in the Princess fleet aimed mostly at the mid to upper market. The ships are deployed all around the globe, calling at more than 200 ports worldwide;

4. **Seabourn Cruise Line (www.seabourn.com)** – a three-ship fleet of luxury all-suite ships carrying just over 200 passengers each (Seabourn Legend, Seabourn Pride and Seabourn Spirit). Seabourn operates a passenger/crew ratio of close to 1/1;

5. **AIDA Cruises (www.aida.de)** – this is the best-known cruise brand in the fast-growing German cruise industry. The company's four ships cruise to the Mediterranean, Baltic, Norwegian fjords, Canary Islands and the Caribbean;

6. **Costa Cruises (www.costacruises.com)** – a ten-ship fleet ranging from the 800-passenger Costa Allegra to their latest three 2,200-passenger ships – Costa Atlantica, Costa Mediterranea and Costa Fortuna;

7. **Cunard Line (www.cunard.com)** – a fleet of three ships comprising the Queen Elizabeth 2, the Queen Mary 2 and the Queen Victoria, which joined the Cunard fleet in summer 2007. A new 92,000-ton liner, Queen Elizabeth, is scheduled to enter service in the autumn of 2010;

8. **P & O Cruises (www.pocruises.com)** – is the largest cruise operator in the UK, with six ships around the 2,000-passenger mark – the Arcadia, Oceana, Adonia, Aurora, Oriana and Artemis. In 2006, P & O offered 130 different cruise holidays to 181 ports in 72 countries, ranging from two to 25 nights in duration, plus one 80-night world cruise;

9. **Ocean Village (www.oceanvillageholidays.co.uk)** – this is a new, two-ship cruise brand in the UK, which has been established to provide informal, contemporary and affordable holidays at sea for younger people;

10. **P & O Cruises Australia (www.pocruises.com.au)** – as its name implies, this company caters for the Australian market with two ships, Pacific Sky and Pacific Sun, offering 7 to 14-night cruises to New Caledonia, Vanuatu and Fiji from the home ports of Sydney, Brisbane and Auckland.

Carnival cruise destinations

With such a huge range of cruise companies under its wing, Carnival operates in a wide range of cruise destinations around the world, including Alaska, the Caribbean, Canada, Eastern USA, the Mediterranean, the Pacific, Western USA and Mexico, plus transatlantic and round-the-world cruises.

Case Study Questions and Activities

1. Explain how Carnival Corporation and plc is an 'integrated' company.
2. Why has Carnival chosen to enter into mergers and takeovers with other cruise lines?
3. Choose one of the Carnival 'brands' and carry out some further research on the company, so that you could advise a customer who wants to take a cruise with that operator.
4. What other sectors of the travel and tourism industry do Carnival's cruise companies work with on a regular basis?

This case study is designed to provide evidence for P1, P2.

Weblink

Check out this website to help answer the questions in this case study and for more information on cruising with Carnival.
www.carnival.com

Links with other sectors of travel and tourism

Like most sectors of the travel and tourism industry, cruise operators work in partnership with many companies and organisations in the course of their work. These 'partners' include:

- Travel agents – these are the retail arm of the industry, advising and selling cruise holidays to customers. The vast majority of UK cruise bookings are made through travel agents – 86 per cent overall in 2004 and 90 per cent for fly/cruises, according to data included in the *World Cruise Review*. A cruise is often an expensive purchase, so many customers prefer the personal contact and reassurance of dealing with an agent. Agents benefit as well, since cruise companies pay good commission on sales;

- Hotels and other accommodation – cruise lines use a variety of accommodation for 'cruise and stay' holiday passengers;

- Attractions – cruise passengers often visit natural and built attractions as part of an excursion on shore;

- Transport operators – coach companies and taxi firms provide transfers to and from destination ports, as well as excursions on shore; some up-

market cruise lines even offer chauffeur-drive and helicopter transfers as options;

- Airlines – cruise lines contract with either scheduled or charter airlines when arranging fly/cruise holidays for passengers.

FOCUS ON INDUSTRY

Thomson Cruises and Leger Holidays

Thomson offers its cruise passengers a return coach service from a variety of UK departure points to one of the company's cruise terminals – currently Southampton, Harwich or Newcastle. Typical fares range from £39 return for an adult travelling from, for example, Sheffield to Newcastle, up to £69 return for a journey from Glasgow to Southampton. The service is operated by Leger Holidays, but does not form part of the holiday arrangement that customers make with Thomson for their cruise. This arrangement makes good sense for both companies – Thomson gains by offering its passengers a useful extra service, while Leger makes revenue from additional sales.

Weblink

Check out this website for more information on Thomson Cruises.
www.thomson.co.uk

Integration in the cruise sector

You have learned in other units on your course that there are many links between different companies and sectors of the travel and tourism industry; this is sometimes referred to as 'integration'. Horizontal integration occurs when a company owns or controls other businesses at the same level of the distribution chain or in the same sector, e.g. TUI owns a wide range of tour operating companies, including Thomson Holidays, Something Special, Simply Travel and OSL. Vertical integration is when a company owns or controls more then one level of the distribution chain, e.g. TUI not only owns a variety of tour operating companies, but also the chain of Thomson travel agencies and its own airline Thomsonfly. Companies get involved in integration via mergers and takeovers as a way of increasing their sales and gaining an advantage over their competitors.

Integration also occurs in the cruise sector. The three major cruise lines – Carnival, Royal Caribbean International (RCI) and Star Cruises – are all integrated companies, i.e. they own other shipping lines that operate under different names. For example, we saw earlier in the case study on Carnival (see page 8) that it owns 10 different cruise companies under different brand names, including Cunard, Ocean Village and P & O Cruises. RCI owns Celebrity Cruises, while Star Cruises own Norwegian Cruise Line and Orient Lines.

Regulatory and trade bodies in cruising

Travel and tourism regulatory bodies exist to make sure that organisations serve the travelling public safely, fairly and efficiently. The International Maritime Organisation (IMO) is a specialised agency of the United Nations with 167 member states and its headquarters in London. It is responsible for measures to improve the safety and security of international shipping, including cruising, and to prevent marine pollution from ships. It is also involved in legal matters, including liability and compensation issues and the facilitation of international maritime traffic.

Trade bodies are set up to represent the interests of companies operating in a particular industry sector. In the UK, the Passenger Shipping Association (PSA) is the principal trade body representing the cruise sector (see case study below). In the USA, there are a number of trade organisations that claim to represent the interests of the cruise sector, e.g. the International Council of Cruise Lines (ICCL) and the Cruise Line International Association (CLIA). Both organisations include the majority of cruise lines in their membership and are actively involved in training, marketing, research, safety and security in the cruising industry. The European Cruise Council (ECC), formed in 2004, promotes and defends the interests of the cruise sector within European Union institutions, collates industry statistics to demonstrate the scale and breadth of the cruise industry, and provides a resource for the promotion of cruises in Europe. The 21 members of the ECC include Fred. Olsen Cruise Line, RCI, Saga Shipping, Thomson Cruises and Costa Cruises.

Case Study

The Passenger Shipping Association (PSA)

Introduction

The Passenger Shipping Association (PSA) is a trade organisation that represents the interests of the leading UK-based cruise and ferry operators. The PSA was originally set up as Ocean Travel

Development (OTD) in 1958 by a group of passenger ship owners. They had seen, for the first time in 1957, the number of passengers travelling across the Atlantic by air exceeding those travelling by sea on the great liners. OTD's main objective was to focus public attention, and that of the travel trade, on sea travel as a holiday and leisure pursuit, and as a modern alternative to transportation from A to B. The shipping lines conceded that they could no longer compete with the developing airlines, both on travel times and cost, and recognised that their future lay in full-time cruising. In 1976, it was agreed by the shipping lines that OTD's name should be changed to the Passenger Shipping Association, to reflect more accurately the aims of the association.

Mission statement and objectives

PSA's mission statement is:

'To provide a service of excellence to the Members and Associate Members of the PSA. To ensure that the PSA is the recognised industry body for the cruise and ferry sectors. To act as a forum for discussion on areas of mutual interest'.

Its objectives are:

1. The promotion of travel by sea by the public;
2. To encourage expansion in the volume of passenger travel, by sea and river;
3. To work towards the removal or prevention of the imposition of restrictions or taxes on passenger travel by sea;
4. To advise member lines to ensure that passengers travel in a safe, healthy and secure environment.

What does the PSA do?

In order to meet its objectives, the Association has a very wide-ranging work programme, including:

- Lobbying the government and officials in the European Union;
- Working with, and through other bodies, notably ABTA (the Association of British Travel Agents), the Chamber of Shipping and the European Community Shipowners' Association (ECSA);
- Providing a forum for the training and education of travel agents through its subsidiary company PSARA (see below);
- Acting as a spokesperson for the industry;
- Co-ordinating activities of its member shipping lines;
- Acting as an information centre for member lines and associate members;
- Acting as a statutory bonding authority for member lines as required;
- Promoting market growth in the passenger shipping industry through public relations campaigns;
- Ensuring that member companies are aware of the best practice and the statutory regulations on safety, the protection of the environment, health, hygiene and security.

Membership of the PSA

Currently, the PSA has 29 cruise line members, including Cunard, Norwegian Cruise Line, Thomson and Royal Caribbean International. Its 17 ferry company members include Brittany Ferries, Stena Line,

Sea France and Condor Ferries. Associate members of the PSA, who work closely with the cruise and ferry sectors, include the Port of Tyne Authority, Eurolines and the Port of Dover.

PSARA

In 1987, the PSA formed a subsidiary company – the Passenger Shipping Association Retail Agents' Scheme (PSARA) – which was entrusted with fulfilling the Association's travel agency educational role. The scheme is self-funding, based on contributions from the cruise industry and retail travel agents. Cruise manuals, newsletters, product information and an extensive programme of training seminars, are the basis of the benefits to members. The PSARA Scheme is an important factor in the growth of cruising traffic in the UK and is steadily increasing its membership in the travel agency world.

Case Study Questions and Activities

1. What are the benefits of being a member of the PSA to an individual shipping company?
2. Over what sort of matters and concerns do you think that the PSA lobbies members of the government and the European Union?
3. Carry out some further research on the PSARA Scheme and make a list of the benefits of membership for travel agents;
4. Log on to the PSA's website and write a summary of two recent press releases concerned with cruising issues.

This case study is designed to provide evidence for P1.

Weblink

Check out this website to help answer the questions in this case study and for more information on the Passenger Shipping Association. www.the-psa.co.uk

---

Know different types of cruises, ships and the facilities they offer

We saw earlier in this unit that cruising now caters for many different types of customers, with the industry offering a wider-than-ever range of products to suit all tastes and budgets. As a consequence, there are many different types of cruises on offer, geared to different segments of the market, using a wide range of ships with an array of on-board facilities.

Types of cruises

The cruise sector has responded to the changing demands and expectations of travellers by developing different types of cruises to suit all tastes, including:

- Fly/cruise;
- Round-the-world;
- Mini-cruise;
- River cruise;
- Luxury cruise;
- Special interest cruise;
- Transatlantic cruise;
- Sail ship;
- All-inclusive;
- easyCruise.

Fly/cruise

Fly/cruise is a popular arrangement that allows cruise passengers to combine their time at sea with a flight to or from the home port of their cruise, thereby beginning their cruise as soon as possible. All major cruise operators offer fly/cruise holidays for an all-inclusive package price. Cruise companies use charter airlines and scheduled services, depending on the destination and type of cruise. Scheduled services with major airlines tend to be offered on the more expensive cruises. Cunard, for example, has an arrangement with British Airways to transport its cruise passengers, offering flight upgrades on payment of a supplement. Wherever possible, passengers on Thomson cruises fly to their cruise home port with Thomsonfly, which is part of the same company. This is an example of vertical integration that we discussed in the first section of this unit.

Round-the-world cruise

A round-the-world trip is most people's idea of the ultimate cruising experience – but you need the money and time to do it! For example, Cunard's 2008 maiden world cruise on the Queen Victoria lasts for 106 nights and the full brochure prices start at £19,689. Not surprisingly, therefore, these types of cruises tend to appeal to retired people with time to spare and a good income or savings. UK passengers wanting a round-the-world cruise can leave from Southampton or fly straight to the sun and start their circumnavigation at a port such as Miami or Los Angeles. Another option is to start the cruise from New York. Passengers who can't spare the time for a full world cruise can sample part of the experience – all world cruises are broken down into fly/cruise segments to allow passengers to select the time periods and destinations that are most convenient for them. One of the most popular options is a

The Queen Victoria's world cruise lasts for 106 nights (courtesy of Cunard)

semi-circumnavigation sailing between the UK and Australia.

Activity 10.3

Plot the route of a round-the-world cruise on an outline map of the world, marking the embarkation port and all ports of call on the journey. Registered tandtONLine users can download a free blank world map from www.tandtonline.co.uk

This activity is designed to provide evidence for P4.

Mini-cruise

Busy, modern lifestyles have created a growing demand for short trips or mini-cruises on board ship, giving passengers the chance to relax and unwind. Nearly one in five cruises booked by British people is of five days' duration or less. Typically, a mini-cruise (a trip of less than seven nights at sea) gives passengers the chance to visit two or three destinations in a short period of time. Short cruises starting and ending in UK ports are growing in popularity, although short trips from Mediterranean ports continue to be in greatest demand.

River cruise

River cruising offers passengers the opportunity of exploring an area at close quarters in a cosy,

Activity 10.4

Carry out some research into three river cruise operators – one operating in the UK, one in Europe and one in the USA. Produce three fact sheets that include information about each operator for use by prospective river cruise passengers, e.g. company history, products on offer, prices, duration of trips, destinations visited, etc. The website www.choosingcruising.co.uk is a good place to start this activity.

This activity is designed to provide evidence for P2.

intimate environment. River ships typically carry up to 200 passengers and can make up to three stops a day, allowing plenty of time for sightseeing and shopping. The ships travel by day and moor up at night, the opposite of a typical ocean cruise. The rivers Rhine and Nile are the most popular river cruise destinations for British people.

Luxury cruise

Most cruise liners offer an element of luxury – indeed the very concept of cruising is closely tied up with luxury and opulence. However, there are only a handful of cruise operators that offer the ultimate luxury cruise experience. Passengers who book a luxury cruise can expect to be greeted on arrival with a complimentary bottle of champagne, to have a spacious cabin with walk-in wardrobe, an elegant bathroom, a well-stocked mini bar and 24-hour room service, with full in-suite dining available during restaurant hours. Passengers never have to queue for food and drink, and never have to wait to use equipment in the gym or to be seated in the dining room, because true luxury ships have more than enough space to accommodate everybody on board in comfort. The small, luxury ships owned by Seabourn Cruise Line and Radisson Seven Seas Cruises are the most exclusive in the world purely in terms of their size.

Special interest cruising

Realising that the interests of potential cruise passengers are very varied, cruise operators try to offer as wide a variety of special interests or 'themes' as possible in their programmes. These cruises give passengers the chance to enjoy a favourite hobby in a different setting, learn new skills or just increase their knowledge. They can choose from a wide variety of subjects – from gourmet cuisine, gardening and music to culture, art appreciation and sculpture. Many special interest cruise operators feature well-known guest speakers, performances by noted entertainers or related shore excursions and the chance to mingle with leading figures in a particular field. Orient Lines is an award-winning ship line operating the Marco Polo, which offers special interest, destination-focused cruises. Celebrity Xpedition, part of the Celebrity Cruises' fleet, carries just 98 passengers and is designed for exclusive, expeditionary cruises to the Galapagos Islands.

FOCUS ON INDUSTRY

Swan Hellenic Cruises

Swan Hellenic has been offering 'discovery cruises' for more than 50 years to a variety of lesser-known locations throughout the world. The itineraries on board its ship Minerva include diverse landscapes, cultures and historical settings – from the mysterious temples and pyramids of the Maya at Chichen Itza, the glacial landscapes of Arctic Norway to the tropical environment of the Amazon interior. After a period of uncertainty about its future, the Swan Hellenic brand was purchased in April 2007 by Lord Sterling to secure its future.

Weblink
Check out this website for more information on Swan Hellenic.
www.swanhellenic.com

'Soft adventure' is the name given to any type of tourist activity that gives people the chance to try out a new experience, but nothing too dangerous! Cruise lines now offer more adventurous shore excursions and have been developing new products geared specifically at those who like to get active on holiday. A prime 'adventure' destination is Alaska, where a number of cruise operators, including Princess Cruises, Norwegian Cruise Line and Holland America Line, have been updating shore tour programmes to include more unusual options like dog sledding, whale watching, hiking in the forest, go-karting, mountain biking and rock climbing. Passengers on Caribbean cruises can try their hand at diving or snorkelling, while Mediterranean cruise activities include abseiling, roller-blading, water rafting and cycling expeditions. Ocean Village is a good example of a cruise brand that appeals to younger, first-time

Ocean Village offers a variety of activities for passengers

cruisers who are keen to take part in activities while on holiday.

Transatlantic cruises

Cruising across the Atlantic appeals to people who like to spend lots of days at sea. Transatlantic cruises may go direct to their destination port or cruise the destination region for a few days before arrival. The majority of transatlantic cruises are 'repositioning cruises', i.e. journeys that allow ships to get to a particular area to begin a new cruise season. As such, they can offer very good value for money. These cruises can take place all year, but most take place from April to October. Weather conditions and the time of year will dictate the route taken.

The classic Southampton to New York (or reverse) 6-night transatlantic voyages offered by Cunard are still available, but there are other cruises from northern Europe to east coast USA or Canada on offer. Many cruise ships are repositioned from Europe to the Caribbean for the winter season. Cruises depart from the major European ports and call at the Canaries, Madeira and/or the Azores before arriving in the Caribbean. A similar repositioning takes place to South America for the northern winter, although there are only a few cruises on offer.

Sail ship

Cruising in a sailing ship is a 'niche' product that appeals to a small number of people who are looking for a more authentic and traditional cruising experience. There are many companies that offer sail cruising, including Monaco-based Star Clippers, Windjammer Barefoot Cruises (the largest operator of tall ships in the world) operating in the Caribbean out of Miami, and Windstar Cruises. Sailing ships are small by cruise standards so the facilities on board are limited, but they do offer the combination of sailing tradition with cruise ship comforts.

All-inclusive

Passengers who choose an all-inclusive cruise have the certainty of knowing that everything is provided for them in the price they pay for their holiday. There are no 'hidden costs' for on-shore excursions, tips for staff, port/airport taxes, on-board activity sessions, drinks, etc. Some cruise operators offer an all-inclusive arrangement as an upgrade for customers, for example Island Cruises.

'Cruise and stay' is an arrangement that allows passengers to combine a fly/cruise holiday with a period of time in a hotel or other type of accommodation, which can be on an all-inclusive basis. For example, a passenger could fly to Florida and spend a week visiting the area and its many attractions, then join a cruise from Miami to the Caribbean for a second week. Cruise and stay is popular with people who are new to cruising and want to try it out before committing to a longer holiday.

easyCruise

easyCruise is a new venture from the easy Group of Companies, whose brands include easyJet, easyCar and easyInternetcafé. easyCruise operates two cruise ships, easyCruise One and easyCruise Life, offering cruise holidays in the Greek islands and Turkey. Unlike traditional cruising, easyCruise sails for just a few hours every morning, arriving at each port around lunchtime, allowing passengers time to explore each destination in the afternoon and evening. Both easyCruise ships feature restaurants and bars, with à la carte dining offering fusion cuisine, as well as a spa. Designed to appeal to younger customers, easyCruise offers cabins that are minimalist in design. Like easyJet, cruise prices vary according to demand and they generally rise as the ship fills up, so early bookers secure the best prices. Online prices are for cruises on a room-only basis, with all meals, drinks, spa treatments, tours and housekeeping services paid for on board. Cruise passengers must make their own travel arrangements to get to and from their easyCruise ship.

Cruise ships

The *Annual Cruise Review* estimates that there are currently 30 new cruise ships on order through to 2010. Almost all are large 'mega-ships', with a much wider range of dining and entertainment facilities to appeal to families and a much broader age group generally. The average maximum capacity of the world's cruise ships has already doubled over the past 10 years, while the average capacity of ships built in the 1990s was just over 1,600 passengers, this decade the average will be more than 2,600.

This trend towards building larger ships not only makes good financial sense for the cruise operators because of the economies of scale, but it also allows the companies to offer ever more elaborate facilities for guests on board ship, e.g. large show rooms with state-of-the-art lighting and sound equipment, shopping malls, ice skating rinks, fitness suites and even rock climbing walls! More restaurants on board have led to the introduction of new dining concepts where passengers are free to choose where and with whom they want to dine. Entertainment on board has developed from shows performed by talented crew members in the 1970s to full scale Hollywood and Las Vegas production shows on today's mega-liners. Last but not least, cabins (often referred to now as staterooms) with balconies, internet access, the latest movies on television and even butler service or 24-hour room service, have been introduced on the new breed of cruise ships.

Many cruise ships now have excellent fitness suites on board (courtesy of Island Cruises)

It is not just new ships that are being designed to appeal to first-time cruisers, families and younger passengers. Cruise lines are now starting to revitalise their existing ships, adding more cabins with balconies, internet cafés and family entertainment areas. Some, like RCI with the Enchantment of the Seas, are even 'stretching' ships by having them cut in half and adding a new central section with more cabins, restaurants, bars and entertainment venues.

On-board facilities

Spending so much time at sea makes the quality, availability and type of facilities on board ship very important to passengers. Cruises vary from very small, intimate experiences with a small number of fellow passengers to mega-cruises with thousands of passengers aboard and a variety of facilities such as shops, bars, restaurants, entertainment venues, internet cafés, currency exchange facilities and children's play areas. The facilities on offer must reflect the number of passengers, type of cruise, target market and the price paid by the passengers.

Perhaps the most important facility on board is the cabin (often referred to as the stateroom). Cabins vary in size and price according to where they are located on the ship. Inside cabins on lower decks tend to be the cheapest, while upper deck cabins and suites with sea views command the highest prices. Cruise brochures and websites include colour-coded deck plans indicating the location and prices of cabins with different facilites (see Figure 10.2).

Activity 10.5

Research and compile two fact sheets that compare and contrast the routes and ship facilities offered by Cunard's Queen Mary 2 and Island Cruises' Island Star.

This activity is designed to provide evidence for M1.

Fig 10.2 – Section from a typical deck plan (courtesy of Royal Caribbean International)

An outside stateroom on Cunard's Queen Victoria

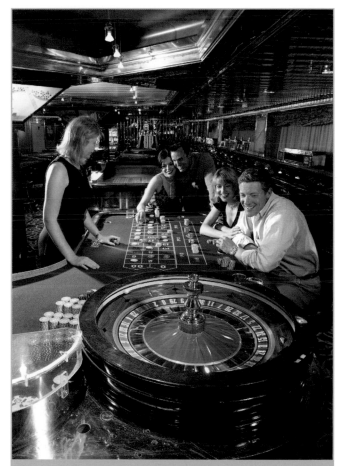

Casino on the Island Escape (courtesy of Island Cruises)

Be able to select cruises to meet specific customer needs

Types of customers

No one cruise company can hope to meet the very different needs of every cruise passenger. Cruise operators target particular customers, providing services and facilities to meet their needs. Customers can be selected by:

- Age – a cruise company may target older customers or young, first-time cruisers;
- Lifestyle – cruise operators can cater for groups, families, singles, etc;
- Income – some cruises are aimed at affluent, up-market clientele, while others appeal to people on a tight budget;
- Special interest – everything from wine tasting, art appreciation and history to sports, cooking and gardening are offered by cruise specialists.

Cruise operators develop products and itineraries to appeal to one of more of these markets and use

Cruise weddings are growing in popularity (courtesy of Island Cruises)

a variety of marketing techniques to persuade them to book with their company, e.g. advertising, direct mail, sales promotions and public relations activities.

Appeal of cruising

The growth in popularity of cruising clearly shows that it has great appeal to many different types of people from all backgrounds and regions of the world. Cruising still appeals to the traditional market that has always enjoyed the product, but there are now many new types of customers attracted to the sector, including younger, first-time cruisers and families.

Customers are influenced by a range of considerations when choosing their cruise holiday, for example:

Activity 10.6

Gather information on three companies that offer cruises for (1) an elderly couple wanting to explore Antarctica; (2) a family with young children looking for a 7-night Mediterranean cruise. Explain how the selected cruises would appeal to the customers.

This activity is designed to provide evidence for P3 and M2.

- Itineraries – factors such as the number and type of on-shore excursions, ports of call, cruise areas visited and variety of sights, influence a passenger's choice of cruise line and itinerary;

- Cruise etiquette – issues such as dress code and tipping policy can influence passenger choice, e.g. a person may prefer a more informal type of cruise with few formalities on an all-inclusive basis to a traditional cruising experience with formal dress code;

- Board – whether to choose an all-inclusive arrangement or pay for extras on board;

- Social – the opportunity to meet and make friends with fellow passengers from a wide variety of social backgrounds and countries;

- Climate – whether to take a cruise in the warm waters of the Caribbean or the Norwegian fjords;

- Cost – selecting a cruise that matches a person's total budget.

- Convenience – starting a cruise from a customer's home country is growing in popularity, whereas fly/cruise holidays are declining in popularity;

- Novelty – some cruise passengers are drawn to new facilities and services offered by cruise companies, for example the maiden voyage of a new ship, a celebrity chef on board or even the launch of a new style of cruising, e.g. easyCruise;

- On-board facilities – shipping companies are actively developing their on-board and on-shore facilities in order to capitalise on the overall growth in the cruise sector and to satisfy the new customers who have been attracted to cruising;

- Passenger/crew ratio (PCR) – the lower the PCR, i.e. the more crew available per passenger, the better the level of service provided and the overall passenger experience;

- Passenger/space ratio (PSR) – the lower the PSR, i.e. the more space available per passenger, the greater the feeling of space on board and less queuing for facilities.

Activity 10.7

Gather information on three companies that offer cruises for (1) a group of students wanting a short cruise in the Mediterranean as part of an overseas study visit; (2) a couple wanting to spend their honeymoon on a Nile cruise. Explain how the selected cruises would appeal to the customers.

This activity is designed to provide evidence for P3 and M2.

SECTION 4 Know the impacts of cruising on the main cruise areas of the world

We have seen that cruising is a global industry that is growing rapidly. In this section we investigate some of the most popular cruise areas of the world and explore the positive and negative impacts of the cruise sector.

Cruise areas of the world

The following is a selection of cruise areas that are popular with the British:

1. The Caribbean and Panama Canal;
2. The Mediterranean;
3. Scandinavia and the Baltic;
4. Alaska;
5. Antarctica/South America;
6. Far East/Australia.
7. UK;
8. The Canary Islands and Madeira;
9. The Nile;
10. Black Sea.

The Caribbean and Panama Canal

There are 7,000 islands in the Caribbean Sea, lying between the southern tip of the eastern USA and the north coast of South America. The area stretches for more than 2,500 miles, so cruising is an excellent way to experience as much as possible of this part of the world. The area has a rich culture and heritage, with many languages spoken and varied geographical features. Nearly all UK passengers opt for a fly/cruise arrangement when buying their Caribbean cruise, allowing them to fit a cruise to a long-haul destination into a normal holiday period. All of the major shipping lines offer Caribbean cruises, including Royal Caribbean International, Carnival, Costa Cruises, Cunard, P & O Cruises, Celebrity Cruises, Orient Lines and Ocean Village.

Caribbean cruises can last anything from three days for a short holiday between Florida and the Bahamas to holidays lasting a month and covering the whole area. Examples of countries that could be visited on a Caribbean cruise include:

- Western Caribbean – Cozumel or Playa del Carmen in Mexico, the Cayman Islands and Jamaica;
- Eastern Caribbean – Puerto Rico, the US Virgin Islands (St Thomas and St Croix), St Martin, Dominica, Barbados, St Kitts and Martinique;
- Southern Caribbean – Puerto Rico, US Virgin Islands, Guadeloupe, Grenada, Barbados, Antigua, St Lucia, Martinique, Venezuela and Aruba.

Activity 10.8

Using an atlas for reference, draw a map of the Caribbean region and locate the above list of cruise ports found in the area.

This activity is designed to provide evidence for P4.

The Panama Canal can also be combined with a Caribbean cruise. Passengers can choose to take a one-way or 'line journey' from Fort Lauderdale, Miami or Puerto Rico through to Acapulco or Los Angeles. Alternatively they can take a cruise that travels half way along the canal before returning.

Figure 10.3 shows an example of a 7-night Caribbean fly/cruise offered by Norwegian Cruise Line (NCL) on board the Norwegian Majesty, starting and finishing in Charleston, South Carolina. Highlights of the cruise include time to visit historic Charleston, the Mayan ruins in the Yucatan, Ernest Hemingway's home in Key West and the fashionable resort of Cozumel.

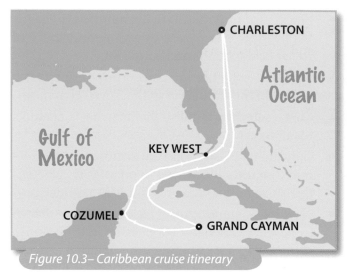

Figure 10.3– Caribbean cruise itinerary

The Mediterranean

The Mediterranean Sea stretches for more than 2,200 miles, from the 22-mile wide straits of Gibraltar to the Black Sea in the east and the Suez Canal in the southeast. It offers cruise passengers a mixture of ancient and modern, with many different cultures, geography and history all set in a beautiful climate. The Greeks, Romans and Egyptians all built their empires around the Mediterranean and have left behind some of the world's best-known tourist attractions, including the Pyramids, the Acropolis and the Coliseum. Most Mediterranean cruise itineraries include a short flight from the UK to Genoa, Palma or Athens, thereby avoiding the sometimes rough waters of the Bay of Biscay and offering instant sunshine. Alternatively passengers can take a coach, train or drive to their Mediterranean departure port. Others may opt for a cruise that starts and finishes in a UK port. All of the major shipping lines offer Mediterranean cruises, including Thomson, Costa Cruises, Cunard, P & O Cruises, Celebrity Cruises, Swan Hellenic, Island Cruises and Ocean Village.

Ports of call that might be visited on a Mediterranean cruise include:

- Spanish mainland ports such as Barcelona, Cadiz, Malaga and Valencia;
- The Balearic Islands of Ibiza, Majorca and Minorca;
- Canary Islands such as Tenerife, Gran Canaria, La Palma, La Gomera and El Hierro;
- French ports of Cannes, Monte Carlo, St Tropez and Ajaccio (Corsica);
- Italian ports such as Genoa, Civitavecchia, Livorno, Venice, Sardinia, Amalfi and Catania;
- Valetta (Malta's main port);
- Cyprus ports of Limassol, Paphos and Larnaca;
- Piraeus, Corfu, Rhodes, Heraklion, Mykonos and Skiathos in Greece;
- Turkish ports of Izmir, Kusadasi, Bodrum and Antalya;
- Israeli ports of Haifa, Tel Aviv and Ashdod;
- Ports in Egypt, including Alexandria, Port Said and Safaga;
- North African ports of Sidi Bou Said in Tunisia and Tangier, Agadir and Casablanca in Morocco.

Figure 10.4 – Mediterranean cruise itinerary

Activity 10.9

Plot the above list of Mediterranean cruise ports on a blank map of Europe, which registered tandtONLine users can download from www.tandtonline.co.uk

This activity is designed to provide evidence for P4.

Figure 10.4 shows an example of a 14-night Mediterranean cruise offered by P & O Cruises on board the Oriana, starting and ending in Southampton. Highlights of the cruise include time to explore the history and culture of a variety of Mediterranean cities, including Barcelona, Valencia, Rome and Naples.

Activity 10.10

Study the itinerary shown in Figure 10.4 and make notes on the type of passengers that you think the cruise would appeal to. Research three of the ports of call and make notes on the tourist attractions that cruise passengers could visit.

This activity is designed to provide evidence for P4.

Scandinavia and the Baltic

Cruises in Scandinavia and the Baltic appeal to people with an interest in history, culture and nature, rather than beaches and hot weather. Baltic cruise itineraries include the great cities of Northern Europe, and the majority of cruises include a visit to the historic port of St Petersburg. Scandinavia offers cruise visitors tranquil fjords and breathtaking scenery.

Cruises that take in the Norwegian fjords and coastline often include the following ports of call:

- Bergen;
- Trondheim;
- Alesund;

- Tromso;
- Hammerfest;
- The North Cape.

Cities that often feature in Baltic cruise itineraries include:

- Amsterdam;
- Copenhagen;
- Helsinki;
- Stockholm;
- Oslo;
- Tallinn;
- Riga;
- St Petersburg.

Activity 10.11

Plot the above list of Norwegian and Baltic cruise ports on a blank map of Europe, which registered tandtONLine users can be download from www.tandtonline.co.uk

This activity is designed to provide evidence for P4.

Alaska

Alaska attracts cruise passengers, from May to October, to see its vast and unspoilt landscape of mountains, forests, glaciers and fjords. Its scenery and wildlife are the main attractions of the area, which covers more than 580,000 miles. There are two basic Alaska cruise itineraries:

1. The classic 'inside passage' – this is a round-trip, one-week cruise, beginning and ending in Vancouver, named because it lies within a long chain of coastal islands that act as a buffer to the open waters of the North Pacific. This type of cruise usually includes visits to tidewater glaciers, such as those at the head of narrow, cliff-sided Tracy Arm, or those found in the many inlets of Glacier Bay;

2. The 'glacier route' itinerary – this includes the Gulf of Alaska in a one-way route between Vancouver and Anchorage. These cruises include some of Alaska's most impressive tidewater glaciers, such as Hubbard Glacier in Yakutat Bay and Columbia Glacier in Prince William Sound.

Cruise companies that feature Alaska include Norwegian Cruise Line, Royal Caribbean International, Crystal Cruises, Holland America Line and Celebrity Cruises.

Figure 10.5 shows an example of a 7-night Alaska fly/cruise offered by Norwegian Cruise Lines on board the Norwegian Sun, starting and ending in Vancouver. Highlights of the cruise include time to explore Vancouver's historic Gastown and cosmopolitan Yaletown, plus cruising by the Sawyer Glacier and viewing all kinds of wildlife.

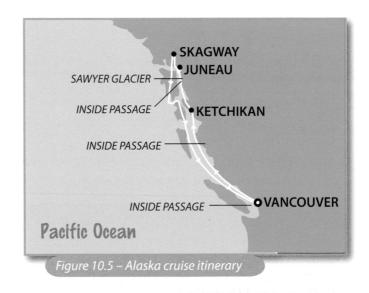

Figure 10.5 – Alaska cruise itinerary

Activity 10.12

Study the itinerary shown in Figure 10.5 and make notes on the type of passengers that you think the cruise would appeal to. You may like to do some further research in brochures and on websites to help you with this task.

This activity is designed to provide evidence for P4.

Antarctica

Cruising the cold waters of the Antarctic appeals to travellers who are looking for the ultimate in natural, wildlife experiences. Cruises are carefully controlled to maintain environmental standards, but passengers can still expect to see penguins, seals, whales and numerous seabirds in a landscape that is dominated by massive ice cliffs and floating icebergs. Companies that offer cruises in Antarctic waters include Hurtigruten, Abercrombie & Kent and Quark Expeditions. Cruising is only possible during the southern hemisphere summer from November to March, when temperatures can still be minus 5°C to minus 8°C and wind chill can be a significant factor. Proper protective clothing is essential for Antarctic cruises, although higher temperatures are found in the northerly islands

Far East

The Far east is a relatively unexplored cruise region, stretching from Thailand, Malaysia, Singapore and Indonesia in the south, through the Philippines, Cambodia, Vietnam, Hong Kong and China to Korea and Japan in the north. South East Asia has a hot and humid tropical climate and is subject to monsoon rains mainly from July to October. November to February is drier and this is when the seasonal cruises along the western Malaysian coast to Phuket take place. Star Cruises sail all year round, but most short season and world cruises in the Far East sail during the northern hemisphere winter or spring, from November to March. Other cruise operators in this region include Royal Caribbean International, P & O, Cunard and Costa Cruises.

The UK

There are a growing number of cruises starting and finishing in UK ports, offering passengers the convenience of beginning their holiday closer to home. Some ex-UK cruises follow the coast line of Western Europe calling at Dutch, UK, French and Spanish ports going as far south as Lisbon in Portugal. Others may circumnavigate the coast of England, Wales, Ireland and Scotland, calling at major cities like Dublin, Liverpool, Glasgow, Belfast and Edinburgh, as well as visiting outlying islands like the Channel Islands and the Isles of Scilly. Hebridian International Cruises specialise in cruising around the Scottish islands. Longer cruises will go as far as the Greenland east coast or volcanic Iceland visiting Reykjavik and calling at the rugged Faroe Islands and the Irish coast en route.

The Canary Islands

The seven Canary Islands are scattered some 70 miles off the coast of Morocco. Gran Canaria offers busy resorts, impressive architecture and a mini Sahara, while Tenerife has mountainous rainforests and impressive beaches. Lanzarote features moon-like landscapes in its Fire Mountain Volcanic Park and is close to the semi-desert Fuertaventura, with its extensive sandy beaches. Further out into the Atlantic are the unspoilt mountainous volcanic islands of La Palma, La Gomera and El Hierro. The climate of the Canaries offers an all-year-round destination, with the majority of cruises taking place between autumn and spring. Cruises to the Canaries can be taken from the UK or Mediterranean ports like Genoa either as return voyages of 7 to 14 days or as a sector of a transatlantic voyage. There are also cruises around the islands leaving from Tenerife or Gran Canaria.

The Nile

The River Nile is the most popular river cruise destination with British people, followed by the Rhine/Moselle. The number of British passengers on the Nile rose by 78 per cent between 2004 and 2005, from 22,700 to more than 40,000. Cruisers are attracted by the thousands of years of history in the region, inspiring monuments such as the Pyramids and Sphinx at Gizeh, the temples at Karnak, Philea and the Valley of the Kings. The majority of British visitors to Egypt include a short cruise on the Nile between Luxor and Aswan during their stay. Cruises of the 140-mile stretch of the Upper Nile typically last for four of five days. A number of Nile cruise operators combine a stay in Cairo with their cruises, giving passengers the chance to visit the Tutankhamun treasures in the Museum of the Antiquities. Companies that feature Nile cruises include Abercrombie & Kent, Discover Egypt and Somak.

The Black Sea

Cruises in the Black Sea are for people who wish to experience the different cultures of eastern bloc countries, like Bulgaria, Ukraine and Rumania, or visit the northern coast of Turkey. Although there are Mediterranean cruises from the UK that include the Black Sea in their itineraries, most are fly/cruises sailing from Athens or Istanbul and many will also include some Greek Islands in the itinerary. Popular cruise ports on the Black Sea include Varna and Nesebur in Bulgaria, Yalta and Odessa in the Ukraine, and Constanta in Romania.

Activity 10.13

Plot the above list of Black Sea cruise ports on a blank map of Europe, which registered tandtONLine users can download from www.tandtonline.co.uk

This activity is designed to provide evidence for P4.

Cruise itineraries

Cruise itineraries are planned to provide passengers with a variety of on-shore experiences and activities to meet their needs. Some cruises visit lively Caribbean and Mediterranean ports, while others specialise in excursions to see wildlife and heritage attractions.

Cruise ports can be divided into four main types:

1. Ports of call – the destinations that a cruise ship visits as part of its itinerary;
2. Ports of embarkation – the ports where passengers begin (and sometimes end) their cruise;
3. Home ports – the ports where a ship has its operating base;
4. Gateway ports – these are major entry, exit and transit points for passengers and freight.

Florida is the cruising capital of the world, with the top three busiest embarkation ports – Miami, Port Everglades and Port Canaveral. The world's top five ports of call for cruise passengers are Cozumel (Mexico), Grand Cayman (Caribbean), Nassau (Bahamas), St Thomas (US Virgin Islands) and St Maarten (Caribbean).

Figure 10.6 shows an itinerary for a typical Caribbean cruise beginning and ending in Miami, Florida. Cruise highlights include visits to the Everglades, Key

Caribbean cruise itinerary					
Day	Date	Port	Country	Notes	Highlights
1	13 February 2008	Outward Flight			
1	13 February 2008	Miami hotel		for one night	
2	14 February 2008	**Miami**	USA, Florida	Embark	City, Everglades
3	15 February 2008	**Key West**	USA, Florida		Mallory Square, Aquarium, Museums, Audubon and Hemingway Houses
4	16 February 2008	**Cozumel**	Mexico		San Miguel, San Gervasio Mayan ruins, Coral reefs
5	17 February 2008	**At Sea**			
6	18 February 2008	**Miami**	USA, Florida	Disembark	City, Everglades
6	18 February 2008	Return Flight		Overnight	

Figure 10.6 – Caribbean cruise itinerary

West and Cozumel in Mexico, plus the opportunity to explore the city of Miami itself.

Impacts of cruising

As with all sectors of the travel and tourism industry, cruising has both negative and positive impacts, particularly on the ports and cruise destinations visited by passengers. As we have discussed earlier in this unit, the cruise sector is growing rapidly, with companies building bigger cruise liners to accommodate the increased demand. This can have serious implications for ports of call on cruise itineraries that have to accommodate increased numbers of tourists and provide them with facilities and services.

Positive economic impacts on cruise ports and destinations include:

- Increased revenue – cruise passengers tend to visit ports in groups on organised excursions.

While in port they spend money in shops, restaurants, attractions and on entertainment, thereby adding to the local economy. Taxi firms and coach companies also benefit financially from cruise passengers;

- Employment – cruising not only provides jobs for people working for the cruise lines, but also for travel and tourism businesses in ports, e.g. in hotels, restaurants, tourist attractions, tour operators and travel guides. Cruising also contributes towards 'indirect employment', i.e. jobs in non-tourism sectors that nonetheless benefit from influxes of cruise passengers, including construction, banking, retail and craft industries.

The sheer scale of the cruise sector, as well as the numbers of passengers carried on each ship, can cause environmental, social and cultural problems, as the following case study on the impact of cruise tourism in Belize explains.

Case Study

The impact of cruise tourism in Belize

Introduction

Belize is a small country situated at the base of the Yucatan in Central America. It borders Mexico and Guatemala, with the Caribbean Sea to the east. The country's area includes many small islands, known as cayes, which straddle a coral reef second only in size to the Great Barrier Reef in Australia. Belize has been developing its tourist industry in recent years based on its natural beauty and ruins associated with the ancient Mayan civilisation. Belize is included in the itineraries of cruise operators in the Western Caribbean, including Carnival Cruises.

The Belize Ecotourism Association (BEA)

The potential harmful impacts of cruise tourism on Belize have been brought to light by the Belize Ecotourism Association (BEA), a body set up in 1993 to:

'Promote environmentally responsible tourism, to be sensitive to the impact of tourism, to promote pollution prevention and environmental concerns, to continually observe the effects of all the above and to promote education for locals and visitors'.

The organisation is particularly concerned about the way that the type of 'mass tourism' associated with cruises may harm the country's economy in the long term, by alienating visitors to the country's small-sale tourism developments that have been nurtured over the last 20 years, based on ecotourism principles. The BEA wants to see a long-term plan for the sustainable development of all forms of tourism to Belize, including cruises.

Environmental concerns

BEA highlights a number of issues concerned with the environmental impacts of cruise tourism, including:

- Ancient Mayan ruins are under pressure from the large, and growing, number of cruise passengers;
- There is evidence of environmental deterioration on the cayes and coral reefs;
- Riverside erosion is increasing due to wash from the high-speed launches taking cruise passengers on adventure trips;
- Road systems are under pressure from the extra volume of traffic generated by cruise tourism;
- Solid waste from cruise passengers is increasing the burden on the area's sanitary infrastructure.

Cultural impacts

BEA believes that tourism should always contribute to cultural exchange between visitors and the people of Belize. Visitors attracted to Belize by the small-scale tourism developments, with the opportunity to learn about the local people and their traditions, are rewarded with warmth and kindness. With mass tourism associated with cruising there is a danger that these experiences may well be reversed. Expectations by street sellers of big sales are often disappointed. Passengers are hustled and their reactions may be seen to be hostile. The interaction, instead of being one of pleasure, can become one of distaste and an unwillingness to return to the country or recommend it to others.

The future

Tourism in Belize is estimated to be worth BZ$270 million to the country's economy, with cruise tourism accounting for some BZ$40 million. The Belize Ecotourism Association would like to see the burden of tourist taxes being spread more evenly amongst all visitors to the country – at present, tourists who stay overnight pay a higher tax than those just visiting for the day, including cruise passengers. They believe this is unfair, since the environmental impacts caused by cruise tourists are greater than long-stay visitors. A rise in the tourist tax for day visitors would give the government extra funds to allow proper monitoring of the impacts of cruise ship tourism. Also, it may attract higher-spending tourists to Belize, thereby benefiting the economy even more. The BEA would also like to see improvements in the country's infrastructure before any future plans for cruise tourism developments are considered and measures are in place to monitor developments for their environmental and cultural impacts.

Case Study Questions and Activities

1. Why is it important for the government of Belize to monitor cruise tourism?
2. What measures could be introduced to reduce the pressure from tourists at the ancient Mayan ruins?
3. How can the government of Belize maximise the benefits from cruise tourism while at the same time minimising its negative impacts?
4. Carry out some further research to find examples of how cruise lines try to reduce their harmful environmental and cultural impacts.

This case study is designed to provide evidence for P5, M3 and D2.

Weblink

Check out this website to help answer the questions in this case study and for more information on the Belize Ecotourism Association.
www.bzecotourism.org

Activity 10.14

Carry out some research on cruises in Antarctica and make notes on the impacts of cruising in the area, its gateway ports and ports of call. Make realistic recommendations about how to maximise the positive and minimise the negative impacts of cruising in Antarctica. The website www.choosingcruising.co.uk is a good place to start this activity.

This activity is designed to provide evidence for P5, M3 and D2.

SECTION 5 — Know the employment opportunities in the cruise sector

The rise in popularity of cruising worldwide means that there are many job opportunities in the sector for people with the right qualifications, skills and personal qualities. In this section we investigate key facts about working in cruising and examine the many job opportunities available on board and ashore.

On-board job opportunities

There are literally hundreds of different on-board jobs on offer with cruise lines. Jobs are offered in different departments on board ship, for example:

- Galley (kitchen);
- Engineering;
- Beauty and hairdressing;
- Hotel (reception);
- Housekeeping;
- Casino;
- Deck;
- Entertainment;
- Medical;
- Food and beverage;
- Tours and excursions;
- Photography;
- Sports, pool and gym.

Some jobs are more technical than others and require specialist qualifications, for example posts in medical, deck, engineering and gym work.

A waiter on the QE2 (courtesy of Cunard)

Activity 10.15

Log on to either of these cruise employment websites www.cruiseworking.com; www.cruiseplacement.com and find details of three jobs in cruising that interest you. Make a note of job roles and responsibilities, salary, contract period, location, etc.

This activity is designed to provide evidence for P6.

Landside job opportunities

Job opportunities with cruise lines on shore include:

- Marketing;
- Reservations and sales (including call centre work);
- Finance;
- Administration;
- Human resources;
- IT;
- Check-in and operations;
- Customer service;
- Baggage handling;
- Catering.

There are many websites that offer advice on getting a job in the cruise sector and some have lists of posts available, for example www.cruiseworking.com and www.cruiseplacement.com

Figures 10.7 and 10.8 give details of two jobs on board a cruise ship – an Entertainments Officer and an Assistant Bartender.

Qualifications, experience and skills required

Not all jobs in the cruise sector require formal qualifications. However, ambitious people who wish to develop their careers in cruising will generally find that their progression will be quicker if they have qualifications that are relevant to their job. Experience counts for a lot in the cruise sector – people who have on-shore experience of, for example retail, entertainment, hospitality and catering, will be more attractive to the cruise lines than applicants with no experience at all.

Personal skills and qualities, such as good appearance and grooming, a positive attitude, enthusiasm and reliability, are of paramount importance in the cruise industry, which is all about meeting and even exceeding passengers' expectations. In general, cruise lines look for people who:

- Are highly-motivated and enthusiastic;
- Are keen to take on a challenge;
- Have a strong desire to work on a cruise ship;
- Get on well with other people;
- Are happy to be away from home for long periods;
- Have a helpful and patient customer service manner;
- Are well-presented.

Summer Cruises plc

Job description

Title of post: **Entertainments Officer**
Post no: SC/08/08
Location: On board
Responsible to: Cruise Director

Job summary

The Entertainments Officer is responsible for assisting the Cruise Director and his/her Deputy in the smooth running of all aspects of the Entertainments division of the Hotel Services and Entertainments Department. The Entertainments Division is responsible for providing a diverse range of entertainment and leisure opportunities during both the day and evening for passengers in order to enhance their cruise experience. This includes production shows, guest lecturers' activities, quizzes, bingo, cabaret, musical programmes, karaoke and deck activities such as quoits, golf, tennis, cricket, football, etc.

Requirements

1. You must possess a warm, outgoing personality to ensure that passengers always have a friendly and understanding person to talk to;
2. Experience in hosting/introducing professional cabaret entertainment;
3. Effective communication skills, both written and oral;
4. You need to be available and visible to passengers at all times and to be easily identifiable as one of the public faces of the on board entertainment product;
5. You will undertake a pro-active role in the various activities delivered by the Entertainments Division.

Salary and benefits

- Competitive salary and benefits package is offered;
- Training and development is delivered mainly through in-house workshops, courses and programmes;
- Contract period of a minimum of 4 months to a maximum of 6 months with a 6-8 week unpaid leave period;
- Concessionary travel after a qualifying period of service.

Application procedure

To apply in the first instance, send a photo and CV to HR Division, Summer Cruises plc, Southampton.

Dated: 1st September 2008

Figure 10.7 – Job description for the post of Entertainments Officer

Summer Cruises plc

Job description

Title of post: **Assistant Bartender**
Post no: SC/09/08
Location: Fleet
Responsible to: Bartender

Job summary

- To ensure the smooth and efficient operation of the bar, under the direction of the bartender, in order to achieve passenger satisfaction;
- To generate and maximise revenue opportunities both individually and as a team;
- To portray a positive and professional image to all outside consultants, agencies, suppliers, passengers, officers and crew;
- To contribute to the creation and maintenance of an enthusiastic, motivated working environment;
- To maintain prescribed systems for the monitoring and control of stock and relevant costs in accordance with company procedures;
- To ensure all revenue is correctly posted to on board accounts;
- To assist with stock takes as required by the Finance Manager.

Requirements

1. Applicants should have attended catering college and obtained a City & Guilds pass in Food and Beverage Service 707;
2. Alternatively, applicants should have had experience in a superior class hotel, club or restaurant;
3. Applicants should have experience of mixing and serving cocktails, and have a thorough knowledge of wines and liquors.

Salary and benefits

- Competitive salary and benefits package is offered;
- Training and development is delivered mainly through in-house workshops, courses and programmes;
- Contract period of a minimum of 4 months to a maximum of 6 months with a 6-8 week unpaid leave period;
- Concessionary travel after a qualifying period of service.

Application procedure

To apply in the first instance, send a photo and CV to HR Division, Summer Cruises plc, Southampton.

Dated: 1st September 2008

Figure 10.8 – Job description for the post of Assistant Bartender

The working environment in cruising

Working on board a cruise ship can be an exciting and rewarding experience, visiting exotic ports of call, working with people from all parts of the world, earning a good living, and having your room and board provided for free. However, like in other sectors of the travel and tourism industry, life on board ship is also demanding and challenging, working long hours (often 7 days a week), sharing accommodation with work colleagues and following the ship's rules and regulations.

Most cruise lines offer an average contract of six months, but depending on the position and the company, it could be as short as four months or as long as ten. Staff are paid only while on contract – holidays are unpaid and usually last two months. Once you've completed a contract you are not obliged to return to the same ship or company, but if you have enjoyed your work and have received a good reference, you are likely to be offered another period of work.

Details of jobs in cruising are available direct from individual cruise lines or through agencies, some of which charge applicants a fee for their services. The cruise sector has a relatively high staff turnover, so companies need to fill vacancies all year round with suitable people. Staff leave for new jobs on different ships, companies or countries. Others leave mid-journey for various reasons, including personal or family circumstances.

Crew having fun with guests on an Island Cruises holiday

Unit summary

This unit has explored the cruise sector of the travel and tourism industry, from the early beginnings in the mid-19th century to the present day global industry. You have seen that cruising is undergoing a period of rapid growth and change, with new ships and facilities being developed to cater for new markets around the world. The links between cruising and other sectors of the travel and tourism industry have been fully examined. You have also explored different types of cruises, ships and the facilities they offer, before examining how cruises are tailored to meet specific customer needs. You have investigated the main cruise areas of the world, including the Mediterranean, Caribbean and Alaska, plus the positive and negative impacts of the sector on cruise destinations. The unit has also looked at the many employment opportunities on offer with cruise lines and the qualifications, experience and personal qualities needed to succeed in the sector. Throughout the unit you have been shown many industry examples, while the case studies on Carnival Corporation and plc, the PSA and the impact of cruise tourism in Belize, highlight key issues in the operation and development of the cruise industry.

If you have worked methodically, by the end of this unit you should:

*   Understand the development and structure of the cruise sector;

- Know different types of cruises, ships and the facilities they offer;
- Be able to select cruises to meet specific customer needs;
- Know the impacts of cruising on the main cruise areas of the world;
- Know the employment opportunities within the cruise sector.

You are now in a position to complete the assignment for the unit, under the direction of your tutor. Before you tackle the assignment you may like to have a go at the following questions to help build your knowledge of the cruise sector.

Test your knowledge

1. Why do you think that cruising has grown in popularity in recent years?

2. Which cruise destination is the most popular with British cruisers?

3. In what ways is the customer profile of cruise passengers changing?

4. Name three companies that offer 'informal cruising'.

5. Which three companies have the biggest share of the global cruise market?

6. Name five cruise brands that are owned by Carnival Corporation and plc.

7. Describe the links that cruising has with other sectors of the travel and tourism industry.

8. What role does the PSA play in the cruise sector?

9. Give two examples of vertical and horizontal integration in the cruise industry.

10. Name ten ports of call used in Mediterranean cruise itineraries.

11. What type of cruise passengers are attracted to cruises in Alaska?

12. Describe some of the environmental impacts of cruise tourism.

13. Describe the features and benefits of five different types of cruises.

14. Describe a variety of external factors that affect the global cruise industry.

15. What personal qualities do the cruise lines look for in new recruits?

Answers to these questions can be found on the Tutor's CD-ROM that accompanies this book. Full details can be found at www.tandtpublishing.co.uk

Unit 10 Assignment

Investigating the Cruise Sector

Introduction

This assignment is made up of a number of tasks which, when successfully completed, are designed to give you sufficient evidence to meet the Pass (P), Merit (M) and Distinction (D) grading criteria for the unit. If you have carried out the activities and read the case studies throughout this unit, you will already have done a lot of work towards completing the tasks for this assignment.

Scenario

As part of a forthcoming open day for prospective students at your college/school, your group has been asked to prepare some presentations, displays and booklets on different sectors of the travel and tourism industry, to give the students and their parents an idea of the type of work you do on your course. You have been chosen to work on the cruise sector and must complete the following tasks.

TASK 1

Research, prepare and deliver a presentation in which you should:

(a) **Explain** the development and structure of the cruise sector.

This task is designed to produce evidence for P1.

To be considered for a Distinction grade for this task, your presentation should also:

(b) **Analyse** opportunities for future growth within the current cruise sector.

This task is designed to provide evidence for D1.

TASK 2

This task is designed to demonstrate your knowledge of the types of cruise ships and the facilities/cruises they offer.

(a) As part of a 'cruise fair', organise a display that describes the facilities and cruises available from different types of ships.

This task is designed to produce evidence for P2.

To be considered for a Merit grade for this task, your display should also:

(b) **Compare** and **contrast** the routes and ship facilities of two different types of cruises. These could be similar cruises offered by competitor companies or two completely different cruises, e.g. a round-the-world cruise and a Mediterranean cruise on board one of the new breed of budget cruises.

This task is designed to produce evidence for M1.

TASK 3

This task is about selecting cruises that would appeal to different types of customers, using simulated role plays.

(a) Having researched the range and variety of cruises on offer, play the role of a travel agent advising two different types of customers on cruises that would meet their needs. The first customer is a young, single male looking for a short fly/cruise in the Mediterranean. He has a limited budget and is looking for a lively nightlife scene. The second customers are a couple celebrating their golden wedding anniversary and looking for a 14-night cruise in the Caribbean, with the chance to visit some interesting heritage and cultural attractions during their holiday. You should **select** appropriate cruises that meet each customer's needs.

This task is designed to produce evidence for P3.

To be considered for a Merit grade for this task, you must also:

(b) **Explain** (in the form of a short written report) how the selected cruises appeal to each customer.

This task is designed to produce evidence for M2.

TASK 4

For this task you must produce a written report that:

(a) **Describes** four cruise areas of the world, e.g. the Caribbean, the Mediterranean, Scandinavia and Alaska;

(b) **Describes** the impacts of cruising on one cruise area, its gateway ports and ports of call.

These tasks are designed to produce evidence for P4 and P5.

To be considered for a Merit grade for this task, your report must also:

(b) **Explain** the impacts of cruising on a selected cruise area.

This task is designed to produce evidence for M3.

To be considered for a Distinction grade for this task, your report must also:

(b) Make realistic **recommendations** about how to maximise positive and minimise negative impacts of cruising.

This task is designed to provide evidence for D2.

TASK 5

For this task you must produce an illustrated booklet that:

Describes three different employment opportunities available in the cruise sector. These must be described in terms of roles, responsibilities and entry requirements. Your booklet should also describe the uniqueness of the working environment in the cruise sector.

This task is designed to produce evidence for P6.

UNIT 12

Tour Operations

Tour operators play a very important role in travel and tourism, by arranging the package holidays that are such an important feature of life in the 21st century. Tour operators are at the forefront of today's travel and tourism industry, seeking out new destinations and holiday experiences to satisfy the ever-changing needs and expectations of travellers. They work in partnership with airlines, hoteliers, car hire companies and a variety of other travel service suppliers to 'package' their products. Tour operators sell holidays through travel agents and direct to the public, with internet bookings showing dramatic rises in recent years.

In this unit you will examine the UK tour operations environment, including links with other sectors of travel and tourism. You will investigate the many challenges facing tour operators, such as integration and the growth in online sales. Different types of tour operators will be identified and you will learn how products and services are developed to meet a variety of customer needs. You will explore how tour operators plan, sell, administer and operate a package holiday programme. Finally, you will have the chance to develop your practical skills by planning and costing a typical package holiday, allowing you to appreciate some of the commercial decisions necessary to be profitable in this sector.

WHAT YOU WILL STUDY

When you have completed this unit you should:

1. **Understand the tour operations environment;**
2. **Know the range of products and services offered by tour operators for different target markets;**
3. **Know how tour operators plan, sell, administer and operate a package holiday programme;**
4. **Be able to plan and cost a package holiday.**

You will be guided through the main topics in this unit with the help of the latest developments, statistics, industry examples and case studies. You should also check out the weblinks throughout the unit for extra information on particular organisations or topic areas and use the activities throughout the unit to help you learn more.

ASSESSMENT FOR THIS UNIT

This unit is internally assessed, meaning that you will be given an assignment (or series of assignments) to complete by your tutor(s) to show that you have fully understood the content of the unit. A grading scale of pass, merit or distinction is used when staff mark your assignment(s), with higher grades awarded to students who show greater depth in analysis, evaluation and justification in their assignments. An assignment for this unit, which covers all the grading criteria, can be found on page 71. Don't forget to visit www.tandtONLine.co.uk for all the latest industry news, developments, statistics and hot links to websites in this unit to help you with your assignments.

Icebreaker

This unit examines the world of tour operations – the sector of the travel and tourism industry concerned with arranging and selling package holidays. Working by yourself, or in small groups under the direction of your tutor, see how you get on with the following tasks to help you make a start on this unit:

- Name five different tour operating companies that you are familiar with;
- Try and come up with a definition of a 'tour operator';
- Make a list of what you think a new tour operator would have to do to organise, plan and sell its holidays;
- Make notes on the range of internal and external influences on a tour operating company that could affect its profits;
- Think about the laws and regulations that tour operators must comply with in the course of their work;
- Name three specific jobs that are offered by the major holiday companies;
- Make a list of the costs that a tour operating company will incur in the course of its work.

When you've finished, show your answers to your tutor and compare your answers with what other students in your class have written.

SECTION 1   Understand the tour operations environment

Tour operations is a dynamic and complex business environment, where companies must work with many different sectors of the travel and tourism industry, comply with laws and regulations, and deal with a variety of external influences and challenges.

Links with other sectors of travel and tourism

Unlike travel agents, who sell holidays and a range of other travel products, tour operators actually assemble the different parts of a holiday, i.e. the type of travel, accommodation, facilities, transfers, excursions and other services. If we consider that travel agents are the retail arm of the travel business, then tour operators are the 'wholesalers', since they buy in bulk from the providers of travel services, such as the hoteliers and airlines, break the bulk into manageable packages and offer the finished product – the package holiday (or inclusive tour) – for sale via a travel agent or direct to the public. The package is sold for an all-inclusive

price, which is generally lower than if the different parts of the holiday had been booked individually by the holidaymaker. Figure 12.1 shows the position of tour operators as intermediaries between the suppliers of travel products and travel agents. There is a growing trend for people to book direct with tour operators rather than booking through a travel agent. This trend is set to continue and gather pace as the popularity of the internet, mobile technology and interactive TV grows.

In working with other sectors of the travel and tourism industry, tour operators develop links with a wide range of organisations, including:

- Travel agents – using agents as a sales outlet for the tour operator's holidays and agreeing commission payments and booking procedures;
- Transport providers – negotiating and agreeing contracts with airlines (charter and scheduled), rail operators, coach companies, taxi operators, etc. to supply transport services for holidaymakers;

Figure12.1 – The position of tour operators

- Hotels and other accommodation providers – negotiating allocations of bed spaces that form the accommodation element of the package holiday;
- Ancillary service providers – contracting with companies to supply representative services, transfers, 'meet and greet' arrangements, insurance, car hire, activities, excursions, etc.

Even the large, vertically-integrated travel groups (see next section) have to liaise on different functions within their own organisations, since individual parts of the group are usually separate companies in their own right, e.g. staff from Something Special Holidays, part of the Thomson/TUI Group, would negotiate with Thomson's own airline Thomsonfly to agree seat allocations for a season.

Horizontal and vertical integration

As competition in the travel and tourism industry has intensified, tour operators have taken over or merged with other travel and tourism businesses as a way of maintaining or increasing their market share and maximising their profits. This is most noticeable in the tour operator/travel agent relationship, where:

- TUI Travel UK owns Thomson and First Choice tour operating businesses, and the Thomson and First Choice travel agency chains (TUI UK is itself controlled by the German company TUI AG);

- Thomas Cook AG (a German group) owns the Thomas Cook and MyTravel tour operating companies (including Airtours), plus the Thomas Cook and Going Places chains of travel agencies.

These 'big two' travel groups were formed in 2007 from the mergers of Thomson and First Choice Holidays, and Thomas Cook with MyTravel. They dominate the sale of package holidays in the UK, accounting for just under 50 per cent of all sales. These are examples of vertical integration in the travel industry, which is when a company has control over other companies that are at different levels in the chain of distribution or in different sectors. Some of the largest tour operators also own their own airlines, giving even greater control over the component parts of package holidays. Figure 12.2 shows how TUI UK is a vertically-integrated travel company, with ownership of tour operators (wholesalers), travel agencies (retailers) and an airline.

Figure12.2 – Vertical integration at TUI UK

Weblink

Check out these websites for more information on each of the 'big two' vertically-integrated travel companies.

www.thomson.co.uk; www.thomascook.com

Vertical integration makes sense for the travel companies since they benefit from bulk discounts and make savings by using their own companies as suppliers. However, there is concern that vertical integration of this sort may not always be in the public's interest, since it can reduce the number of companies and give customers less choice. Also, customers may not know that a tour operator is owned by the travel agency that is selling their holiday. Since 2000, all vertically-integrated travel companies have been obliged to make their links to other travel companies clear by, for example, having notices in their travel agencies and printed in brochures.

FOCUS ON INDUSTRY

Disclosure of industry links

Travel businesses must comply with the following regulations concerning their links with other companies:

- Travel agents must display a prominent notice in the front window of each shop outlining its ownership links;
- A notice must be displayed on the front cover of every in-house tour operator's brochure explaining its links with the agency;
- The name of every tour operator that is part of the same group must be listed inside the shop;
- All company stationery must outline the ownership links of the agent;
- All joint advertisements between a tour operator and an in-house agent must spell out the link between the two. This includes internet and Teletext pages that direct customers to book through a sister company, e.g. a Thomson-owned site that refers people to a Thomson travel agency must explain the connection.

Horizontal integration is when a company owns or has control over a number of companies at the same level in the distribution chain or the same industry sector. For example, many tour operating businesses that are now part of the 'big two' were originally independent companies, e.g. Neilson and Club 18-30 (now part of the Thomas Cook Group), and Something Special and the Holiday Cottages Group (now merged with Thomson). Large travel companies take over smaller independents as a way or reducing competition in the marketplace, but this is not always a benefit for customers who may have less choice.

Activity 12.1

To give yourself an example of integration in travel and tourism, carry out some research into either Thomas Cook or TUI UK and design a chart that shows all the different companies it owns across tour operations, travel agencies and transport operations.

This activity is designed to provide evidence for P1.

Links with trade and regulatory bodies

Trade bodies and associations are established to represent the interests of companies in a particular industry sector.

Trade bodies

ABTA – The Travel Association, is the main trade body for both travel agents and tour operators in the UK. Its members are responsible for the sale of over 90 per cent of package holidays and 45 per cent of independent travel arrangements in the UK. ABTA's role is to ensure that customers benefit from high standards of trading practice in the travel industry and that the standards of service and business throughout its membership are of the highest calibre. All ABTA members – travel agents and tour operators – adhere to a strict code of conduct (there is a full case study on ABTA in Travel and Tourism for BTEC National Book 1).

AITO (the Association of Independent Tour Operators) is a trade organisation representing more than 150 of Britain's specialist tour operators. Its members are independent companies, most of them owner-managed, specialising in particular destinations or types of holiday (there is a full case study on AITO in Travel and Tourism for BTEC National Book 1).

UKinbound (formerly BITOA – the British Incoming Tour Operators' Association) is a trade association representing the interests of companies specialising in inbound tourism to the UK.

The European Tour Operators' Association (ETOA) was founded in 1989 as a direct result of the introduction of the EU Package Travel Directive, which made tour operators aware of the power the European institutions had to influence policy and legislation affecting tour operators. ETOA now has 400 members and has established a track record of influencing travel and tourism legislation at both national and European levels. It promotes greater awareness of the benefits provided by the travel industry in Europe, particularly the increased income and employment.

The International Federation of Tour Operators (IFTO) is a grouping of trade associations representing tour operators' interests in the various regions of the world. Its vision is to 'ensure the continued long-term success of the organised holiday by influencing legislators and civil servants in the EU, originating and destination countries, as well as other opinion formers, on the benefits to consumers and other public and private stakeholders of organised holidays'. The secretariat for IFTO is provided by the UK-based Federation of Tour Operators (FTO), one of the most influential of all trade associations in the UK tour operations sector and the subject of the following case study.

Case Study

The Federation of Tour Operators (FTO)

Introduction

The Federation of Tour Operators (FTO) works on behalf of its members to ensure the continued, long-term success of the air-inclusive holiday business. It does this by influencing governments and opinion formers on the benefits to consumers and other stakeholders of air-inclusive holidays compared to other forms of holiday arrangements.

FTO's activities

The following is a brief overview of the activities FTO undertakes:

- Bring about change and improvement in all areas affecting overseas holidays;
- The point of contact for government (UK, EU and destinations) on all UK-outbound tour operating issues;
- Co-ordinate members' activities in key areas of operational delivery – crisis handling, health and safety, sustainable tourism, operational issues, and establishing best practice;
- Co-operation and co-ordination with other trade associations and interested parties;
- Lobby to ensure that the tax burden on holidaymakers is as low as possible;
- Promote the professional and positive image of the industry;
- Provide public relations support;
- Currently acts as a regulator of financial protection on behalf of its members in relation to their non-ATOL business;
- Represent its members at meetings of the International Federation of Tour Operators (IFTO), the European trade association for tour operators.

FTO membership

Full membership is by invitation and subject to the agreement of all existing FTO members. Prospective members must sign up to a set of 'core values':

1. Able to recognise the benefit of working with others in the industry to achieve common objectives, which are of a non-competitive nature, and willing to give appropriate attention and resource to achieving those objectives;
2. Customer-focused – will aim to prioritise product quality and service delivery;
3. A responsible business with effective implemented standards of health and safety, and a balanced approach to environmental issues;
4. Trades in a way that attempts to ensure long-term financial stability.

FTO members companies account for over 70 per cent of all package holidays sold in the UK. Current (February 2008) members include some of the best-known names in the travel and tourism industry, including:

- British Airways Holidays – a fully-owned subsidiary of British Airways plc;
- Cosmos – an independent UK tour operator;
- Inghams – tour operator offering skiing, lakes and mountains, and city holidays and short breaks;
- Kosmar – UK tour operator to Greece;
- Kuoni – a market leader in long-haul travel;
- Libra Holidays – tour operator offering holidays, flights and hotels to Cyprus, Greece, Spain, Egypt and Turkey;
- RCI Travel – serving the timeshare vacation market;
- Thomas Cook – tour operator and high street travel retailer;
- Thomas Cook Signature – tailor-made holiday solutions' company;
- TUI UK – the UK's largest holiday company;
- Virgin Holidays – long-haul and ski tour operator.

FTO and responsible tourism

Responsible tourism is about making a positive difference when we travel, by:

- Enjoying ourselves and taking responsibility for our actions, respecting local cultures and the natural environment;
- Giving fair economic returns to local people, helping to spread the benefit of our visit to those who need it most;
- Recognising that water and energy are precious resources that we need to use carefully;
- Protecting endangered wildlife and preserving the natural and cultural heritage of the places we visit for the future enjoyment of visitors and the people who live there.

Members of the FTO are becoming increasingly aware of the socio-cultural, environmental and economic impacts of their products and services. In 2003, they formed a Responsible Tourism Committee and are developing a series of initiatives to assist tour operators to integrate responsible tourism practices into their core business.

Case Study Questions and Activities

1. What are the 'core values' that prospective FTO members must agree to adhere to?
2. Outline the work that the FTO does in the area of health and safety in the air-inclusive tour operating sector;
3. How is the FTO structured and funded?
4. What is 'responsible tourism' and what activities do the FTO and its members undertake to promote this type of approach to tourism?

This case study is designed to provide evidence for P1.

Weblink

Check out this website to help answer these questions and for more information on the FTO. www.fto.co.uk

Regulatory bodies

Regulatory bodies exist to make sure that tour operating companies operate in a fair, honest, efficient, safe and secure manner, for the good of the companies, their customers, suppliers and society at large. There are many regulatory bodies whose rules and regulations must be followed by all companies, including tour operators, e.g. Companies House and HM Revenue and Customs. Specific regulatory authorities concerned with tour operating include:

- The Civil Aviation Authority (CAA) – the UK's independent aviation regulator and controller of air traffic services. It manages the UK's largest system of consumer protection for travellers, the Air Travel Organisers' Licence (ATOL) used by tour operators;

- The Health and Safety Executive (HSE) – responsible for many aspects of the safe operation of tour operators' products and services;

- Trading Standards Officers – enforce the Package Travel Regulations (see page 46);

- The Foreign and Commonwealth Office (FCO) – advises on travel to and from all parts of the world, including those seen as a risk to UK travellers.

Weblink Check out these websites for more information on the work of the CAA, HSE and FCO
www.caa.co.uk; www.hse.gov.uk; www.fco.gov.uk

Legal framework

Tour operators must follow a variety of consumer protection and contract laws and regulations when carrying out their business activities, as the following sections of this unit explain.

Package Travel Regulations

The Package Travel, Package Holidays and Package Tours Directive was adopted in June 1990 and came into operation on 1 January 1993 in the then 12 Member States of the European Union as the Package Travel, Package Holidays and Package Tour Regulations. The main aim of the Regulations is to give people buying package holidays more protection and access to compensation when things go wrong, while at the same time harmonising the rules covering packages operated throughout European Union countries. The provisions of the Directive did not replace national laws and, in the case of the UK, simply consolidated existing legislation and industry codes of conduct. The Package Travel Directive has, nonetheless, caused something of a stir in the UK travel and tourism industry, given its wide-ranging powers and scope. Up to the introduction of the Regulations, tour operators had been able to disclaim responsibility when holiday arrangements went wrong, for example overbooking at a hotel or the failure of a coach transfer to arrive, on the grounds that they had no control over these unfortunate events. Under the terms of the Package Travel Regulations, tour organisers must accept legal responsibility for all the services they offer to travellers. Exceptions would be made in circumstances which could

The Package Travel Regulations are designed to protect holidaymakers

neither have been foreseen nor overcome, although in such circumstances, organisers must give all necessary assistance to consumers.

The Package Travel Regulations place a number of duties and responsibilities on the organisers of packages, namely:

- Providing information to customers on who is responsible for the package they have booked. That person or organisation is then liable in the event of failure to deliver any elements of the package;

- Providing clear contract terms;

- Giving emergency telephone numbers;

- Providing proof of the organiser's security against insolvency and information on any available insurance policies;

- Giving immediate notification with explanation of any increase in prices permitted within the terms of the contract;

- Providing a variety of compensation options if agreed services are not supplied;

- Producing accurate promotional material including brochures.

The Regulations apply to packages sold or offered for sale in the UK, regardless of the operator's place of establishment. They do not apply to packages sold in other countries by operators established in the UK, although similar provisions apply in other member states of the European Union and in those countries that are part of the European Economic Area (EEA). The Regulations do not apply to packages sold in the Channel Islands or the Isle of Man, although the regulations do apply to organisers based in these areas, or anywhere else in the world, who sell their packages within the UK.

Trade Descriptions Act 1968

This Act protects consumers against false descriptions made knowingly or recklessly by anybody selling products and services, including holidays and other travel products. Any description

of, for example, a hotel or resort must be truthful at the time it was written (if circumstances change, then the company must inform the customer of the nature of the changes). The Act places a duty on owners and operators of travel and tourism facilities to produce brochures, websites and other promotional materials that are not intended to deceive customers.

Supply of Goods and Services Act 1982 (as amended by the Sale and Supply of Goods Act 1994)

This legislation states that any contract for a holiday should be carried out using 'reasonable care and skill'. The tour operator and travel agent should ensure that the booking is carried out correctly and that the holiday itself should be of a generally satisfactory standard, complying with any descriptions made. Tour operators must take great care when selecting accommodation, transport and any services they provide as part of their package holidays.

Consumer Protection Act 1987

The Consumer Protection Act makes it a criminal offence for an organisation or individual to give misleading price information about goods, services, accommodation or facilities they are offering for sale. The Act defines a 'misleading' price as one which:

- Is greater than the price given in any promotional material;
- Is described as being generally available, but in reality is only available in certain circumstances;
- Does not fully state what facilities are included in the price and the fact than surcharges will be payable after booking.

The Act has special significance for tour operators, which must ensure the accuracy of any price information in their brochures and other online publicity material. This is because it is an offence to include incorrect price information even if the inclusion was innocently undertaken, but is later shown to be misleading.

Unfair Contract Terms Act 1977 and Unfair Contract Terms in Consumer Contracts Regulations 1999

These laws allow customers to challenge any terms in a contract that they consider to be unfair or unreasonable, unfairly weighted against them, or that are ambiguous. Standard contract terms should be written in clear, understandable language. It is illegal to have a contract term that attempts to restrict the customers' statutory rights or avoids responsibility for death or personal injury. In certain cases, the Office of Fair Trading (OFT) may be able to prevent a company from using an unfair contract term in the future.

Contract law

Contrary to popular belief, most contracts do not need to be in writing. From a lawyer's standpoint, a contract is any agreement that the law will enforce, whether in writing, verbal or implied, i.e. assumed from the conduct of the parties. Contracts range from the very simple, e.g. buying a drink at a resort complex, to the very complex, e.g. building a cruise ship. The law of contract is principally concerned with promises that constitute part of an agreed exchange. It governs such questions as which agreements the law will enforce, what obligations are imposed by the agreement and what will happen if the obligations are not carried out.

The following conditions must be satisfied if a contract is to be legally enforceable:

1. There must have been agreement between the parties on all material aspects of the contract;
2. The parties must have intended to create a legally binding contract;
3. There must be at least two parties to the contract.

It is an essential requirement of English law that, for a contract to be legally binding, each party must have agreed to provide something of value to the other. For example, when a customer books a package holiday, but the booking has yet to be confirmed, the contract between the customer and the tour operator may still be legally binding even where he or she has not yet paid for it. The important point is that the customer has promised to pay the price for the holiday when required to do so. The tour operator, by the same token, promises that the holiday is available.

It is important to remember that when a holidaymaker books a package holiday through a travel agent, the contract is between the customer and the tour operator, with the travel agent merely acting as an intermediary. It is against the tour operator that the customer must seek legal redress in the event of a breach of contract, although the travel agent may be liable to the customer for any other extras that are not part of the brochure holiday, such as currency exchange, airport car parking, travel insurance, etc.

Licensing and bonding

All tour operator members of ABTA must provide a bond securing their liability in respect of all forms of transportation, accommodation, travel and holiday arrangements, whether outside or within the UK. The bond is a formal undertaking from an approved bank or insurance company to pay a sum of money to ABTA or the Civil Aviation Authority (CAA) in the event of the company's financial failure. The bond monies are used primarily for the purpose of reimbursing customers who would otherwise lose money that they had already paid, so that:

- Clients whose holidays are actually taking place when a tour operator ceases trading can continue with their holiday as planned or be brought back to the UK;
- Clients who have yet to travel on holidays already paid for can get their money back when an operator fails;
- Alternative holiday arrangements can be made for clients, who have paid for trips that have yet to take place, when a tour operator ceases trading.

For bonding purposes, tour operators are classed as either 'licensable' or 'non-licensable'. Licensable activities are those that require the operator to hold an Air Travel Organisers' Licence (ATOL); all other tour operations are classed as non-licensable. The CAA bonds provided by ATOL holders provide the first line of defence for licensable activities when things go wrong, whereas ABTA bonds provided by members fulfil the same function in respect of non-licensable activities.

Weblink

Check out this website for more information on ATOLs.

www.caa.co.uk

FOCUS ON INDUSTRY

Air Travel Organisers' Licence (ATOL)

An ATOL is a licence issued by the Civil Aviation Authority (CAA) and is required by all individuals and companies selling holidays and seats on charter flights. Applicants must show that they are fit to hold an ATOL, have adequate financial arrangements and must lodge a bond with the CAA. In the event of company failure, the bond money is used to repatriate clients who might otherwise be stranded overseas and to refund, as far as possible, passengers who have paid in advance but have yet to travel. Where the bond is insufficient to meet all claims, the Air Travel Reserve Fund, managed by the CAA, meets the shortfall.

External influences on tour operators

The tragic natural and human events that have occurred around the world since the start of the new millennium serve to illustrate the uncertain conditions that all tour operators face in the course of their work. They have to take into account a range of external influences as shown in Figure 12.3 and described in the following sections of this unit.

Environmental factors

Natural disasters, such as hurricanes, floods and avalanches, can have serious consequences on an area's travel and tourism industry. The tsunami of 26 December 2004 was one of the world's most devastating natural disasters of recent times, killing

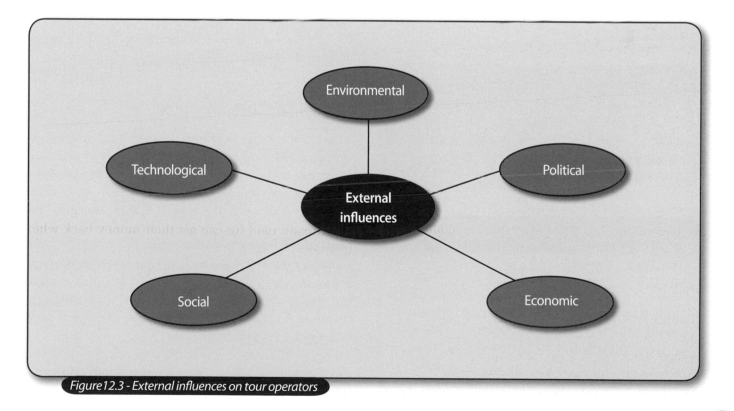

Figure 12.3 - External influences on tour operators

nearly 300,000 people across a range of countries, including Indonesia, the Maldives and Sri Lanka. Reports from the World Tourism Organisation (WTO) suggest a drop in tourism of as much as 70 per cent in the Maldives, when January 2003 figures are compared with those of the same month in 2004. The people in these countries rely heavily on the foreign currency that tourism generates and have worked hard to restore the tourism industry to its former state.

Accidents or deliberate acts of vandalism that lead to oil spillages and chemical leaks can have localised impacts on tourism. The Sea Empress oil spill off the coast of Pembrokeshire in February 1996 had a devastating impact on the county's tourism industry in that year and in subsequent summer seasons. The outbreak of foot and mouth disease (FMD) in 2001 had a devastating impact on tourism in many rural parts of Britain. Research carried out for the Countryside Agency estimated a loss of £2-3 billion in tourism revenue in 2001.

Although it is impossible to predict when disasters of the type described above will occur, tour operators must have contingency plans in place should they be needed.

Weblink

Check out this page of the Federation of Tour Operators' website for advice on crisis management for tour operators.
www.fto.co.uk/operators_factfile/uk_operational_support/

Activity 12.2

Log on to the Travel Foundation's website (www.thetravelfoundation.org.uk) and produce an information sheet on the Foundation's aims, work, structure, partners, etc.

This activity is designed to provide evidence for P1.

Political factors

Political acts such as war and terrorism can have devastating impacts on a destination and its travel and tourism industry. This is particularly true when the destination is heavily reliant on tourism and has few other economic activities. The effects of the 9/11 disaster on world travel still persist today, while recent bombings in Bali, Nairobi, Madrid and Cairo, have immediate impacts on tourism, although most destinations eventually recover lost trade. Strikes and industrial disputes, for example at airports and railway stations, can also disrupt travel and tourism.

Economic factors

Tour operations can be a risky business! A sudden change in world currency exchange rates can wipe out a company's profit margins overnight. Similarly, rises in the cost of oil and other natural resources can push up a tour operator's costs and affect its profitability. Holiday companies use a number of mechanisms to try and reduce the impacts of these situations. They can pay for foreign currency and commodities in advance when rates are favourable and sometimes pass the extra costs on to travellers in the form of extra taxes and duties, e.g. in the form of an aircraft fuel surcharge or holiday supplement.

Social factors

Tour operating companies have to keep abreast of social changes and adapt their products to reflect a changing society. The fact that people are generally living longer, are choosing to have children later in life (or not have children at all), changes in the composition of families, working methods and the home/life balance, all impact on the products and services that tour operators offer their customers. For example, Ocean Village have introduced a greater number of 3-person berths on their cruise ships in response to the growing numbers of lone-parent families buying their holidays.

Tour operators are becoming increasingly aware of the impacts (good and bad) that their activities have on the destinations they use in their tour programmes, in particular how tourism can have harmful effects in areas such as exploitation, poverty, corruption and unemployment. A number of initiatives have been established to try to make tourism in developing countries a force for good, by attempting to alleviate poverty and by promoting sustainable principles and practices. These include the work of the Travel Foundation, Tourism Concern and the Tearfund charity.

Technological factors

The travel and tourism industry has always been at the forefront of new technological developments. The dramatic growth in the use of the internet for researching and booking holidays is having a major impact on the way that tour operators sell their holidays. Trends such as the rise in 'dynamic packaging' (see below) and the computerised reservation systems (CRS) used by travel agents are changing the way that tour operators work.

Challenges to tour operators

We have seen that tour operators work in a very challenging and fast-moving business environment, sometimes having to react to changing circumstances at very short notice. Tour operators also face a range of challenges, as the next sections of this unit describe.

Dynamic packaging

'Dynamic packaging' is when travellers use the internet to research their holidays and make their own travel arrangements direct with airlines, hotels, car hire companies, etc. It offers people greater flexibility than buying standard holidays from a travel agency and can sometimes work out cheaper as well. Dynamic packaging is a serious threat to tour operators and travel agencies, since they stand to lose business to these 'DIY travellers'. ABTA estimates that there were 1.5 million dynamically packaged holidays in summer 2006. Many tour operators, traditional and online, are fighting back by offering customers a more 'tailor-made experience', using new web-based technologies. In effect, tour operators are themselves getting involved in dynamic packaging to maintain their market share.

Distribution channels and integration

New technologies, especially the internet, are having major impacts on the way that holidays are distributed to customers. Traditionally, a person would visit their local travel agency to get advice and book their holiday. This, of course, still happens up and down the country, but travellers are increasingly using the internet to research their holidays and make their own travel arrangements direct with airlines, hotels, car hire companies, etc., the process known as 'dynamic packaging' that we discussed above. The major integrated travel companies are changing the way that they sell their holidays, with fewer high street travel agencies and more investment in internet technologies.

We saw earlier in this unit when discussing integration that many tour operators are part of much bigger travel groups, which own their own their own travel agencies and even airlines. Travel companies become integrated to improve their competitive position in the marketplace and increase their market share by having more control and benefiting from 'economies of scale', e.g. when a travel agency and tour operator are owned by the same organisation, company functions such as purchasing, finance and human resource management can be carried out by fewer staff, thereby reducing costs.

Budget airlines

One of the most important developments in the transport sector in recent years has been the introduction of budget or low-cost airlines, helped by the growth in internet use. The budget airlines, including easyJet, Ryanair, flybe and bmibaby, offer a cheap, 'no frills' service to people looking to travel on a budget. They are able to offer cheap fares by keeping support services to a minimum and selling direct to travellers via the internet and telephone, thereby saving travel agents' commission charges.

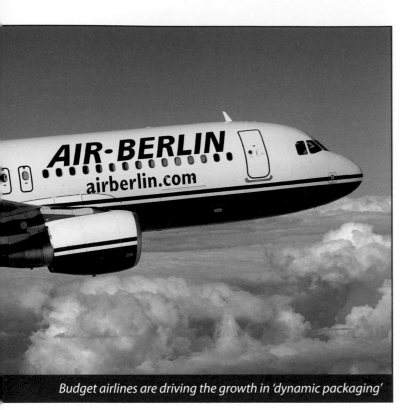
Budget airlines are driving the growth in 'dynamic packaging'

is to do with the fact that travellers are using the low-cost airlines to put together their own holidays – dynamic packaging – by-passing the need for a tour operator's services.

Maintaining market share

'Market share' in tour operations refers to the percentage sales of holidays that a single company achieves. For example, if a tour operator specialising in safari holidays to an African country sells £10 million pounds worth of holidays per year and the total sales of safari holidays to that country is £100 million, the company is said to have a market share of 10 per cent. Maintaining market share is difficult in the competitive travel and tourism industry. Competitor companies offering similar holidays will be constantly looking for ways to increase their market share. Tour operators try to maintain or even increase their market share in a number of ways:

- Through mergers and takeovers – buying a competitor company that offers similar holidays will immediately increase market share and reduce competition;
- By reducing prices – this can increase business and is often used when new companies start up ;
- Increasing promotion – can raise awareness of a tour operator and lead to increased sales;
- Improving quality – this can improve customer satisfaction and increase repeat business and recommendations to friends/family;
- Training staff – allows tour operators to improve customer service.

They also use smaller regional, airports that charge lower landing fees and the airlines sell ranges of add-on products, such as travel insurance, 'phone cards, car hire, rail tickets and accommodation on a commission basis. The low-cost carriers are having important impacts on the work of tour operators, some positive and some negative. On the positive side, tour operators are able to use the network of routes offered by the budget airlines when developing their holidays, thereby offering a greater variety of destinations at reduced prices. The negative impact

Year	Total no. of holidays	% independent	% packaged
2002	39.9m	48	52
2003	41.2m	53	47
2004	42.9m	54	46
2005	44.2m	57	43
2006	45.3m	59	41

Fig 12.4 – Independent travel versus package holidays taken by the British 2002 – 2006

Source: Adapted from www.statistics.gov.uk

Trend towards independent travel

There has been a gradual increase in recent years in the proportion of overseas holidays taken by the British that are arranged independently, rather than taken as package holidays. The data in figure 12.4 shows this trend, with the proportion of package holidays falling from 52 per cent in 2002 to 41 per cent in 2006, while independent holidays grew from 48 per cent to 59 per cent over the same time period. This is linked to the growth in the use of the internet, development of budget airlines and the introduction of dynamic packaging.

Activity 12.3

Write a 500-word newspaper article that explains the challenges facing the tour operating sector and evaluates the effectiveness of two named tour operators that are responding to the challenges.

This activity is designed to provide evidence for M1 and D1.

SECTION 2

Know the range of products and services offered by tour operators for different target markets

This section investigates the different categories of tour operators found in the UK, the products they offer and the different types of customers (target markets) they cater for.

Categories of tour operator

Tour operators come in all shapes and sizes! Most people are familiar with the big, well-known holiday companies that sell millions of holidays abroad every year, e.g. Thomas Cook and Thomson Holidays. Not so well-known are the many specialist operators that provide packaged and tailor-made holidays to meet particular needs, and the domestic operators that sell holidays and short breaks in this country. Incoming/inbound tour operators service the needs of overseas visitors to Britain.

We will look in detail at types of tour operators in the following categories:

1. Outbound – companies that offer holidays for British people travelling abroad;
2. Inbound – tour operators that service the needs of overseas visitors to the UK;
3. Domestic – companies that develop and sell holidays in Britain;

4. Independent – tour operators that are not part of a large, integrated travel company;
5. Specialist – holiday companies that specialise in a particular type of holiday or destination, for example golfing trips or expeditions to the Himalayas.

Activity 12.4

Find out some detailed information on one tour operating company in each of the following categories:

1. Outbound;
2. Inbound;
3. Domestic;
4. Independent;
5. Specialist.

Produce a fact sheet on each company that describes the products and services it provides for its target market(s).

This activity is designed to provide evidence for P2.

Outbound tour operators

Outbound tour operators develop and sell holidays for British people wanting to travel abroad. Some are very big companies that sell millions of holidays every year, the so-called 'mass-market' tour operators, while others are small and medium-sized enterprises (SMEs), employing just a few people.

The mass-market tour operators are amongst the best-known names in the travel and tourism industry, courtesy of their big advertising budgets! In many respects they are the 'supermarkets' of the travel industry, since they sell large volumes of value-for-money holidays to millions of customers every year. The following data from the Civil Aviation Authority (CAA) shows that four tour operators dominated the sale of package holidays for ex-UK tourists in 2006 (numbers of passengers carried):

1. TUI UK/Thomson   4,473,705
2. First Choice   2,445,344
3. Thomas Cook   2,438,244
4. MyTravel   1,802,547

Between them, these four tour operators organised package holidays and flights for just over 11.1 million UK travellers in 2006, accounting for 42 per cent of all such products sold. As we discussed earlier in this unit, TUI and First Choice joined forces in 2007, while Thomas Cook merged with MyTravel in the same year, meaning that TUI UK and Thomas Cook now have an even greater hold on the package holiday market.

As well as offering popular Mediterranean holiday destinations, tour operators are selling more packages to long-haul destinations, such as Florida, the Caribbean, Australia, New Zealand and the Far East, as travellers seek out new destinations and experiences. In recent years, there has also been a gradual move away from traditional package holidays and an increase in demand for more individualised, tailor-made holidays as people become more sophisticated and discerning. This is reflected in the numbers of passengers carried by the mass-market operators, whose numbers have fallen recently.

Another trend is the rise in popularity of internet-based tour operators (e-operators), which offer 24/7 access for customers and the chance for people to put together their own holidays. Leading operators in this field are lastminute.com, Expedia and ebookers. Tour operators are also developing new sales outlets for their products, such as interactive TV and telephone call centres. These trends are making the distinction between tour operators and travel agents less clear.

Case Study

Thomson Holidays

Introduction

Thomson Holidays is Britain's biggest tour operator, selling more package holidays and flights than any other travel company – a position it has held since 1974. It is part of TUI Travel plc, which was formed in 2007 from the merger of TUI UK Ltd, which included Thomson, with another mass-market, UK-based tour operator, First Choice Holidays. TUI UK is the UK's largest holiday company and part of the German-based TUI AG Group, the largest tourism and services group in the world, employing 80,000 people in 500 companies. TUI AG owns many of Europe's best-known holiday brands, including Thomson Holidays in the UK. It has leadership positions in airline, inclusive tour operations and travel agency sectors. The group employs 17,500 people in the UK, Ireland, Sweden, Norway, Denmark and Finland. TUI UK employs around 9,000 people, 7,000 of whom work overseas in some 40 holiday destinations.

History

In 1965, at the height of the boom in demand for package holidays to the sun, entrepreneur Lord Thomson bought three travel and tourism companies – the charter airline Britannia Airways and the tour operators Riviera Holidays and Universal Skytours. His companies continued to trade successfully, as demand for package holidays continued to rise. By the late 1960s, Thomson had introduced winter sun, cruise, and lakes and mountains package holidays to the UK mass market.

It was not, however, until 1972 that the brand name Thomson Holidays was created, when Lord Thomson combined his tour operating brands into one company. The package holidays market was continuing to grow rapidly and Thomson Holidays grew with it. By 1974, two more companies, Sunair and the high street travel agency Lunn Poly, had been brought into the Thomson fold. Thomson Holidays had now become the UK's largest vertically-integrated travel company, carrying out tour operator, transport principal and travel agent functions.

Today, Thomson Holidays sells more package holidays than any other UK-based tour operator, making it the market leader in the air-inclusive holiday sector. Its head office is in London, but the majority of its 3,000 employees work overseas.

Distribution and branding

Thomson's UK retail distribution channels include:

- Thomson travel agencies – more than 730 retail stores;
- Thomson UK's call centre operation;
- Thomson's website www.thomson.co.uk, where customers can research, book and pay for holidays online.

Through these channels, Thomson sells around 5 million holidays and flights per year.

As well as the main Thomson tour operating brand, Thomson's portfolio also includes several specialist and niche holiday brands, including Jetsave, Jersey Travel, Simply Travel, Headwater Holidays, the Magic Travel Group, Crystal Holidays, Thomson Ski and Snowboarding, and Thomson Lakes and Mountains.

Airline operations

For more than 40 years, Britannia Airways has been TUI UK/Thomson's charter airline and the world's leading holiday airline. This changed on May 1st 2005 when TUI UK's aircraft fleet was renamed and re-branded as Thomsonfly, to reflect the single Thomson name that now applies to all parts of the group's operations. This one brand now runs through the company's charter service and its growing low-fares airline Thomsonfly.com. Thomsonfly operates flights from 24 UK airports to over 80

Thomsonfly is a Thomson Holidays' sister company

destinations around the world. Based at London Luton Airport, the airline carried 5 million passengers in 2006 and is now the UK's third largest carrier.

Case Study Questions and Activities

1. What are the advantages to TUI UK of owning its own tour operations, travel agency and airline companies?
2. Log on to the Thomson website (www.thomson.co.uk) and make a list of the different tour operating brands that it offers in the UK. Why do you think it has so many brands available to customers?
3. Analyse how TUI/Thomson's portfolio of products and services meets the needs of its target markets.
4. Recommend how TUI/Thomson could expand its range of products and services for its current target markets or adapt its range of products and services to appeal to a new market.

This case study is designed to provide evidence for P1, M2 and D2.

Weblink

Check out this website to help answer these questions and for more information on Thomson Holidays/TUI Travel.
www.thomson.co.uk

Some material in this case study is reproduced with permission from Travel & Tourism Case Studies by Stephen Rickerby (ISBN 9780955019067).

Inbound tour operators

Inbound, or incoming, UK tourism is concerned with meeting the needs of the increasing numbers of overseas visitors who choose to visit Britain; outbound tourism, on the other hand, deals with UK people taking holidays abroad. Just as we might visit a travel agency to book our annual overseas holiday or business trip abroad, many overseas visitors do the same in their own country when they want to come to Britain. A travel agent in the USA, for example, who has a client wanting to spend a week in Scotland, has to contact a tour operator to make all the arrangements. This operator, who may be based in the USA or in Scotland, is known as an incoming tour operator, since it is providing a service for incoming visitors to Britain. Many incoming tour operators in the UK are members of UKinbound, formerly BITOA – the British Incoming Tour Operators' Association.

Domestic tour operators

Domestic tour operators are companies that specialise in holidays in the UK for British people.

FOCUS ON INDUSTRY

UKinbound

UKinbound was founded in 1977 as BITOA (the British Incoming Tour Operators' Association) and was renamed UKinbound in November 2004. Its main aim is to represent the interests of companies deriving a substantial part of their income from the provision of tours and tourism services for overseas visitors within Britain. UKinbound is concerned with helping its members to manage successful, profitable businesses that are part of a vibrant and sustainable inbound tourism industry. It does this by focusing on three key areas:

- Advocacy – to champion the interests of UKinbound members with government;
- Professionalism – to promote best practice and encourage lifelong learning through training and staff development;
- Networking – to provide opportunities for its members to develop relationships with suppliers, buyers and partners in the UK and overseas.

UKinbound members include Hilton Hotels, Evan Evans Tours and Tours International.

They offer a very wide range of holiday products, from packages in holiday centres such as Center Parcs and Butlins, to coach holidays in all parts of Britain. Many domestic tour operators deal directly with their customers rather than selling through travel agents. This is partly to do with the fact that small, domestic operators are sometimes reluctant to pay commission to agents and also because many British people see travel agents as a place to go to book a holiday abroad. However, there are some domestic tour operators that sell packages through travel agents and pay commission, for example Superbreak, Hoseasons Holidays and Shearings.

FOCUS ON INDUSTRY

Shearings Holidays

Shearings Holidays is a major UK domestic tour operator specialising in coach holidays, aimed primarily at older people – the so called 'grey market'. Shearings is a diversified business providing cruise and air travel holidays as well as coach-based trips. In addition to its 300 coaches, the company's assets include a chain of 44 hotels and 8 high street travel agency shops. Shearings Holidays' core business is in operating coach tours, in the UK, the Irish Republic and continental Europe. In the British Isles, their destinations include London, traditional seaside resorts such as Newquay and Great Yarmouth, countryside areas such as Galway in Ireland and heritage destinations like Stratford-upon-Avon. Shearings also operates coach holidays to 17 different countries on the continent. The company employs approximately 3,000 people and serves a customer base of around three million, mostly in the over-50 age group. About a million passengers travel with the company every year.

Independent tour operators

Independent tour operators are usually small businesses that are not part of larger, integrated companies, such as TUI Travel and Thomas Cook. Because of their size and the experience of their staff, independent tour operators are often able to provide a more personalised service to their customers. Successful independent tour operators are sometimes taken over by larger travel firms, which are looking to expand their operations and reduce competition in the marketplace.

Specialist tour operators

There is a growing demand for specialist tour operators from a travelling public that is looking for something more than the mass-market companies offer. There are literally hundreds of specialist tour operators in the UK travel and tourism industry, including:

- Companies offering holidays and other travel arrangements to a particular geographical region or destination, e.g. Magic of Spain and Magic of Italy;
- Those that cater for a particular segment of the market, e.g. PGL Adventure Holidays for young children and Saga Holidays which specialises in the 'senior' market;
- Operators that specialise in a particular type of activity, e.g. walking holidays offered by HF Holidays and Susi Madron's 'Cycling for Softies', which offers all-inclusive cycling packages to rural France;
- Tour operators that cater for the special interests of their clients, e.g. wine tasting holidays in the Loire and art history tours to Italy;
- Those that specialise in sporting holidays and breaks, e.g. Longshot Golfing Holidays and tours to see the Formula One Grand Prix around the world;

- Companies that use a specific type of accommodation or form of transport, e.g. Eurocamp, which organises self-drive camping holidays in the UK and on the Continent, and operators that offer tours on steam railways, e.g. Ffestiniog Travel.

Many specialist operators join the Association of Independent Tour Operators (AITO) to help their businesses grow and to develop the interests of the sector (there is a case study on AITO in Travel and Tourism for BTEC National Book 1).

Activity holidays are growing in popularity

Activity 12.5

Visit the AITO website (www.aito.co.uk) and choose one tour operator that offers holidays to Europe. Compile a fact sheet that describes the products and services offered by the tour operator, analysing how these meet the needs of its target market(s). Recommend, with justification, how the tour operator could expand its range of products and services for its current target market(s) or adapt its range of products and services to appeal to a new market.

This activity is designed to provide evidence for P2, M2 and D2.

Special interest groups are well catered for by domestic operators. Activity holidays are growing in popularity and tour operators, large and small, are emerging to cater for the demand, for example YHA Holidays, Acorn Adventures, PGL, HF Holidays and Cycleactive. Companies offering specialist services and facilities, ranging from sketching holidays to ballooning breaks, are being increasingly sought by people looking for something unusual to do in their leisure time.

Products

Figure 12.5 shows a breakdown of the main products sold by the four main categories of UK-based tour operators. They all sell package holidays of one type or another, although the mass-market operators we discussed earlier in this unit offer the standard packages that are so familiar today.

Package holidays

The introduction of the package holiday, with its standard arrangement of accommodation, flight and the services of a representative, has been one of the great success stories of the travel and tourism industry in the last 50 years. Sales of package holidays really took off in the early 1970s and have continued to grow ever since, with a slight tailing off in recent years (see Figure 12.6). Low prices have given millions of British people the chance to travel abroad for the first time.

Today, however, package holidays are under threat from the growth of low-cost airlines and the internet, which allow people to assemble their own holidays, bypassing travel agents and tour operators altogether. Increasing numbers of people are looking for the 'unpackaged holiday', individually tailored to their particular needs and desires.

Tailor-made holidays

Tailor-made travel arrangements involve designing all aspects of a customer's holiday on an individual basis rather than selling a ready-assembled package

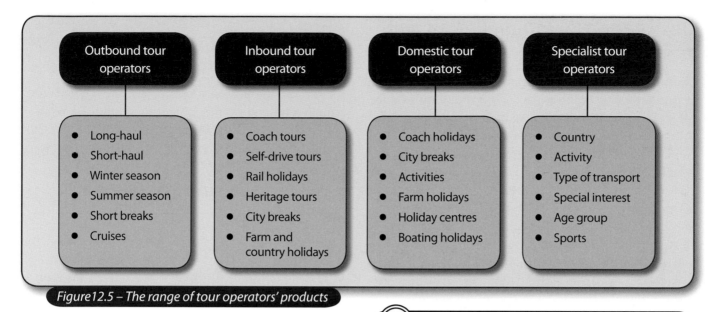

Figure12.5 – The range of tour operators' products

holiday. The customer benefits by getting a holiday that is individually tailored to their needs, but it does mean more work for the tour operator. This type of arrangement is growing in popularity as more people seek out holidays and destinations that offer something different.

More tour operators are using internet-based systems to help them assemble tailor-made travel solutions for

Weblink
Check out this website for more information on National Holidays.
www.national-holidays.co.uk

FOCUS ON INDUSTRY

Tailor-made arrangements at National Holidays

National Holidays specialises in coach-based holidays and short breaks in the UK and Continental Europe. For groups of 30 or more, the company offers tailor-made travel and accommodation arrangements. Members of the group choose the resort, hotel, meal arrangements and excursions, and the company designs the holiday to meet the needs of the group. The group organiser can either discuss arrangements with a member of National Holidays' staff or complete an online form for a quotation.

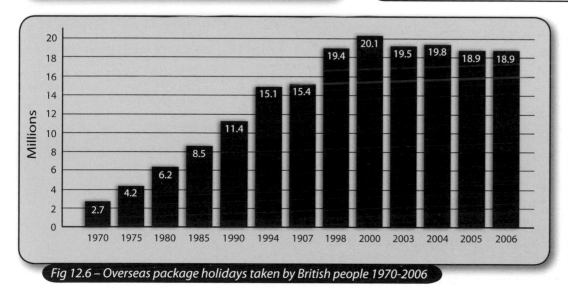

Fig 12.6 – Overseas package holidays taken by British people 1970-2006

customers. This is known as 'dynamic packaging', since it is totally driven by the needs of the customer. This is a trend that will grow as travellers look for a more personal service from tour operators and the companies themselves react to developments in new technology.

Destination, accommodation and transport options

Tour operations has developed a great deal since the introduction of the first package holiday more than 50 years ago. Developments in aircraft technology and reductions in prices have opened up new, long-haul destinations, including Florida, the Caribbean, Brazil, Mexico, Dubai, the Far East, Australia and New Zealand. At the same time, tourist boards have helped businesses to improve accommodation standards by introducing quality grading schemes in destinations. New board arrangements, such as the introduction of 'all-inclusive' hotels and resorts, have given visitors greater holiday choices. In addition to aircraft developments, high-speed rail services, that cut travel times between major cities, continue to be developed across the world. The growth of low-cost airlines, firstly in the USA and Europe but now spreading to India and Asia, is having a considerable impact on travel patterns and the development of new holiday destinations.

Ancillary products and services

The very competitive nature of the tour operations sector means that profit margins on holidays are often very low (and sometimes non-existent!). This means that tour operators look for ways of supplementing their income through sales of ancillary products and services, either in-resort or before their clients travel. The income they make on the sale of add-ons, such as car hire, excursions and travel insurance, can be greater than the profit margin on a holiday, so they are very important to the company.

Target markets

A 'target market' refers to the customers that a tour operator is trying to attract to buy its holidays. Typical target markets for which tour operators develop holidays include:

Activity 12.6

Look through a variety of tour operators' brochures (outbound and domestic) and draw up a list of the different types of ancillary products and services they offer. Make a note of the similarities and differences you find between operators.

This activity is designed to provide evidence for P2.

- Singles;
- Families;
- Couples without children;
- Groups;
- Special interest market;
- Business travellers;
- Youth market;
- Activity market;
- Senior market.

A tour operator may concentrate on a single target market or develop holidays that appeal to a variety of customers. Himalayan Kingdoms, for example, has a very clearly-defined target market – people wanting a trekking holiday in the Himalayas. Thomas Cook, on the other hand, offers a wide variety of holidays to suit a range of target markets, as shown in Figure 12.7.

Product	Brand
Package holidays (upper market range)	Thomas Cook
Package Holidays (lower market range)	Airtours
Direct sell packages	Direct Holidays
Scheduled flight packages	Thomas Cook Signature
Specialist products	Club 18-30/ Neilson/Tradewinds
City breaks	Bridge/Signature/Cresta
Self-catering	Style Villas
Family market	Holiday Resorts/Disneyland Paris
Special occasions	Thomas Cook weddings

Figure12.7 – Thomas Cook holiday products

Companies carry out market research to find out the precise needs of their particular customers and tailor their holidays to meet these needs.

Know how tour operators plan, sell, administer and operate a package holiday programme

All tour operators have to carry out a variety of inter-related functions in order to plan, sell, administer and operate their package holiday programmes successfully. The same basic functions are carried out whether the company is a large, mass-market operator or a small, specialist firm employing just a few people.

Planning a package holiday programme

There are four key elements to planning a package holiday programme:

1. Research and product development;
2. Contracting;
3. Costing and pricing;
4. Brochure production.

The next sections of this unit look at each of these in turn, based on how the functions are carried out in a typical mass-market tour operator.

Research and product development

A great deal of background research is carried out to make sure that tour operators' products have the best chance of meeting their sales potential. Sources of market research data available to help tour operators with this process include:

- Internal sales data – gives a tour operator a clear idea of which products and destinations are in demand and which may need to be scrapped or revised;

- External sales data – available from commercial sources, this information gives a tour operator a 'benchmark' against which to measure its own performance;

- Analysis of competitors' programmes – can be very helpful in identifying new themes, destinations or product opportunities;

- Market research reports – from companies such as Deloitte & Touche, Mintel and Nielsen give useful information on future trends in the tour operating sector;

- Government data – is a useful tool for analysing past visitor numbers to particular destinations overseas, for example using the International Passenger Survey (IPS);

- Analysis of customer satisfaction questionnaires – provides a tour operator with valuable feedback on a range of issues, such as quality of accommodation, customer service standards, price, etc;

- Financial analysis – essential for forecasting future revenue streams and profitability.

Tour operators' research staff work with marketing department colleagues to identify potential new market opportunities, as well as assessing the changing needs, expectations and tastes of past customers. This is achieved by studying sales statistics and market research surveys. They particularly look at the feedback collected from existing customers via CSQs (customer satisfaction questionnaires). Staff try to predict what holidaymakers will want, in terms of which resorts, what type and length of holiday, what standard of accommodation, which departure airports and what price they are prepared to pay.

In large tour operating companies, it is staff employed in the marketing department who are responsible for 'product development', i.e. planning and designing new holidays based on market research findings. They focus on the selection of resorts, choice of accommodation and selection of regional UK departure airports. Planning and

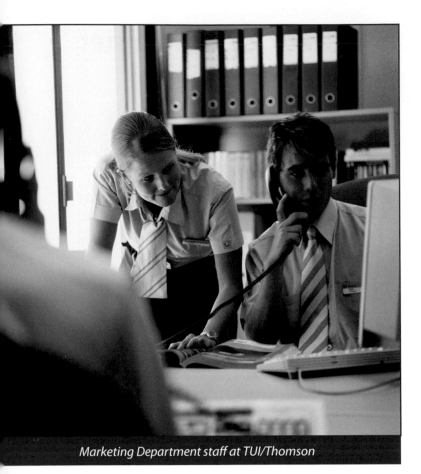
Marketing Department staff at TUI/Thomson

Activity 12.7

Draw a flow chart of the main tasks involved in developing a package holiday programme to a new long-haul destination in South America. Include timescales and staff/departmental responsibilities in your chart.

This activity is designed to provide evidence for P3.

organising a holiday programme does not happen overnight. Staff in the marketing department often start making plans for a season 12-18 months before the holidays go on sale. The first task is to assess the total number of holidays that will be taken during a season by all UK holidaymakers. Having calculated this total market figure, individual Brand Managers or Product Managers decide what share of the market it is realistic to sell – the programme capacity. Having decided on the capacity of the programme, detailed planning on how many holidays should be arranged in each resort and what accommodation and flights are needed can begin. Marketing staff are also responsible for the key activity of pricing the holidays, which can be very risky given the advance planning necessary before the launch of a programme and the potential for fluctuations in currency exchange rates and fuel prices.

Contracting

Once the structure of a tour operator's programme is finalised, staff in the contracts department negotiate with accommodation providers over the number of beds and type of accommodation required. This function is often the responsibility of senior management, under the direction of the Overseas Regional Manager, who may be assisted by specific Product Managers. The staff involved in contracting the accommodation and related services have to negotiate on price, quantity and quality, within a very competitive environment. It is likely that other mass-market operators will be using the same hotels in their programmes. An operator may try to negotiate exclusive use of particular accommodation, but this will involve a financial commitment on behalf of the operator that it may not be willing to risk.

There are three main types of contracts used in tour operating:

- Commitment/guarantee – where the tour operator guarantees to pay for a certain number of bed spaces;
- Allocation and release back – where the tour operator agrees an allocation of a certain number of bed spaces with the hotel and agrees to give back any that it has not sold by a certain date;
- Ad hoc – this is the most flexible arrangement, when a tour operator agrees a contract (discounted) rate with a hotelier and makes bookings as and when required.

Negotiations on contract terms usually start a year before the holidays are sold.

At the same time as accommodation contracting is under way, the flight programmes have to be

Tour operators negotiate contract rates with hoteliers

negotiated, either with their own in-house airline in the case of the large operators, or with charter or scheduled airlines in the case of smaller tour operators. In large tour operating companies, teams working on different programmes and products liaise with the flight or aviation department over how many seats they will need, which regional airports are to be used and whether day or night flights are required. The flight department must make optimum use of its resources, which includes selling spare capacity in the flight-only market. Contracts are generally agreed more than 12 months in advance

Costing and pricing strategies

Section 4 of this unit looks in detail at the process of costing a package holiday (see page 68). Pricing holidays has to be based on the best available knowledge and experience. A mass-market tour operator that sets the prices of its main summer programme holidays too high in relation to its

competitors will not achieve optimum levels of sales. Too low, on the other hand, and it will find it difficult to produce an adequate profit.

There are two basic methods that can be adopted to arrive at the cost of a package holiday programme:

- Cost-based pricing;
- Market-based pricing.

Cost-based pricing involves calculating all the fixed and variable costs of a tour product, including any commission payments to agents, and setting the price at a level which covers all these costs and allows a profit margin. This is the method adopted by small, specialist operators who are unlikely to be operating in such a competitive environment as the mass-market holiday companies and whose products will have a degree of uniqueness. In large tour companies, it is not always easy to work out the exact proportion of fixed costs that should be levied on a tour programme.

Sometimes referred to as 'what the market will bear', market-based pricing sets pricing in a wider context by taking account of what competitors are charging when determining prices. Reissuing brochures with revised prices is now commonplace among tour operators that are constantly checking competitor activity and making adjustments to maintain their market share. Following the market leader's pricing is a risky business, if a company has not fully taken into account its own costs of operation. The hope is that the economies of scale involved in tour operating will enable the larger operators to reduce their costs, but still allow a profit margin at the end of the day. In reality, pricing a typical package holiday programme is often a combination of both market-based and cost-based approaches.

We have seen that tour operators rely on obtaining the elements of their tour programmes at discounted rates, from suppliers such as hoteliers and airlines, which are happy to negotiate a discount in return for releasing an agreed amount of stock. Discounting is also prevalent at the other end of the distribution chain, namely discounted holidays offered for sale in travel agencies, via the internet and on TV channels. In the past, tour operators often frowned on travel agents that offered cut-price holidays, but in today's very competitive holiday industry discounts are a common way for a travel agent to attract custom and for tour operators to shift unsold stock.

Brochure production

Brochures are amongst the tour operator's most important sales tools, although they often cause storage problems for travel agents! Brochures provide clients with detailed information, images and prices designed to persuade them to make a booking. In particular, brochures aim to:

- Accurately present products and services to the reader;
- Supply product information to travel agents;
- Convey an image of the company;
- Offer a means of booking a holiday;
- Explain booking and contractual conditions;
- Present the information within the bounds of current UK and European Union legislation.

Above all, brochures should be designed in such a way that they have the best chance of converting enquiries into sales. Teams working in a tour operator's marketing department will liaise with brochure production staff to finalise design, copy (the words that are written) and photographs.

Figure 12.8 lists the main stages in the brochure production process for tour operators, starting with the design brief that is given to the in-house or agency designers and ending with the final product distributed to travel agents. It is common for new editions of brochures to be issued with revised prices, but this can cause confusion with travel agents and clients. A lot of brochure printing takes place outside the UK to save on costs.

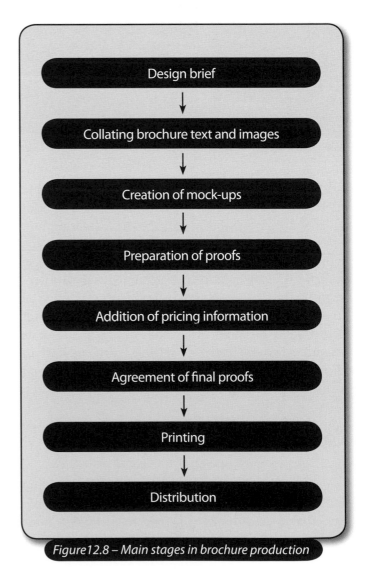

Figure 12.8 – Main stages in brochure production

The ABTA Tour Operators' Code of Conduct lays down the minimum standards for brochures, requiring that they contain clear, comprehensive and accurate descriptions of facilities and services offered. It details rules that govern booking conditions in brochures as they relate, for example, to the cancellation or alteration of tours, holidays or other travel arrangements by the tour operator. The Code also contains strict rules concerning the prompt handling of complaints and regulations relating to the business relationships between tour operators and travel agents.

Weblink

Check out this website for more information on the ABTA Tour Operators' Code of Conduct. www.abta.com

Activity 12.8

Carry out an analysis of six summer sun brochures from different tour operators and rate them on

(1) Overall quality and content;
(2) Use of images;
(3) Style of copy;
(4) Ease of use.

Make suggestions as to how the shortcomings you identified could be put right.

This activity is designed to provide evidence for P3.

Selling package holidays

Tour operators can sell their holidays through a variety of distribution channels, including:

- High street travel agents;
- Online travel companies, e.g. Expedia, lastminute. com, etc;
- Direct to customers via the internet, telephone, television and brochures;
- In conjunction with newspapers and magazines.

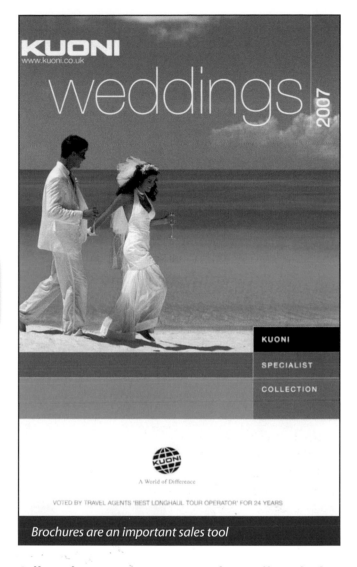

Brochures are an important sales tool

Selling direct to customers tends to offer a higher profit margin for the tour operator, since there are no agents or 'middle men' to pay. Travel agents and online travel bookers require a commission for every sale they make on behalf of the tour operator, i.e. a percentage of the total selling price – normally in the region of 10 per cent.

Promotions

Tour operators must promote their products well if they are to reach their sales targets. In large tour operating companies, marketing department staff plan and co-ordinate a range of promotional activities including advertising in newspapers, magazines, on the internet and Teletext, direct mail, product launches, sponsorship and sales promotion, to ensure that the operators' products are given maximum exposure and sales opportunities. This may be long-term brand support or short-term advertising and promotion. It may involve advertising in both the consumer and trade press, or special point-of-sale (POS) materials in travel agencies to raise awareness of particular products. Sales representatives will regularly visit travel agencies and offer product training and POS materials, such as posters and window displays, in order to maximise sales opportunities. The travel agencies that sell the most holidays will receive particular attention, including enhanced incentives for management and staff to encourage and reward high-volume sales.

Reservations

Tour operators employ reservations staff to handle bookings from travel agents and direct from the

Call centres are growing in popularity

public. Most tour operators, whether large or small, use computerised reservation systems to process bookings, offer alternatives if a first choice of holiday is not available and generate the paperwork associated with a sale. With the growth in the use of the internet for online bookings, which are often confirmed electronically, many reservations staff are now found in call centres, handling high volumes of 'phone calls from agents and the public. Call centre staff are fully trained in the details of the products included in a tour operator's brochure or on its website. Large tour operators have separate reservations teams handling, for example, group bookings, winter ski holidays, cruises and last-minute sales.

Administration

The tour operator's administration department is responsible for producing invoices, receiving payments and issuing tickets and other documentation. Staff also produce passenger lists, known as manifests, for distribution to airlines, hoteliers, ground handling agents and resort representatives, plus carry out the full range of everyday administrative duties associated with the operation of a commercial concern.

Activity 12.9

Working as part of a small group, list the main tasks that would be undertaken by staff in the administration department of a major outbound tour operator. Use your list as the basis for drawing up a job description and person specification for the permanent post of Administrative Assistant for a mass-market operator based in Manchester.

This activity is designed to provide evidence for P3.

Operations

As well as being responsible for researching, planning, costing, promoting and selling package tour programmes as described earlier in this unit,

UK-based tour operations staff have a number of important duties to perform to ensure that holidays run as smoothly as possible, including:

- Managing changes – to travel arrangements and bookings, e.g. overbooking, cancellations, errors, name changes, flight/coach transfers, consolidations (when a flight is cancelled and its passengers are transferred to another), etc;

- Duty office – this is the main link between resorts and UK operations, manned 24 hours a day in case of problems. In extreme cases of emergency, duty office staff can charter aircraft to repatriate customers as the need arises;

- Customer service – handles all aspects of the customer/tour operator interface before departure, in-resort and post-holiday.

In addition to these functions, the UK operations side of the tour operator handles personnel/human resource issues, including all recruitment for the UK and overseas operations, job evaluation, employee appraisal, training, payments to staff and pensions' management, plus all administrative matters related to employees and their welfare. Staff in the finance department handle the flow of revenue into the business and payments to suppliers in the UK and overseas. Senior staff will be responsible for meeting planned sales and revenue targets and managing budgets. The legal department advises on a range of matters, such as the content of contracts, health and safety matters, accuracy of brochure copy and statutory regulations concerning the company and its relationship with customers and suppliers.

Overseas operations

As well as having a general duty to provide a high standard of service to the tour operator's customers while abroad, staff in the overseas office of a major UK tour operator will have a number of specific responsibilities, including:

- Checking passenger manifests (lists of customers travelling);

- Organising transfers to and from the accommodation and airport;

- Selling and arranging excursions and other 'extras' such as car hire;

- Finalising contracts with hoteliers and transport operators;

- The well-being, training and deployment of representatives;

- The handling of complaints and emergencies;

- Crisis management in the event of a major incident;

- Ensuring health and safety procedures are followed by staff and customers;

- Feeding back to the UK office any formal or informal research findings.

Smaller, specialist UK operators may have a small number of permanent employees based in overseas resorts, but will also use the services of seasonal and part-time UK staff. They also rely on the services of specialist individuals and companies in the resorts to provide a range of ground handling services, such as a 'meet and greet' service, coach transfers and welcome meetings for clients.

Activity 12.10

Design an illustrated chart that shows the different roles carried out in the UK and overseas by a major, mass-market tour operator.

This activity is designed to provide evidence for P4.

Be able to plan and cost a package holiday

The final section of this unit gives you practice in planning and costing a typical package holiday, while gaining an appreciation of some of the factors that affect a tour operator's profitability.

Planning a package holiday

Section 3 of this unit has shown that a great deal of time and effort goes into planning a package holiday programme (see pages 61 to 66). Tour operators have to make decisions on:

- Destinations – how many and which to include in a tour programme;

- Transport – what types to offer, plus which departure and arrival points to use;

- Accommodation – location, type, quality and quantity needed;

- Excursions – whether included or optional, what type to meet customer needs;

- Additional services – for example, travel and accommodation upgrades, insurance, car hire, airport parking, etc.

Costing a package holiday

Calculating prices of package holiday programmes is one of the most difficult and risky aspects of the tour operating business. Tour operators have to consider a number of important factors when determining the final selling price of a holiday, including:

- The contracted rates that have been agreed with accommodation providers, airlines, car hire companies, transfer service providers, etc;

- Seasonal adjustments, e.g. low prices for the 'shoulder season' (either side of the peak) and higher prices for peak season demand;

- Load factor on the aircraft, i.e. the percentage of seats that need to be filled before the tour operator breaks even and begins to make a profit;

- Fixed costs, e.g. the cost of hiring a transfer coach is the same regardless of the number of passengers aboard;

- Variable costs, e.g. credit card charges, which will increase as the number of holidays sold increases;

- Indirect costs, e.g. head office overheads;

- Direct operating costs, e.g. the cost of accommodation;

- Profit margins, i.e. the percentage added to the net selling price, covering all indirect costs and allowing for a profit.

Fixed costs are costs that do not alter with changes in the level of business activity, whereas variable costs alter in direct proportion to the volume of business generated by the tour operator. Examples of both types are given in Figure 12.9.

Fixed Costs	Variable Costs
• Rates	• Postage
• Rent or mortgage	• Telephone, fax and internet
• Interest on loans	• Computer and equipment hire
• Bonding monies	• Printing and stationery
• Maintenance	• Advertising and publicity
• Cleaning	• Part-time staff
• Insurance	• Professional fees and charges
• Staff salaries	• Bank charges
• Lighting and heating	• Transaction charges, e.g. credit cards
• Market research	

Figure 12.9 – Fixed and variable costs in tour operations

Costing a package holiday to the Corfu – 14 nights half-board		
Flight costs	£	
26 return flights during the season @ £18,000 per flight	468,000	
Empty leg at beginning and end of season	18,000	
Total flight costs	486,000	
Cost per occupied flight (£486,000 divided by 26)	18,692	
Cost per seat based on 90% load factor on Boeing 737 with capacity of 168 passengers		123.62
Hotel costs per person for 14 nights		190.00
Transfers and handling fees per person		10.75
Total costs of package per person		£324.37
Final selling price (+20% mark-up)		**£389.24**

Figure 12.10 – Costing a package holiday to Corfu

Figure 12.10 shows a detailed costing for a package holiday to Corfu. The direct costs of the holiday are £324.37 per person. The tour operator uses this figure to determine a selling price that covers these costs plus an additional amount (mark up) to cover (1) a proportion of the fixed costs of the holiday; (2) any commission payments to travel agents and (3) a profit margin. The exact price charged will depend on a number of factors, including prices of similar holidays offered by competitors, the cost of the holiday last year and the season in which the holiday is taken.

If we assume a mark-up of 20 per cent, the final brochure price of the holiday to Corfu would be £324.37 + £64.87 = £389.24 per person.

Profitability

The secret of a profitable tour operating business is to keep costs to a minimum while at the same time maximising income – the bigger the difference between the two, the higher the profit! Senior managers must monitor all the costs shown in Figure 12.9 and try to negotiate the lowest possible rates with suppliers, whether they be telephone companies, office equipment companies or banks. Also, they must negotiate the best rates when agreeing contracts with hotels and transport companies. Changes in currency exchange rates can have a serious impact of profitability. Some tour operators buy currency in advance when rates are favourable to offset this. Savings can also be made in the level of commission paid to travel agents. Lowering these commission rates will save the tour operator's costs, but will not be welcomed by the agents. Tour operators can use a variety of techniques to maximise income, for example selling 'extras' such as car hire, airport parking, travel insurance, etc., and investing any surplus funds they may have to earn interest.

Activity 12.11

Your uncle has always wanted to set up a business offering walking holidays in the Pyrenees, after many years of enjoying similar holidays with HF Holidays, Headwater and Ramblers' Holidays. He has asked you to help him research the idea and put together a programme for six week-long tours in May and September. If these go well, he hopes to expand the number of weeks in future years. He will lead the tours himself and take no more than 12 walkers on each tour.

You will need to carry out some in-depth research to address the following points:

1. Which destination(s) to use in the Pyrenees;
2. What transport arrangements to get to the Pyrenees would suit best;
3. What type of accommodation is needed and on what accommodation basis;
4. What excursions and activities should be included in the package;
5. What precise dates and timescales should be agreed.

You can assume that all suppliers will give you discounted, inclusive tour (IT) rates for accommodation, travel, excursions, etc., but as this is a new venture you are only likely to be offered a discount of 25 per cent off their brochure rates, e.g. you will be charged £37.50 for a room that would appear in a hotel's tariff as £50.

Having designed and planned your package, you are now in a position to cost it. As with the example of the package holiday to Corfu on page 69, you will need to calculate all the direct costs of the holiday and add a mark-up of 20 per cent to cover fixed costs and a margin for profit. If you choose to fly your holidaymakers to the destination, you need not worry about load factors as you will be using a scheduled carrier (which could be one of the low-cost airlines).

Points to be bear in mind when costing include:

1. Variations in accommodation and travel prices depending on the season;
2. How your final prices compare with similar packages offered by other operators.

Present your planning and costing of the package as a short feasibility study, including all the information you have collected. Include a section that explains ways of maximising the profitability of the planned package holiday.

This activity is designed to provide evidence for P5 and M3.

Unit summary

This unit has examined the important role that tour operators play in the UK travel and tourism industry. You have examined the links between tour operators and other travel and tourism organisations, and considered the work of trade associations and regulatory bodies. Different categories of tour operators and the products they offer to target markets have been explored in detail. You have seen that planning, selling, administering and operating a package holiday programme is a complex business, often giving only small profit margins. The impact of environmental, political, economic, social and technological factors was discussed in detail, showing how tour operators can have both positive and negative impacts on destination areas. Finally, you were given the chance to plan and cost a package holiday of your own. Throughout the unit you have been shown examples of good industry practice in UK tour operations. The case studies on the FTO and Thomson Holidays gave an insight into the activities of a trade association and a mass-market, integrated tour operator.

If you have worked methodically, by the end of this unit you should:

- Understand the tour operations environment;
- Know the range of products and services offered by tour operators for different target markets;
- Know how tour operators plan, sell, administer and operate a package holiday programme;
- Be able to plan and cost a package holiday.

You are now in a position to complete the assignment for the unit, under the direction of your tutor. Before you tackle the assignment you may like to have a go at the following questions to help build your knowledge on tour operations.

Test your knowledge ❓

1. Why are tour operators sometimes thought of as 'wholesalers'?
2. What is the difference between horizontal and vertical integration?
3. What is UKinbound and what activities does it undertake?
4. Name six members of the Federation of Tour Operators.
5. What is 'consolidation'?
6. What is an outbound tour operator?
7. Why are ancillary sales important to tour operators?
8. Why has the popularity of package holidays fallen in recent years?
9. What is an ATOL?
10. What sources of research are available to tour operators to help them plan their programmes?
11. What is the difference between a tour operator's fixed and variable costs?
12. List the main stages in the production of a tour operator's brochure.
13. Name three environmental and political events have affected tour operators in the last 5 years?
14. What impact is the internet having on the work of tour operators?
15. How do you think the tour operations sector will change in the next 10 years?

Answers to these questions can be found on the Book 2 Tutor's CD-ROM that accompanies this book (ISBN 9780955019050). Full details can be found at www.tandtpublishing.co.uk

Unit 12 Assignment

Tour Operations

Introduction

This assignment is made up of a number of tasks which, when successfully completed, are designed to give you sufficient evidence to meet the Pass (P), Merit (M) and Distinction (D) grading criteria for the unit. If you have carried out the activities and read the case studies throughout this unit, you will already have done a lot of work towards completing the tasks for this assignment.

Scenario

Your local Business Advisory Service has been in touch with your tutors to see if you can help out with a project they are just starting. Staff at the advice service are getting lots of requests for information on setting up travel and tourism businesses, and they would like some students to carry out research and produce some business advice materials. You have been selected to do the work on the tour operations sector.

TASK 1

(a) Produce an illustrated booklet **describing** the UK tour operations environment. Your booklet should be divided into the following sections.

1. Links with other sectors of travel and tourism;
2. Links with trade and regulatory bodies;
3. The tour operators' legal framework;
4. External influences on tour operations;
5. Challenges facing tour operators.

This task is designed to provide evidence for P1.

To be considered for a Merit grade for this task, your booklet should also:

(b) **Explain** the challenges facing the tour operating sector.

This task is designed to provide evidence for M1.

To be considered for a Distinction grade for this task, your booklet should also:

(c) **Evaluate** the effectiveness of tour operators in responding to challenges facing the sector.

This task is designed to provide evidence for D1.

TASK 2

Staff at the Business Advisory Service would like you to design and produce a display that:

(a) **Describes** the products and services provided by different categories of tour operator for different target markets. You must select one tour operator from each of the following categories to complete this task – outbound, inbound, domestic, independent, specialist – and identify their target markets and provide a review of the products and services they offer.

This task is designed to produce evidence for P2.

To be considered for a Merit grade for this task, your display should also:

(b) **Analyse** how a selected tour operator's portfolio of products and services meet the needs of its intended market(s).

This task is designed to produce evidence for M2.

To be considered for a Distinction grade for this task, your display should also:

(c) **Recommend**, with justification, how a selected tour operator could expand its range of products and services for its current target market or adapt its range of products and services to appeal to a new market. You should use the same tour operator that you selected for Task 2 (b) to complete this task.

This task is designed to provide evidence for D2.

TASK 3

Produce two fact sheets that cover the following:

(a) A **description** of how tour operators plan, sell and administer a package holiday programme;

(b) A **description** of how tour operators operate a package holiday programme;

These tasks are designed to provide evidence for P3 and P4 respectively.

TASK 4

Staff at the Business Advisory Service are particularly keen to alert potential new business start-ups to the processes involved in planning and costing a package holiday for inclusion in a tour operator's programme and explaining ways of maximising profitability. They would like you to write a report that includes the following:

(a) An example of a **planned** and **costed** package holiday for inclusion in a tour operator's programme;

(b) An **explanation** of ways of maximising the profitability of the planned package holiday.

These tasks are designed to produce evidence for P5 and M3 respectively.

UNIT 13

Special Interest Tourism

INTRODUCTION TO THE UNIT

Special interest tourism is growing rapidly throughout the world, giving people the chance to enjoy their hobby, learn about cultures or take part in an activity in a holiday setting. Special interest tourism is very wide-ranging and can include a number of different activities – everything from white-water rafting in New Zealand and trekking holidays in the Himalayas to cookery courses in France and art appreciation holidays to Italy. Changes in society, such as the ageing of the population, a greater desire for self-fulfilment, more use of technology, increased concern for the environment and a desire to learn more about different cultures, are fuelling an increased demand for special interest tourism.

In this unit you will learn about the relationship between special interests and tourism, focusing on key motivators in the development of tourism and the interests of consumers. You will also explore the factors that affect participation in special interest tourism, from the industry and participant perspectives. You will investigate the nature of special interest activities in different locations. The unit gives you the opportunity of examining one specific area of special interest tourism in detail, investigating both the providers, locations and the range of services offered.

WHAT YOU WILL STUDY

When you have completed this unit you should:

1. **Understand the relationship between special interests and tourism;**
2. **Know the factors that affect participation in special interest tourism;**
3. **Know the nature of special interest activities in different locations;**
4. **Understand the factors affecting and influencing the tourism provision for a special interest.**

You will be guided through the main topics in this unit with the help of the latest developments, statistics, industry examples and case studies. You should also check out the weblinks throughout the unit for extra information on particular organisations or topic areas and use the activities throughout the unit to help you learn more.

ASSESSMENT FOR THIS UNIT

This unit is internally assessed, meaning that you will be given an assignment (or series of assignments) to complete by your tutor(s) to show that you have fully understood the content of the unit. A grading scale of pass, merit or distinction is used when staff mark your assignment(s), with higher grades awarded to students who show greater depth in analysis, evaluation and justification in their assignments. An assignment for this unit, which covers all the grading criteria, can be found on page 105. Don't forget to visit www.tandtONLine.co.uk for all the latest industry news, developments, statistics and hot links to websites in this unit to help you with your assignments.

Icebreaker

This unit examines special interest tourism, which combines hobbies and interests, social and cultural encounters, sport and adventure activities with tourism. Working by yourself, or in small groups under the direction of your tutor, see how you get on with the following tasks to help you make a start on this unit:

- Try and come up with your own definition of 'special interest tourism';
- List five different types of special interests that people can follow while on a holiday or short break;
- Name three different companies that offer special interest holidays in the UK;
- Make a list of why you think special interest tourism has grown in popularity in recent years;
- Name four regions that are popular for adventure holidays – two in the UK and two overseas;
- Think about the different reasons why people choose to go on a special interest holiday rather than a standard 'sun, sand and sea' package;
- Consider the role of the internet in the growth of special interest tourism;
- Name three different companies that offer special interest holidays abroad.

When you've finished, show your answers to your tutor and compare your answers with what other students in your class have written.

SECTION 1 # Understand the relationship between special interests and tourism

Special interest tourism is one of the fastest-growing sectors of the travel and tourism industry. People are becoming better educated, have more spending power and are seeking out new holiday experiences in their leisure time – cultural, educational, social and adventurous. At the same time, the travel and tourism industry is responding by offering an ever-wider choice of holidays and activities to meet this growing demand, both in the UK and overseas. In the opening sections of this unit we look at the relationship between special interests and tourism, starting with just what we mean by 'special interest tourism'.

What is special interest tourism?

Given that there are so many different interests and activities that people can take part in while on holiday or a day visit, finding a suitable definition of 'special interest tourism' is not an easy task! A simple definition is that special interest tourism is 'tourism with a purpose' – rather than just sitting on a beach or beside a pool, special interest tourists are looking to add something more to their holiday experience. Taking this a little further, we can say that it is a type of tourism that appeals to people who have a particular interest that they with to pursue in a holiday setting – it is often the hub around which their total holiday experience is built.

Special interest tourism covers many different types of tourism, for example:

- Cultural tourism – e.g. visiting a cathedral;
- Rural tourism – e.g. staying on a farm in Devon;
- Activity tourism – e.g. a walking holiday in the Alps;
- Adventure tourism – e.g. bungee jumping in South Africa;
- Food tourism – e.g. visiting the Ludlow Food Festival;

- Wildlife tourism – e.g. whale watching in the Antarctic;
- Health tourism – e.g. staying at a spa hotel in Austria;
- Sports tourism – e.g. travelling to Australia to watch a cricket match;
- Educational tourism – e.g. students on a study visit to Barcelona;
- Ecotourism – e.g. volunteering on a coral reef project in Belize
- Event tourism – e.g. visiting the Olympic Games.

It is important to remember that there is often overlap between these different categories of special interest tourism. For example, a family may visit the Scottish Borders for a cycling holiday – this will be both activity tourism and rural tourism.

Activity 13.1

Using the bullet point list above, draw up a chart that includes the 11 categories of special interest tourism and your own suggestions for three examples of each category.

This activity is designed to provide evidence for P1.

Development of special interest tourism

The 'mass tourism' that exists in many parts of the world today has its origins in the years immediately following the end of the 1939-1945 Second World War, but throughout history, people have travelled the world for purposes of trade, education, religion and to fight in battles. The early origins of tourism can be traced back to pre-Egyptian times, when there was a limited amount of travel associated with festivals and celebrations of a religious or spiritual nature. The early Egyptian civilisation displayed a primitive social structure and rewarded the privileged classes with leisure time to enjoy activities such as dance, music, drama and archery. So, even in Egyptian times, taking part in special interests and activities was an important part of life for some.

The Greeks and Romans

The Greek civilisation was the first to promote the benefits of a healthy balance between work and leisure. There is evidence of travel for purely recreational purposes, with the Greeks hosting international visitors during the first Olympic Games held in 776 BC.

The Romans were keen to promote 'leisure with a purpose' to their citizens. Roman engineers built public leisure facilities for the masses living in urban areas, who practised recreation for physical fitness and in preparation for war. The extensive road network developed by the Romans allowed faster and more convenient travel for business and leisure purposes. There was growth in international travel within the Roman Empire for trade, while the wealthier Romans made visits to friends and relations, and began to appreciate the healing powers of near and distant spa waters for the first time.

The 'Grand Tour'

From 1670 onwards, young gentlemen of the aristocracy were sent on the 'Grand Tour' of the great cultural cities of Europe to widen their education and experiences of life, prior to seeking positions at court on their return home. Cities such as Paris, Venice, Rome and Florence gave these young tourists the opportunity of sampling different cultures and societies. The popularity of the 'Grand Tour' reached its peak in the mid-18th century, but was halted abruptly by the onset of the French Revolution and the Napoleonic Wars.

The rise of spa resorts

Although the medicinal benefits of spa waters had been recognised in Roman times, it was not until the 16th century that their full tourist potential began to be exploited and spa resorts grew in popularity. The healing potential of spa waters became widely accepted amongst the aristocracy, leading to the development of spa resorts in Britain and on the Continent. Towns such as Buxton, Cheltenham, Leamington Spa, Llandrindod Wells and Bath prospered until well into the 18th century. Baden-Baden in Germany was one of the most popular spa destinations in Europe.

Early transport developments

In 1841, Thomas Cook organised his first excursion by train from Leicester to Loughborough for his local Temperance Association. Within 15 years, spurred on by the success of his first trip, Cook was running a fully-commercial travel company arranging tours and excursions both at home and overseas, including visits to the Great Exhibition in London in 1851 and inclusive tours to the Paris Exhibition in 1855. The completion of the Suez Canal in 1869 provided Cook with the opportunity of organising his first tours to Egypt.

In the early 19th century, just as steam power on land was radically changing the patterns of tourism and travel, the same was true at sea, with the introduction of a new generation of steam-powered ships serving North America, the Continent and the Far East. The Peninsular and Oriental Steam Navigation Company (P & O) introduced the first, regular, long-distance services to India and the Far East in 1838. The Cunard Steamship Company started services to North America in 1840. Following his successes in Britain and on the Continent, Thomas Cook organised the first steamship excursion to America in 1866.

The Industrial Revolution

The 1938 Holidays with Pay Act gave a stimulus to mass tourism in the UK, with 80 per cent of workers being entitled to paid holidays by 1945. Holiday camps flourished immediately before the outbreak of the Second World War, the first having been opened by Billy Butlin in 1936 at Skegness. Two years later, there were around 200 camps offering self-contained 'package' holidays to 30,000 people per week. In the early 1950s, two-thirds of all domestic holidays were taken at the seaside and the majority of holidaymakers travelled to their destinations by coach or train.

Tourism developments post-World War Two

The type of 'mass tourism' that is such a prominent feature of life in the 21st century began to develop after the end of the Second World War. Three important elements of post-World War Two society in the UK – the development of jet aircraft, the growth of the overseas package tour and increasing car ownership – were to have far-reaching implications on the UK domestic tourism scene.

Activity 13.2

Read through the first sections of this unit up to this point and make a list of the main factors that you think have had an impact on the development of special interest tourism. One example could be the rise in car ownership in the 20th century.

This activity is designed to provide evidence for P1.

Current developments in travel and tourism

The travel and tourism industry of the 21st century is going through a period of rapid change, influenced by a number of factors, including:

1. Developments in technology – the internet is having a dramatic effect on the way people gather information on holidays and buy travel and tourism products. Technology is also influencing developments in different types of transport;
2. Demographic changes – e.g. the ageing of the population, more lone-parent households, marriage later in life, etc;
3. Lifestyle changes – e.g. more part-time working, search for enlightenment, desire to learn about different cultures and take part in new experiences;
4. Globalisation – the move towards ever-larger corporations with influence that stretches across continents;

The Eden Project is a good example of sustainable tourism

rail networks, growth of low-cost airlines, bigger cruise ships, etc;
- Increase in popularity of long-haul destinations;
- Development of 'niche' products to meet the needs of particular types of holidaymakers, including those with special interests;
- Restructuring of the travel and tourism industry into smaller numbers of larger companies, offering a range of 'brands';
- Higher quality products and better service standards for customers;
- Greater demand generally for travel and tourism products, especially short breaks and additional holidays;
- Development of 'responsible' holidays and travel products that are respectful of the environment and local communities in destination areas.

5. Consumer behaviour – people are demanding higher standards of service and higher quality products;
6. Economic changes – e.g. lower inflation rates, higher levels of disposable income, lower unemployment levels, free movement of people across borders;
7. Environmental issues – e.g. greater concern for the environment, management of the earth's resources and sustainability.

The effects of these factors on the travel and tourism industry in general, and special interest tourism in particular, include:

- Growth in online sales of holidays and other travel products – and the impact this is having on traditional sales outlets, including travel agencies;
- New developments in transportation, e.g. high-speed

Sea kayaking is growing in popularity (courtesy Exodus Travel)

Self-actualisation

The growth in special interest tourism has gone hand-in-hand with a general trend towards people wanting to make something more of their lives, become better people and 'give something back' to the world – this is known as self-actualisation or self-fulfilment. Tourism can help people to achieve their inner-most, spiritual goals.

There are complex psychological influences within individuals that affect their motivation for travel and sway their choice of holidays. Probably the most widely-quoted work on how motivation affects people's actions is that of Maslow, who developed his 'hierarchy of needs' (see Figure 13.1).

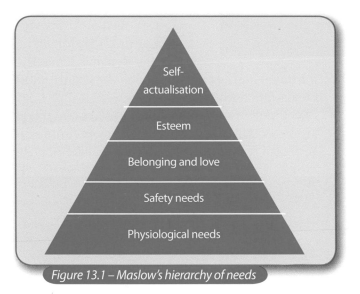

Figure 13.1 – Maslow's hierarchy of needs

In Maslow's model shown in Figure 13.1 there are five levels of needs that an individual seeks to satisfy, from physiological needs at the base of the pyramid to self-actualisation at the pinnacle. Maslow argues that individuals must satisfy certain physiological needs, such as shelter, warmth, water and food, plus safety needs before moving on to the need for belonging and love, esteem and ultimately self-actualisation. Applying Maslow's hierarchy of needs to tourists' motivation for special interest tourism, it is clear that, depending on the particular circumstances of the individual, tourism can satisfy their needs at every level. A holidaymaker, for example, will choose accommodation, hospitality and travel arrangements that meet his or her physiological and safety needs. Special interest holidays can certainly provide opportunities for developing social relationships, thereby contributing towards the need for belonging and love. Tourists sometimes use their travel experiences as a way of boosting their esteem among peers and the fashionable nature of some special interest tourism activities, such as paragliding and kite surfing, can contribute to this. Particular types of special interest tourism experiences may also contribute to a person's achievement of self-actualisation or self-fulfilment, perhaps becoming spiritually enlightened, helping communities in the developing world or learning a new language while on holiday, or taking part in health and spa tourism.

Growth of special interest tour operators

The UK tour operating business has come a long way in the last 50 years, from offering just Mediterranean package holidays to the vast array of specialist holidays right across the world available today. New companies have entered the market to develop special interest tourism, while the long-established, mass-market tour operators have changed their holiday products to reflect the growing demand for specialist interests. It is not uncommon for mass-market tour operators to offer holidays that include cultural visits, activity tourism, wildlife tourism and other special interests, alongside their more traditional 'sun, sand and sea' holidays.

You have learned in other units on your course that the sale of traditional package holidays is in decline, while 'unpackaged holidays', which are tailor-made to individual needs, are growing in popularity. Many of these holidays are based on special interests. This trend towards independent rather than packaged travel is, in part, a reflection of the move for self-actualisation discussed in the last section of this unit.

Integration in the travel and tourism industry, both vertical – where a single organisation owns a range of companies at different levels in the chain of distribution – and horizontal – when an organisation merges with companies at the same level or in the same industry sector – is influencing the way that special interest tourism develops. Large integrated tour operators, like Thomas Cook and TUI/Thomson, buy up smaller, specialist tour companies to increase their market share and reduce competition. TUI/Thomson, for example, has taken over a number of specialist tour operators that used to operate independently, including Headwater Holidays, Simply Travel and Jetsave. This is an example of horizontal integration, since the companies are all in the same sector of travel and tourism. Integration is not always in the best interests of travellers since their holiday choices may be limited.

Role of budget airlines

Budget airlines, such as Ryanair, easyJet and flybe, offer cheap air fares to all parts of Europe. They influence the growth in special interest tourism, since people often combine a cheap flight on a low-cost airline with an activity or other special interest, e.g. taking an easyJet flight to Geneva to ski or mountain bike in the Alps, flying with Ryanair to Knock in the west of Ireland to visit the religious site of Croagh Patrick or travelling with flybe to enjoy the cultural sights of Paris. As the budget airlines continue to grow in popularity, with new destinations being added all the time, so their influence on special interest tourism will increase.

Special interest tour operators

We saw earlier in this unit that the large, integrated tour operators often buy up smaller, independent business to increase their share of the holiday market. Most special interest tour operators are, however, small and medium-sized enterprises (SMEs), employing relatively small numbers of people. Many special interest tour operators are members of the Association of Independent Tour Operators (AITO), a trade organisation that represents their interests and helps to publicise their holidays through brochures, press work and its website.

Weblink
Check out this for more information on AITO and its member companies.
www.aito.co.uk

Most of today's special interest tour operators have an 'online presence', i.e. a website that allows customers to research holidays, sign up for e-mail reminders, browse destinations and book holidays online. The power on the internet means that not having such a presence is a major disadvantage to a travel business, as people come to rely more and more on web-based services. Some specialist travel companies are 'virtual tour operators', only working online and having no face-to-face contact with customers; examples include lastminute.com, ebookers and Expedia.

Kuoni

Introduction

Kuoni is an international tour operating company. Although it operates some short-haul holidays, Kuoni is perhaps best known in the UK as a specialist, long-haul tour operator. Figure 13.2 lists the Kuoni brochures available in the UK marketplace in 2007-8.

Despite major restructuring in 2006-7, Kuoni has maintained its previous level of staffing. Altogether, Kuoni employs more than 7,500 staff in its 300 offices worldwide. This includes 1500 employees in its destination management operations around the world.

History

Kuoni was founded by Alfred Kuoni in Switzerland in 1906 when he added a travel agency to the family freight transport business. Since 1966, Kuoni has been a

Long-haul	Short-haul	Specialist/niche
Worldwide	Swiss Summer	Weddings
World Class *luxury long-haul*	Italy	Wisden Cricket Supporters Tours
Tropical Sun *3-star*	World Class Europe	H2O *water-centred*
Southern Africa		Sandals *Sandals all-incusives*
Dubai		Beaches *Beaches all-incusives*
Sri Lanka		
China		Taj *Taj hotels*
Indo-China		Limited Editions
Seychelles		Lakes and Mountains
Morocco		Sport Abroad: Rugby
Florida		Sport Abroad: Motorsport
Africa and Indian Ocean		Sport Abroad: Cricket
Egypt		Snow
America and Canada		Selections *holidays with Emirates flights*
Australia, New Zealand and South Pacific		

Figure 13.2 – Kuoni's product range in the UK

major long-haul tour operator in the UK market. More recently it has diversified into 'niche markets' by acquiring previously independent specialist tour operator businesses. These have included Voyages Jules Verne, Travel Collection and Sport Abroad – brands which continue to operate autonomously within the wider Kuoni Group. Kuoni UK underwent a major restructuring in 2006-7 (its centenary year) and broadened its product range by purchasing two upmarket touring holiday brands – Journeys of Distinction and Kirker Holidays. This was in line with Kuoni's current strategy of focusing on high quality travel products. It won the 'World's Leading Tour Operator' award in 2006 (for the eighth time) and has been voted 'Best Long-haul Tour Operator' by UK travel agents for 24 years (to 2007).

Distribution and branding

Kuoni owns a range of specialist brands which trade in the UK as autonomous businesses. These include:

● Kuoni Sport Abroad – a specialist sports brand offering supporters tours to major sporting events, such as cricket, rugby, motor sport, horse racing, fishing and golf;

● The Travel Collection – operating tours that are designed to provide unusual travel experiences;

● Voyages Jules Verne – specialising in small group travel to destinations which have special cultural appeal, for example Egypt, China and Italy;

● Journeys of Distinction – up-market, escorted tours to long-haul destinations.

Corporate social responsibility

The Kuoni Group has published its first group-wide Sustainability Report. The report describes the results of several years of commitment to sustainable tourism, and features the results of the Kuoni Corporate Responsibility Strategy, which has been implemented in steps since September 2006. Kuoni's approach is rooted in enhancing the positive impacts of tourism, whilst mitigating tourism's negative aspects. The report includes descriptions of projects, partners and problems, as well as the achievements made so far and the company's plans for the future. Further details are available at the Kuoni Group website www.kuoni-group.com.

? Case Study Questions and Activities

1. Why do you think Kuoni concentrates on providing high quality holidays to the upper end of the market?
2. Log on to Kuoni website www.kuoni.co.uk and make notes on the full range of special interest activities the company offers its customers.
3. How do you think the growth in the use of the internet will affect Kuoni and the sales of its holidays?
4. Assess the current market for special interest tourism, identify gaps in provision and suggest potential new products that Kuoni could develop.

This case study is designed to provide evidence for P1, M1 and D1.

Weblink
Check out this website to help answer these questions and for more information on Kuoni.
www.kuoni.co.uk

Some material in this case study is reproduced with permission from Travel & Tourism Case Studies by Stephen Rickerby (ISBN 9780955019067).

Special interests

As people become better educated, have more disposable income and make more use of new technology, the range of special interests that many want to experience grows all the time. Taking part in special interests in their leisure time gives people a sense of achievement, may help to keep them fit and can forge new friendships. Special interests can be categorised into three different types, as shown in Figure 13.3.

Figure 13.3 – Types of special interests in tourism

Passive activities are those that require very little physical effort from those who take part and include:

- Painting;
- Cooking;
- Reading;
- Arts and crafts;
- Taking part in drama;
- Spiritual experiences;
- Sports spectating;
- Watching television and listening to the radio.

Active pursuits, where physical effort is required from the participants, include:

- Team events such as playing football and cricket;
- Walking;
- Cycling;
- Camping and caravanning;
- Youth camps;
- Orienteering;
- Sailing;
- Horse riding.

Adventurous activities take active pursuits one stage further, by adding a degree of danger when taking part. These 'extreme sports' as they are sometimes known include:

- Climbing and abseiling;
- Airsports, e.g. paragliding, parascending, flying, sky diving;
- Canoeing;
- Diving;
- White water rafting;
- Canyoning;
- Surfing and kite surfing;
- Bungee jumping;
- Mountain biking;
- 4 X 4 motorised activities.

Popularity of special interests

It is difficult to estimate the total numbers of people taking part in special interests and activities in the UK, given that there are so many different types. The Office for National Statistics collects data on participation in leisure and sports activities as part of the General Household Survey (GHS) and, in 2002, the survey found that 75 per cent of all adults had taken part in some type of sport, game or physical activity during the 12 months prior to interview. Another measure of the popularity of special interests is the growth in membership of organisations such as the National Trust, Royal Society for the Protection of Birds (RSPB), English Heritage, Ramblers' Association, Cyclists' Touring Club and the many wildlife trusts and local conservation groups across the country.

Diving (courtesy Exodus Travel)

Passive activities

Figures from the General Household Survey show that participation in passive activities in 2002 by those interviewed was as follows:

- 99 per cent watched television;
- 88 per cent listened to the radio;
- 83 per cent listened to records/tapes;
- 65 per cent read books;
- 11 per cent sang or played a musical instrument;
- 11 per cent danced;
- 9 per cent painted or did drawing, printmaking or sculpture;
- 4 per cent wrote stories, plays or poetry;
- 3 per cent helped with the running of an arts/cultural event or organisation on a voluntary basis;
- 2 per cent performed in a play, drama or rehearsed for a performance.

The trend over a 30-year period shows that participation in most passive activities has increased, but dressmaking, needlework and knitting have decreased in popularity.

Active pursuits

Statistics from the same GHS survey indicate that the five most popular activities undertaken in 2002 (with participation rates in brackets) were:

1. Walking   (43 per cent)
2. Swimming   (35 per cent)
3. Keep fit/yoga   (22 per cent)
4. Cycling   (19 per cent)
5. Billiards/snooker/pool   (17 per cent)

Compared with the other activities, keep fit/yoga was the most likely activity to be done regularly. Eight per cent of adults said that they had taken part in keep fit/yoga four or more times over a four-week period, while three per cent said that they participated in it twelve or more times over the same period. Swimming was the next most frequent activity. For the first time in 2002, interviewees in the General Household Survey were asked which activity that they currently do not take part in would they like to try. The most popular activities mentioned were:

1. Swimming   (13 per cent)
2. Keep fit/yoga   (12 per cent)
3. Golf   (5 per cent)
4. Skiing/snowboarding   (5 per cent)
5. Horse riding   (5 per cent)

Adventurous activities

Adventurous activities combine active pursuits with an element of danger. We saw earlier that these include airsports, land and water-based activities. There are no comprehensive figures on participation in adventurous activities in the UK. The United Kingdom Tourism Survey (UKTS) includes data on participation in some types of adventurous activities, including watersports and climbing. Figures for hill walking and mountain biking are, however, included in more general walking and cycling categories, and UKTS includes no data on motorised adventure sports. An article in the March 2003 edition of Insights (VisitBritain) points out that the UKTS data that is available indicates that:

- Over 10 per cent of UK holiday trips involve participation in adventurous activities (15 per cent in Scotland and 17 per cent in Wales);
- At least 11 million UK holidays each year include taking part in some type of adventurous activity;
- Annual spending by UK holiday visitors who take part in adventurous activities during their stay is at least as much as £2 million;
- Adventure holidays currently account for approximately 4 per cent of all UK holidays.

Research quoted in the same article suggests that hill walking, non-motorised watersports (in particular canoeing, surfing, windsurfing and dinghy sailing), climbing and mountain biking are currently the most popular adventurous activities in the UK. Other types of adventurous activities (caving, motorised watersports, motorised land sports, diving, airsports and other land-based activities) appear to be much more 'niche' products, appealing to very specific sectors of the market. Some adventurous activities,

Adventure tourism in action (courtesy Outward Bound Trust)

- The growth of budget airlines – leading to new opportunities for special interests in different destinations;
- Increases in leisure time and longer paid holidays – resulting in a general growth in tourism and travel;
- Rise in car ownership – giving people the chance to explore new destinations independently and gain access to a wider range of special interests;
- Growth in the use of the internet – allowing people to investigate new interests and holiday products, and take part in 'dynamic packaging' – assembling the different parts of a holiday (accommodation, travel, car hire, insurance, excursions, etc.) independently rather than buying a standard package;
- Changes in education – offering young people the chance to take part in UK and overseas educational trips, resulting in the growth of educational tour operators;
- The rising interest in self-actualisation – leading to new holiday experiences, e.g. spa and health tourism.

such as rope courses and quad biking, often have more appeal as part of a multi-activity holiday or as incidental holiday activities.

Relationship between special interests and tourism

Having considered key aspects of the development of tourism and identified a range of special interests, we are now in a position to bring these together by examining the relationship between special interests and tourism. It is perhaps not surprising that people want to carry on their special interest or activity while on holiday, particularly if it is in a warmer climate! People who participate in specialist interests and activities can be very inquisitive by nature, wanting to learn about different areas, meet new people and take part in new experiences. All the available evidence on special interest tourism is that it is a major growth area of the travel and tourism industry – meeting the specialist needs of increasing numbers of travellers. There is a general trend away from traditional package holidays to more specialist holiday experiences, witnessed by an increasing number of specialist tour operators.

Specific relationships between special interests and tourism include:

The wide variety of special interest tourism products on offer is the result of the industry responding to the very different motivations of individuals – it is a very customer-led sector of the travel and tourism industry. For example, special interest tourism can be associated with somebody wanting to:

- Learn a new skill or activity;
- Attend a sports event;
- Take part in adventures;
- Relax and investigate self-improvement;
- Learn about nature, wildlife and the environment;
- Investigate different cultures.

These motivations, with examples of associated special interest tourism products, are shown in Figure 13.4. The examples of special interest tourism products given in the table are by no means exhaustive, but give a flavour of how different motivations are satisfied by particular products and services.

Motivation	Special interest tourism products
Learning a new skill or activity	Watercolour painting holidays Spinning and weaving tours Wine tasting tours Cookery holidays Pottery holidays
Attending sports events	Motor racing Grands Prix trips Tours to football matches in Europe Wimbledon Lawn Tennis Championships Corporate hospitality at the FA Cup Final Holiday packages to the Ryder Cup
Taking part in adventures	Mountain trekking holidays Quad biking events Canyoning Bungee jumping Kite surfing
Self-improvement and relaxation	Spa tourism Pilgrimages Yoga holidays Health breaks Retreats
Learning about wildlife, nature and the environment	Wildlife safaris Conservation holidays Whale watching tours Walking holidays Bird watching tours
Investigating heritage and culture	Cultural holidays Industrial heritage tours Art appreciation holidays Garden tours Farm holidays

Figure 13.4– Motivations and products in special interest tourism

The great majority of the types of special interest tourism products shown in Figure 13.4 are provided by private sector enterprises – companies that are in business to make a profit for their owners and/or shareholders. These are a mixture of small, independent tour operators and large, integrated travel companies. Public and voluntary sector providers also play a role in special interest tourism by, for example, organising conservation holidays, educational trips, heritage holidays and garden tours.

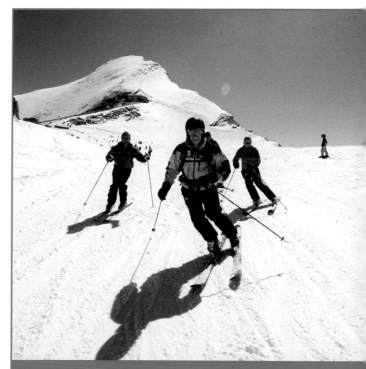

Skiing is a great way to keep fit (courtesy Ski Club of Great Britain)

Activity 13.3

Research and write a newspaper article of 750 words that assesses the current market for special interest tourism, identifies gaps in provision and suggests potential new products that could be developed.

This activity is designed to provide evidence for D1.

Know the factors that affect participation in special interest tourism

Special interest tourism is a very dynamic sector of the travel and tourism industry. New products are being developed all the time and people are keen to try out new experiences as soon as they are developed. In this section we look at the factors that influence whether or not people take part in special interest tourism and, if they do, what affects their choice of special interest or activity. Some of these factors are specific to the industry (industry factors), while others are concerned with the characteristics of the tourists themselves (participant factors).

Industry factors

Factors that organisations working in the special interest tourism sector need to take into account include:

1. Market segmentation;
2. Developing attraction and appeal;
3. Social changes and trends;
4. Consumer behaviour;
5. Flexible provision in new locations.

Market segmentation

Market segmentation is the process of dividing the total market for a product or service, i.e. all the people who could buy it, into different 'segments', each with broadly similar characteristics. Holiday companies carry out segmentation because it allows them to focus more clearly on the needs and expectations of particular groups, for example older people, young people wanting an activity holiday of high spenders looking for the ultimate in luxury while on holiday. Special interest tourism lends itself particularly well to market segmentation, since it is made up of very many specialised interests and activities. Figure 13.5 shows how market segmentation can be applied to the special interest tourism sector – six popular areas have been selected, each made up of providers that try to match the segments' needs to the products they offer.

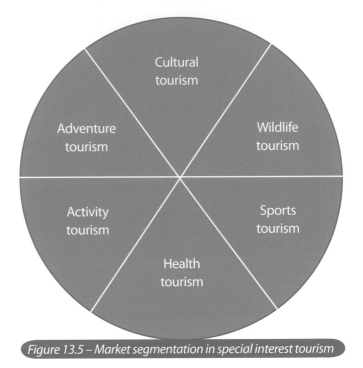

Figure 13.5 – Market segmentation in special interest tourism

The 'wildlife tourism' segment, for example, offers products such as whale watching tours, wildlife safaris and jungle expeditions to a variety of clients. Segmenting the market for special interest tourism is not always straightforward and there is often overlap between sectors. For example, taking part in a tour of spa towns in Europe could be both health tourism and cultural tourism. The important point is that companies are clear about the products they offer and the needs of their particular customers.

Developing attraction and appeal

Special interest tourism is in many respects an 'unpackaged holiday' – companies often tailor holidays to customers' particular requirements rather than selling something 'off the shelf'. The specialist nature of some activities often makes it impossible to offer a standardised holiday product. Companies work hard to make their products as appealing as possible to their target audience, using a variety of promotional techniques, including brochures with high quality images of activities and special interests. The internet is a particularly useful tool for providing information and selling special interest tourism holidays and breaks, given that the customers for special interest tourism tend to be very computer-literate.

The media plays an important part in stimulating demand for special interest tourism. The growing numbers of terrestrial and digital TV channels showing programmes covering a variety of special interests, from gardening and watercolour painting to custom cars and cookery, are partly responsible for the increasing popularity and appeal of special interest tourism. Specialist magazines and newspaper articles also play an important role in stimulating demand.

Social changes and trends

'Demographics' is the term used to describe the characteristics and trends of the population, for example age, family composition, gender and ethnicity. It is important for special interest tourism companies to monitor changes in demographics and changes in society so that they can either adapt their products to changing circumstances or even introduce new products in a growth area. Some of the most important demographic and social changes that are occurring in the UK include:

- The ageing of the population;
- More lone-parent households – the proportion of children living in lone-parent families more than trebled between 1972 and 2004;
- Marriage later in life – the average age for first marriages in 2003 was 31 for men and 29 for women, compared with 26 and 23 respectively 40 years ago;
- More part-time and flexible working;
- Increased working from home.

The ageing of the population is perhaps the most significant of all the demographic changes taking place in the UK today. Figures from the Office for National Statistics (ONS) show that the proportion of the population aged 65 and over has increased over the last 30 years, while the proportion below 16 years of age has fallen. The percentage of people under 16 fell from 25 per cent in mid-1971 to 19 per cent in mid-2004, whereas the proportion of people aged 65 and over rose from 13 per cent to 16 per cent over the same time period. Also, older people are living longer – the proportion of people aged 85 and over increased from 7 per cent in mid-1971 to 12 per cent in mid-2004. These figures are important for the special interest tourism sector, which can look to the future in the knowledge that there will be more older people with the time to take part in all types of special interests and activities while on holiday. It is not such good news for companies that offer special interest products aimed at children and young people, since the proportion of the population in younger age categories is falling.

Activity 13.4

Carry out some research into three companies that offer holidays aimed at older people. Make notes on the types of products they offer, destinations used and activities/special interests catered for. Explain how the companies meet the needs of this particular group of tourists in their products and services.

This activity is designed to provide evidence for P2.

Consumer behaviour

We have seen that society is changing rapidly in the UK, with greater use of new technology, increased disposable incomes, changes in population characteristics and different work patterns. These changes are altering the purchasing behaviour of consumers in many ways. People expect to be able to buy products easily and quickly, whether in a shop or online, they are looking for high quality products and services, good value for money and 24/7 access to facilities whenever possible. These same requirements apply equally well to all types of tourist products, including special interest tourism. Companies must strive to meet customer needs at all stages of the holiday experience, from initial enquiry through to the departure for home.

Flexible provision in new locations

We discussed earlier in this unit that special interest tourism lends itself well to independent travel rather than package holidays. As the nature of special interest holidays become more specific and complex – in order to meet travellers' changing demands and expectations – so the industry must provide more flexible arrangements rather than 'off-the-shelf' packages. This increasingly involves 'dynamic packaging', when customers use the internet to assemble their own holidays or ask a travel agent to do it on their behalf.

Special interest tourists who are looking for something new on their travels often seek out new locations around the world that have not previously been popular as tourist destinations, including the following from ABTA's list of 'hot destinations for 2008':

- China;
- Singapore;
- Columbia;
- Israel;
- United Arab Emirates;
- Dubai;
- Oman;
- Syria;
- Canada;
- Botswana;
- Siberia.

Encouraging tourism to new destinations is good for the countries concerned, since it helps the local economies. However, tourism must respect local cultures and traditions in these host destinations if it is to be sustainable in the long term.

Participant factors

Factors that can influence special interest tourism from the customers' point of view include:

1. Socio-economic factors and new challenges;
2. Political stability and security;
3. Motivation and self-actualisation.

Skydiving is an extreme type of special interest tourism (courtesy High & Wild Adventure Travel)

Socio-economic factors and new challenges

A person's disposable income, i.e. what is left over after all necessary expenses have been met, influences their choice of holiday, short break or day trip. Clearly, the more disposable income a person has, the more they have available to spend on their holiday. We saw earlier in this unit that special interest tourism is a 'niche' product, i.e. it appeals to small, specialist groups of people with particular interests. Research shows that people who take part in specialist interest tourism generally have higher levels of disposable income than the population as a whole, tend to be younger and are in professional occupations. Some people say they are 'money rich, but time poor' because although they earn good salaries, they have little leisure time in which to spend their money. They tend to take part in challenging, active pursuits for short periods of time. Retired professional people are also attracted to special interest tourism and, as well as having the time, also have reasonable levels of disposable income.

Some types of special interest tourism activities are considered to be very fashionable and appeal to people who relish a challenge, value status symbols and like to impress their friends! Activities like sky diving, bungee jumping, kite surfing and paragliding fall into this category. The introduction of outdoor clothing into high street fashion, the growing numbers of adventure sports magazines and increasing coverage of special interests and activities on TV, all illustrate the fashionable image associated with some types of special interest tourism.

Political stability and security

As with all kinds of tourist activity, special interest tourism needs a secure and stable political situation in a country or destination in order to prosper. Areas that have been the scene of terrorist attacks or civil wars cannot hope to attract and retain special interest tourists. Some types of special interest tourism, particularly adventure and exploration activities, take place in remote parts of the world that are prone to political unrest. Companies that operate in these areas, as well as their customers, need to be kept fully aware of the situation at all times and follow the advice from the Foreign and Commonwealth Office (FCO) on whether or not it is safe to travel.

Weblink
Check out this website for the latest information on safe travel abroad.
www.fco.gov.uk

Motivation and self-actualisation

Motivation to take part in an activity or special interest is clearly a very important aspect of special interest tourism – the more motivated a person is, the more likely that he or she will follow their interest. Figure 13.4 on page 87 gave some examples of what motivates people to take part in special interest tourism, but motivation is a complex subject. There are complex influences at work within individuals that affect their choice of holidays, as the section of this unit on self-actualisation, including Maslow's hierarchy of needs, demonstrated (see page 80).

Activity 13.6

Choose one of the special interest tourism products from Figure 13.4 on page 87 and write a short report on the factors (industry and participant) that influence participation in the activity.

This activity is designed to provide evidence for P2.

Know the nature of special interest activities in different locations

This section investigates the nature of special interest tourism activities and where they take place. It includes case studies on two specific types of special interest tourism – cycling tourism, and health and spa tourism – which you will find useful when completing your assignment for this unit. You can also find a case study on adventure tourism on page 101 As well as considering the nature and location of these activities, each case study includes information on companies and organisations that operate in each of these specialist markets.

Nature of activities

We saw earlier in this unit that people take part in many different activities during their leisure time – some passive, some active and some involving a degree of risk or danger (see pages 83 to 86). The types of activities included in special interest tourism can be divided into three categories – those that take place on water, land-based activities and airsports, as shown in Figure 13.6.

People can take part in these activities in many different circumstances – on an individual basis, as part of a group or as a member of a team or club, for example:

- Individual – completing a long-distance cycle ride for charity;
- Group – some friends on a sailing holiday in Greece;
- Team – members of a hockey team visiting Germany for a tournament.

Activity 13.7

Choose three different types of special interest tourism and describe the occasions when a person may take part in each activity (1) on an individual basis; (2) as part of a group; (3) as a member of a team or club. Name companies or organisations that provide products and services for each of the activities and circumstances that you have described. Present your findings as a chart.

This activity is designed to provide evidence for P3.

Purpose

We saw earlier in this unit that there are many different reasons why people want to take part in special interest tourism (see Figure 13.4). These motivations include:

- For educational reasons – e.g. a group of garden enthusiasts visiting the Royal Horticultural Society's gardens at Wisley in Surrey to learn about varieties of fruit;
- To explore different cultures – e.g. a backpacker spending a gap year in Thailand to work and learn about Thai culture;
- For reasons of discovery – e.g. a couple going on a cruise in the Norwegian fjords;
- To pursue a hobby – e.g. a person attending a watercolour painting course in Provence;

Land-based	Water-based	Airsports
Visiting historic sites	Canoeing	Hang gliding
Quad biking	Kayaking	Paragliding
Mountain trekking	Sailing	Sky diving
Art appreciation	Surfing	Gliding
Pottery	Windsurfing	Flying
Cycling	Kite surfing	Parachuting
Walking	Canyoning	Bungee jumping
Bird watching	Scuba diving	
Visiting spas	Jet skiing	
Visiting gardens		

Figure 13.6 – Types of activities in special interest tourism

- To face a challenge and danger – e.g. abseiling in the Swiss Alps or sky diving in the USA;
- For excitement – e.g. a family holiday to the theme parks in Florida;
- For relaxation – e.g. a family enjoying a short break at a health spa.

Location of activities

Special interest tourism takes place in many different indoor and outdoor settings, in the UK and abroad. Adventure and activity tourism often makes use of natural resources, so is usually located in countryside and coastal areas. Access to locations is important, both from the point of view of guest convenience in reaching the facility and the need for swift access by the emergency services in the event of an accident or incident. Distance from major centres of population is a consideration for special interest tourism providers, with those located close to cities benefiting from increased trade. Climatic considerations are important in some types of special interest tourism, for example winter sports, sailing, surfing, flying, gliding, etc.

Some adventure tourism activities take place under cover, for example in centres with 'all weather' facilities, such as indoor climbing walls. Special interest tourism concerned with hobbies or learning a new skill, for example cooking, painting, pottery, stained-glass making, spinning and weaving, may need purpose-built facilities.

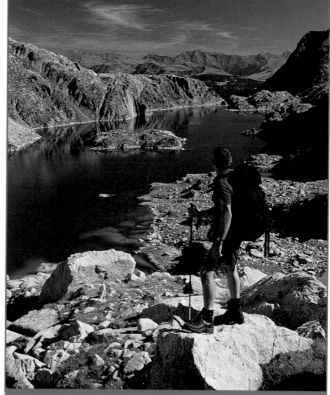

The High Pyrenees is a spectacular location for special interest tourism (courtesy Exodus Travel)

Activity 13.8

Carry out some research on three different special interest tourism activities – one passive, one active and one adventurous – and locate on a map of the world 10 key destinations where the activities are offered by tour operators.

This activity is designed to provide evidence for P4.

Case Study

Cycling tourism

Introduction

Cycling tourism can be defined as a holiday or day visit that involves participation in cycling, either as a primary or secondary purpose of the visit. It is an environmentally sustainable type of tourist activity, which has minimal negative impact on the environment and local communities. It can also make a positive contribution towards encouraging visitors to use their cars less and makes good use of under-utilised and redundant resources, such as by-roads and disused railway lines. It also generates income for a variety of tourism businesses and destination areas, helping to create jobs and contribute to economic development. A recent study in Scotland has shown that cycling is worth £39 million to the economy of the Highlands and Islands region, while in Wales, cycling currently contributes £18 million to the economy, a figure that is forecast to double by the end of the decade.

Nature of the activities

There are a number of different types of cycling tourism 'products', for example:

Cycling on the NCN route 64 near Lincoln(courtesy Sustrans/Paul Rea)

1. Family cycling – all members of a family can enjoy the benefits of cycling while on holiday or a day trip;
2. Off-road cycling – tends to appeal to younger people looking for a challenge on mountain biking routes;
3. Cycle touring – holidays covering long distances in the UK and overseas, with overnight stays en route, perhaps using the National Cycle Network (NCN);
4. Cycle racing – combining racing with a holiday, for example a group of UK enthusiasts following the route of the Tour de France.

Cycling tourism products take different forms, for example:

- A cycling holiday or short break – where cycling is the main purpose of the trip;

- Cycling for a short period while on holiday – perhaps hiring a bike for half a day;

- A day visit that involves cycling – for example, visiting a forest area with mountain biking trails.

Location and destinations

The great appeal of cycling is that it can take place virtually anywhere. In the UK, cycling tourism takes place along country lanes, disused railway lines and canal towpaths, as well as in forests and moorland areas. It is particularly popular in National Parks, where many authorities promote cycling as way of reducing the number of cars in the parks. The National Cycle Network is a countrywide series of signed cycling routes linking communities to schools, stations and city centres, as well as to countryside areas. Co-ordinated by the charity Sustrans, the network currently extends to 10,000 miles of routes throughout the UK, with further expansion planned.

There are increasing numbers of companies that offer cycling holidays in European countries, especially France and Spain. Regions such as the Loire, Dordogne, Brittany and northern Spain are popular with cycle tourists from the UK. Mountain bikers travel to areas such as the French Alps in the summer, riding on the runs that are used for skiing in the winter. Outside of Europe, cycling tourism is more of a specialist activity, but it is possible to book a cycling holiday to South America, Africa, Thailand, India and even cycle across Russia! Many charities organise long-distance bike rides to attract sponsorship.

Cycling in France (courtesy Headwater Holidays)

Cycling tourism providers

The increasing popularity of cycling in recent years has led to an increase in the numbers of providers. Most are private companies offering a specialist service on a relatively small scale, but many of the large, well-known tour operators now offer activities, including cycling, as part of their holiday packages. Examples of specialist cycling tourism providers offering holidays in the UK and overseas include:

- Bicycle Beano Cycling Holidays (www.bicycle-beano.co.uk);
- Cycleactive (www.cycleactive.co.uk);
- Susi Madron's Cycling for Softies (www.cycling-for-softies.co.uk);
- Headwater Holidays (www.headwater.com);
- Breton Bikes Cycling Holidays (www.bretonbikes.com);
- CTC Cycling Holidays, part of the Cyclists' Touring Club (www.cyclingholidays.org.uk);
- Neilson Holidays (www.neilson.co.uk);
- Sherpa Expeditions (www.sherpa-walking-holidays.co.uk);
- Exodus Travel (www.exodus.co.uk);
- Explore Worldwide (www.explore.co.uk);
- Bents Bicycle Tours (www.bentstours.com).

Cycling often forms part of multi-activity holidays for children at holiday activity centres and outdoor pursuit centres operated by local authority education departments.

Case Study Questions and Activities

1. What is the National Cycle Network and what is it trying to achieve?
2. Choose one of the cycling tourism providers listed above and carry out some further research into the products and services it offers, including destinations visited, types of holidays, costs, travel details, etc.
3. Research the provision for cycling tourism in one of the UK's National Parks.
4. Provide details of three companies that offer cycling tours in France, including the areas visited, types of holidays on offer, costs, travel arrangements and special requirements.

This case study is designed to provide evidence for P4 and P5.

Weblink

Check out these websites to help answer the questions in this case study and for more information on cycling tourism.
www.ctc.org.uk; www.sustrans.org.uk; www.aito.co.uk

Case Study

Health and spa tourism

Introduction

The healing power of spa waters was recognised as long ago as Roman times and in the 18th century spa towns such as Bath, Buxton and Tunbridge Wells were welcoming visitors to sample the waters. Today, spas across Europe offer a range of facilities from casinos and leisure pools to luxury hotels and beauty salons. Over the last 10 years, the word 'spa' has broadened out in new directions to encompass virtually any place, facility, treatment or product that is connected with physical, mental or spiritual health. Over the same time period there has been a rapid growth in spa facilities of all types, to meet the growing demand from customers who need guidance on wellness and well-being, as well as somewhere to escape from the pressures of modern life and re-energise their physical and mental processes. This demand has resulted in health and spa tourism becoming one of the fastest-growing sectors of the UK travel and tourism industry.

Nature of the activities

Health and spa tourism can be divided into five distinct categories:

1. Destination spas;
2. Day spas;
3. Hotel spas;
4. Spa towns;
5. Spa travel.

Destination spas

Sometimes known as 'health farms' or hydros, these are popular with clients who need a relaxing break to take time out from their busy lives, to be pampered, to experience new therapies and activities, to eat healthily and possibly to lose weight or 'detox'. Destination spas provide comfortable accommodation and a wide range of spa facilities, e.g. steam rooms, bubble-jet pools, sauna and relaxation areas. They are often located in a countryside setting and offer clients tailor-made packages to suit their needs. Companies in this sector of the health and spa market include Ragdale Hall Health Hydro in Leicestershire and the Celtic Manor Resort near Newport in south Wales.

Day spas

These cater for people who want to take a few hours out of their busy schedule or demanding home life to 'recharge their batteries'. Day spas can be located in a historic building, a new purpose-built facility or within an existing health club. They offer steam rooms and sauna, relaxation areas, some gym facilities and classes such as yoga or pilates with qualified instructors. Companies offering day spa facilities include Aqua Sana at Center Parc's Oasis Whinfell Forest centre in the Lake District and the Academy Spa in Harrogate, North Yorkshire.

Hotel spas

More and more hotels are adding spas and spa treatments to their leisure facilities and some of the best are of a very high quality. Clients can expect steam rooms, bubble-jet pools, sauna and relaxation areas, a range of therapeutic treatments and some gym or fitness equipment. Weekday business guests in the hotel can make use of the spa facilities, while spa breaks help to fill rooms at weekends with leisure tourists. Companies offering hotel spa facilities include Chewton Glen Hotel, Spa and Country Club in Hampshire and Calcot Manor Spa in the Cotswolds.

Hotel spas are growing in popularity (courtesy St Davids Hotel and Spa, Cardiff)

Spa towns

Britain's spa towns are undergoing something of a revival in popularity. Places as far apart as Llandrindod Wells in Wales, Leamington Spa in Warwickshire, Moffatt in Scotland and Harrogate in North Yorkshire are using their long association with spa waters to encourage tourism. All have a water source, often rich in minerals and legend, and sometimes credited with specific healing properties. Many spa towns are rejuvenating their spa architecture, renovating historic facilities and staging cultural activities and festivals to attract visitors.

Spa travel

Holidays are for leisure, pleasure and relaxation – three ideals that are in keeping with the philosophy of spas and spa treatments. Increasing numbers of people are using their holidays and short breaks to concentrate on improving their well-being using health and spa tourism facilities. Companies that specialise in spa travel include Erna Low and Thermalia Travel, both operating tours in a wide variety of destinations across the world.

1. What factors – industry and participant- are likely to influence the future development of the health and spa tourism sector?
2. Choose one of the spa travel companies listed above (Erna Low or Thermalia) and carry out some further research into the products and services it offers, including destinations visited, types of holidays, costs, travel details, etc.
3. What changes in society have led to increased demand for health and spa tourism products and services?
4. What are the objectives of the Spa Business Association?

This case study is designed to provide evidence for P2 and P3.

Weblink

Check out this website to help answer the questions in this case study and for more information on health and spa tourism. www.britishspas.co.uk

---

SECTION 4 # Understand the factors affecting and influencing the tourism provision for a special interest

This final section of the unit looks in detail at the factors affecting a specific type of special interest tourism, including locations, types of providers and special requirements, using adventure tourism as a case study.

Locations

We saw in the previous section of this unit that special interest tourism can take place in a variety of different locations, for example on land, water and even in the air (see Figure 13.6). This type of tourism can also be domestic – people following a special interest in their own country, e.g. a couple from Birmingham enjoying a gourmet weekend break at a Devon hotel, or international – travelling abroad to follow a special interest, e.g. a family from Belfast taking a boating holiday on the Canal du Midi in the south of France. Climatic considerations are also important in special interest tourism, with some activities being more seasonal than others, e.g. whale watching, winter sports and mountain expeditions.

Provision for special interest tourism

The increasing popularity of special interest tourism has resulted in a growing number of UK-based providers of products and services. Most are tour operators of all sizes – large, integrated travel companies, small and medium-sized operations and web-based tour operators. They offer a complete service to their customers, e.g. booking flights and transfers, arranging accommodation, providing guides and tutors, etc. Some offer budget-priced package holidays, while others offer a more personalised service that tends to be more expensive. Other companies just offer a 'meet and greet' service or other 'ground-only arrangement' when customers arrive in a destination, e.g. acting as a tour guide, leading an expedition or assisting customers with access and transfer arrangements at airport/port gateways and border crossings.

Himalayan Kingdoms

Himalayan Kingdoms is a UK-based specialist tour operator offering worldwide, small group adventure travel. A holiday with the company can range from climbing a trekking peak in Nepal, a classic trek to Everest base camp or Machu Picchu, to a gentle walking adventure through rolling foothills. Himalayan Kingdoms also offers a selection of gentle treks in Nepal, Bhutan, Peru and Cambodia. The company is the leading provider of tours and treks to Bhutan, having pioneered most of the trekking routes in this Himalayan kingdom. It places an emphasis on quality, personal service and small group travel, as well as being committed to responsible tourism. The company feels strongly that its holidays should benefit the local communities in the destinations it visits, protect the environment by minimising pollution and respect local traditions, religion and heritage.

Weblink
Check out this website for more information on Himalayan Kingdoms.
www.himalayankingdoms.com

Special interest tourism providers are found in the private sector, public sector and voluntary sector. There is sometimes overlap between these sectors – the Ramblers' Association, for example, is a voluntary sector organisation, but it operates a commercial (private sector) division known as Ramblers' Holidays.

Private sector providers

Private sector special interest tourism providers are either companies running facilities such as outdoor activity centres and walking tours, or tour operators selling special interest holiday packages in the UK and overseas. Many of the tour operators are small, specialist companies offering a limited number of tours to small groups of travellers. However, the rising popularity of special interest tourism has persuaded the major, integrated holiday companies to enter the market. Thomas Cook, for example, has a number of special interest products including Neilson (skiing, sailing and mountain biking), Thomas Cook Signature and Thomas Cook Sport. Thomson/TUI owns Headwater Holidays and Crystal Holidays, both operating in the special interest tourism sector. Even mid-size tour operators have a variety of special interest tourism products, as the case study on Kuoni on page 81 illustrates.

Activity 13.9

Carry out some research and describe the tourism provision for diving holidays in the UK, including locations offered and special requirements. Analyse and evaluate the provision for diving holidays in the UK and justify recommendations for development.

This activity is designed to provide evidence for P5, M3 and D2

Many of the holiday companies offering special interest and activity products are members of AITO, the Association of Independent Tour Operators. They offer packages based on a variety of themes and interests, and most can produce tailor-made itineraries based on customers' individual requirements.

Weblink
Check out this website for more information on AITO and its member companies offering special interest tourism products and services.
www.aito.co.uk

Public sector providers

The public sector's role in special interest tourism is mainly concerned with local education authorities (LEAs) providing outdoor activity centres for use by schools under their control. Many inner city councils run centres in National Parks and other countryside areas in England, Wales, Scotland and Northern

Ireland. Safety is a key concern at these centres and, at present, all LEA centres, as well as those in the private sector, that cater for people under the age of 18 are required by law to be licensed by the Adventure Activities Licensing Authority (AALA).

Weblink

Check out this website for more information on the Adventure Activities Licensing Authority and the activities that it licenses.
www.aals.org.uk

FOCUS ON INDUSTRY

Grangewaters Outdoor Education Centre

Grangewaters is a typical outdoor education centre run by a local authority, in this case managed on behalf of Thurrock Council in Essex. It is licensed by the AALA and offers a wide range of activities, including dingy sailing, canoeing, high ropes, camp craft, orienteering and climbing. The centre caters for school and college groups, youth groups and visitors with special needs.

Weblink

Check out this website for more information on Grangewaters Outdoor Education Centre in Essex.
www.thurrock.gov.uk/grangewaters

Voluntary sector providers

The voluntary sector plays an important role in special interest tourism provision, through organisations such as:

- The National Trust – offers working holidays in the UK, covering a range of activities, from dry stone walling to planting trees;

- Youth Hostels Association – with more than 220 hostels in England and Wales;

- British Trust for Conservation Volunteers (BTCV) – organises around 250 conservation holidays each year in the UK and in 25 countries worldwide. Tasks include pond clearing, beach cleaning and hedge laying;

- Outward Bound Trust – has centres in more than 30 countries offering special interest and activity holidays;

- Royal Society for the Protection of Birds (RSPB) – offers a range of leisure breaks in association with tour operators.

Local communities also contribute to special interest tourism provision by organising events and courses that attract visitors as well as local people.

Special requirements

By their very nature, special interest tourism activities often need specialist equipment. This includes safety equipment for many of the adventure activities we have mentioned elsewhere in this unit.

Many special interest tourism holidays involve companies providing tuition and instruction to guests at a range of levels – beginner, intermediate and advanced. Depending on the type of special interest or activity concerned, staff need to be to be fully trained to deliver the activities in a safe and efficient manner. Many staff at activity and adventure centres have to be trained to the National Governing Body standards of their respective sports and activities. It is common for staff working with children to have to undertake a Criminal Records Bureau (CRB) check and for the companies concerned to follow the guidelines set out in the Children Act. First aid training for staff is important in many companies offering activity and adventure tourism, while all companies operating in travel and tourism have to comply with the requirements of the Disability Discrimination Act (DDA) and are advised to take out public liability insurance.

Adventure Tourism

Introduction

Adventure tourism is a growing 'niche' sector of the UK travel and tourism industry that is capitalising on people's increased interest in fitness and desire to accept a challenge. It consists of holidays, short breaks and day visits that involve taking part in active or adventurous outdoor activities, either as a primary or secondary purpose of the visit. Adventure tourism is particularly popular in Scotland and Wales, but also in many English destinations such as the Lake District, Peak District, Yorkshire and the south west, especially Cornwall. Adventure tourism activities involve a degree of risk and danger and appeal particularly to young, professional people, who have sufficient disposable income to buy the (often expensive) equipment needed to take part in the activity.

Nature of the activities

Adventure tourism includes a wide range of outdoor activities, such as:

- Mountain biking;
- Canoeing and kayaking;
- Caving and pot-holing;
- Rock climbing of all types;
- Surfing, windsurfing and kite surfing;
- Hang-gliding, paragliding, parascending, sky diving and microlighting;
- Mountain trekking, gorge walking and canyoning;
- Motorised land sports, e.g. 4 X 4 driving, rally driving and quad biking;
- Scuba diving;
- Orienteering, snowboarding, land yachting, bungee jumping and other land-based activities.

Adventure tourism products can take different forms, for example:

- Adventure holidays or short breaks – where taking part in adventure activities is the main purpose of the trip, e.g. a trekking holiday in the Himalayas;
- Taking part in adventure activities as part of a holiday, e.g. having a half-day kite surfing lesson while on a family holiday in mid Wales;
- Adventure day visits – where taking part in adventure activities is the main purpose of the visit, e.g. a group from Exeter taking part in multi-activity adventure day course on the south Devon coast.

Trekking in the Himalayas (courtesy Himilayan Kingdoms)

Location and destinations

Adventure tourism takes place in the UK and overseas. In the UK, many adventure holidays take place in National Parks and other areas of outstanding natural beauty. Part of the experience of an adventure tourism holiday is being in close contact with nature and the environment, so these areas are well-suited to adventure tourism activities. The precise location will depend on the requirements of the activity, e.g. access to water for canoeing and kayaking, access to crags for climbing, access to beaches for surfing, kite surfing and windsurfing, etc. As for adventure tourism destinations abroad, the sky is literally the limit! Every world continent has destinations that are popular with adventure tourists, for example:

- Europe – e.g. the Alps, Scandinavia and the Mediterranean islands;
- Asia – e.g. the Himalayas, Cambodia, Thailand and Vietnam;
- South America – e.g. the Amazon rainforest, the Andes and coastal regions;
- North America – e.g. the Rocky Mountains, National Parks and British Columbia;
- Africa – e.g. game reserves, Sahara Desert and the Victoria Falls;
- Australia/New Zealand – e.g. the Great Barrier Reef, Tasmania and South Island New Zealand;
- Antarctica and the South Pole.

Adventure tourism providers

The UK adventure tourism industry is made up of mainly small activity businesses catering for a specialist adventure activity or offering a multi-activity experience for customers. Some have their own self-catering or serviced accommodation, while others use nearby hotels, guesthouses, campsites, bunkhouse barns and hostels. There are increasing numbers of tour operators offering adventure holidays in the UK and to all parts of the world, usually taking small numbers of travellers in groups under the direction of an experienced tour leader. Examples of larger adventure tourism providers offering holidays in the UK and overseas include:

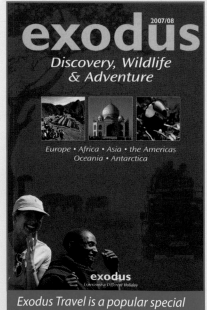

Exodus Travel is a popular special interest tourism company

- PGL (www.pgl.co.uk);
- Acorn Adventure (www.acornadventure.co.uk);
- Dragoman Overland (www.dragoman.com);
- Exodus Travel (www.exodus.co.uk);
- Explore Worldwide (www.explore.co.uk);
- Guerba Worldwide (www.guerba.co.uk);
- Himalayan Kingdoms (www.himalayankingdoms.com);
- Adrift (www.adrift.co.uk);
- Discover the World (www.discover-the-world.co.uk);
- Audley Travel (www.audleytravel.com);
- Naturetrek (www.naturetrek.co.uk).

Adventure activities sometimes form part of multi-activity holidays for children at holiday activity centres and outdoor pursuits' centres operated by local authority education departments.

Special requirements

Adventure tourism can involve dangerous activities, so the correct equipment, clothing and instruction are vital. Some people who take part in activities prefer to use their own equipment and clothing, while others are happy to use what is supplied by the company or hire equipment from specialist suppliers. Some adventure tourism companies have age restrictions for customers, given the dangerous nature of their activities.

Case Study Questions and Activities

1. Choose one of the adventure tourism providers listed above and carry out some further research into the products and services it offers, including destinations visited, types of holidays, costs, travel details, special requirements, etc.
2. Provide details of three companies that offer trekking holidays in the Himalayas, including the areas visited, types of holidays on offer, costs and travel arrangements.
3. Analyse the provision for mountain biking holidays in the UK, covering providers, product details, locations, costs, travel and accommodation options, etc.
4. Evaluate the provision for adventure tourism and justify recommendations for development.

This case study is designed to provide evidence for P5, M3 and D2.

Weblink

Check out this website to help answer the questions in this case study and for more information on adventure tour operators. www.aito.co.uk

Unit summary

This unit has investigated the growth area of special interest tourism. You have seen that the term 'special interest tourism' covers a variety of activities and special interests that people carry out while on holiday or on a day visit, either in the UK or overseas. You have investigated the relationship between special interests and tourism, delving back in history to illustrate key points. The many factors that affect participation in special interest tourism – both industry factors and participant factors – have been explored in detail. Factors such as the ageing of the population, changing social structures and increasing disposable incomes were seen to be important in affecting the development of special interest tourism. You have considered the location of special interest tourism activities and the nature of the activities themselves. Finally, the unit has examined the factors affecting the tourism provision for a special interest, such as locations, types of organisations and special requirements. Throughout the unit you have been shown many industry examples, while the case studies on Kuoni Travel, cycling tourism, health and spa tourism, and adventure tourism provide in-depth examples of the nature of different aspects of special interest tourism.

If you have worked methodically, by the end of this unit you should:

- Understand the relationship between special interests and tourism;
- Know the factors that affect participation in special interest tourism;
- Know the nature of special interest activities in different locations;
- Understand the factors affecting and influencing the tourism provision for a special interest.

You are now in a position to complete the assignment for the unit, under the direction of your tutor. Before you tackle the assignment you may like to have a go at the following questions to help build your knowledge of special interest tourism.

Test your knowledge ?

1. What is 'special interest tourism'?
2. Which points about the historical development of tourism have had an impact on the development of special interest tourism?
3. What are 'niche' tourism products and why is special interest tourism considered to be one?
4. List five passive and five adventurous activities that can form part of a special interest tourism holiday.
5. Which is the most popular active pursuit in the UK?
6. How do adventurous activities contribute to economic development in the destinations where they take place?
7. List three motivations of people who take part in special interest tourism.
8. What are 'demographics' and how do they affect special interest tourism?
9. Name six different market segments found in special interest tourism.
10. Which socio-economic factors affect participation in special interest tourism?
11. Explain how Maslow's hierarchy of needs relates to special interest tourism.
12. Describe the locations of three different types of special interest tourism.
13. Name six companies that offer cycling tourism holidays and breaks.
14. Describe the range of organisations that provide special interest tourism in the UK.
15. Name six UK-based adventure tourism companies that offer holidays within the UK and overseas.

Answers to these questions can be found on the Book 2 Tutor's CD-ROM that accompanies this book (ISBN 9780955019050). Full details can be found at www.tandtpublishing.co.uk

Special Interest Tourism

Introduction

This assignment is made up of a number of tasks which, when successfully completed, are designed to give you sufficient evidence to meet the Pass (P), Merit (M) and Distinction (D) grading criteria for the unit. If you have carried out the activities and read the case studies throughout this unit, you will already have done a lot of work towards completing the tasks for this assignment.

Scenario

In your first job since leaving college you are working in the Marketing Department of a medium-sized tour operator that has been selling villa holidays to Spain, Greece and Turkey for the last six years. The Head of Marketing, Jenni Frost, has been asked by senior management to investigate the possibility of introducing special interest tourism holidays into the company's programme to capitalise on the growth in popularity of activities and special interests amongst clients. Jenni has asked you to help out on the project, which focuses on four main areas:

1. The relationship between special interests and tourism;
2. The factors which affect participation in special interest tourism;
3. The nature of special interest activities in different locations;
4. The tourism provision for a specific special interest that the company may wish to introduce.

She wants you to complete the following four tasks.

TASK 1

Jenni needs some background evidence on special interest tourism and would like you to produce a written report in which you must:

(a) **Describe** the development of the relationship between special interests and tourism;

This task is designed to provide evidence for P1.

To be considered for a Merit grade for this task, your report should also:

(b) **Explain** how two relationships between special interests and tourism have developed;

This task is designed to provide evidence for M1.

To be considered for a Distinction grade for this task, your report should also:

(c) **Assess** the current market for special interest tourism, identify gaps in provision and suggest potential new products.

This task is designed to provide evidence for D1.

TASK 2

(a) Jenni would like you to prepare and deliver an illustrated presentation in which you must describe three industry factors and three participant factors (six in total) that affect participation in passive, active and adventure special interest tourism;

This task is designed to produce evidence for P2.

To be considered for a Merit grade for this task, your presentation must also:

(b) **Analyse** how two key factors have affected participation in each of passive, active and adventure special interest tourism (six in total – two from each category).

This task is designed to produce evidence for M2.

TASK 3

For this task, Jenni would like you to produce three special interest tourism case studies – one water-based, one land-based and one airsport. Each case study must:

(a) **Describe** the nature of the activities in this particular type of special interest tourism. You should consider the scope for individual, group and team participation in each type of special interest tourism, plus the purpose, degree of danger and risks (real and perceived) associated with each activity.

This task is designed to produce evidence for P3.

(b) As a separate piece of work, **identify** and **show** the location on a map of the world of 20 key worldwide destinations that offer passive, active and adventure activities – four of these must be in the UK.

This task is designed to produce evidence for P4.

TASK 4

Finally, Jenni would like you to carry out a thorough investigation into one area of special interest tourism. She would like you to compile a portfolio in which you should:

(a) **Describe** the tourism provision for a specific special interest, including locations and special requirements;

This task is designed to produce evidence for P5.

To be considered for a Merit grade for this task, your portfolio must also:

(b) **Analyse** the tourism provision for the special interest that you chose in task 4 (a);

This task is designed to produce evidence for M3.

To be considered for a Distinction grade for this task, your portfolio must also:

(c) **Evaluate** the provision for the special interest that you chose in task 4 (a), describing and justifying recommendations for development.

This task is designed to produce evidence for D2.

UNIT 14

Roles and Responsibilities of Holiday Representatives

INTRODUCTION TO THE UNIT

Holiday representatives play a vital role in the successful operation of a tour operator's programme of holidays. A holiday representative ('rep') is the holidaymakers' first, and probably only, direct point of contact with the tour company. Working as a holiday rep is a very appealing job to many people thinking of a career in travel and tourism. It offers the chance to work in all parts of the UK or abroad and help all types of customers enjoy their holidays to the full, but it is a very demanding and responsible job. Reps have to work long hours, deal with a host of enquiries from customers and sort out problems in a professional and efficient manner. Time off in the resort is very limited during the season and the job involves a certain amount of administration and basic accounting.

In this unit you will learn about the roles and responsibilities of different types of holiday representatives who work overseas. The unit also gives you the opportunity to examine the legal responsibilities of reps and the part they play in providing a healthy and safe holiday environment for customers. You will also have the chance to practise your social, customer service and selling skills when dealing with a range of situations that reps encounter, such as organising a welcome meeting for guests.

WHAT YOU WILL STUDY

When you have completed this unit you should:

1. **Know the roles and responsibilities of different categories of holiday representatives;**
2. **Understand the legal responsibilities of a holiday representative;**
3. **Understand the importance of health and safety in relation to the role of the holiday representative;**
4. **Be able to apply social, customer service and selling skills when dealing with transfers, welcome meetings and other situations.**

You will be guided through the main topics in this unit with the help of the latest developments, statistics, industry examples and case studies. You should also check out the weblinks throughout the unit for extra information on particular organisations or topic areas and use the activities throughout the unit to help you learn more.

ASSESSMENT FOR THIS UNIT

This unit is internally assessed, meaning that you will be given an assignment (or series of assignments) to complete by your tutor(s) to show that you have fully understood the content of the unit. A grading scale of pass, merit or distinction is used when staff mark your assignment(s), with higher grades awarded to students who show greater depth in analysis, evaluation and justification in their assignments. An assignment for this unit, which covers all the grading criteria, can be found on page 135. Don't forget to visit www.tandtONLINE.co.uk for all the latest industry news, developments, statistics and hot links to websites in this unit to help you with your assignments.

SECTION 1 — Know the roles and responsibilities of different categories of holiday representatives

Working as a holiday representative is many people's idea of the perfect job – the chance to work abroad in the sun, socialise while you work and visit exciting places all sound very appealing, particularly to many young people. However, working as a rep is very hard work and may not suit everybody, as the advice from Thomson Holidays shown in Figure 14.1 explains.

Tour operators look for people who have a responsible and sensible outlook when recruiting holiday reps. Applicants need to be tactful, flexible and patient,

---

Living and working overseas

Working and living in a different country is a completely different experience to being at home. The food, the language, the culture and the working hours, to name but a few, will all be new to you. Taking a big step and leaving all your friends and family behind is therefore not for the faint-hearted!

The nature of the holiday business also requires a large degree of flexibility. You will work six out of seven days. However, you may be contacted at any time if there is an emergency, so you will need to be willing and available to help if the need arises. We do our best to place you in the country of your choice, especially if you speak the language; however, this is not always possible, so you will need to be prepared to work anywhere in our programme.

Although leaving your home to work in a different country is a big step, it is also a completely different life experience and on offer is great job satisfaction and excellent career opportunities. So if you want adventure in your life, take a small step towards making a big leap!

Figure 14.1 – Advice from Thomson Holidays

with a lot of drive, enthusiasm and stamina, plus excellent organisational skills.

Although the image of a person working in a sunny Mediterranean resort is the one that comes most readily to mind when you think about the work of a holiday representative, there are actually many different types of reps working in the UK and abroad, serving all types of customers in many different kinds of accommodation and various resort areas. Reps can be classified into:

1. Resort representatives, e.g. property, 18-30s, over-50s, etc;
2. Ski representatives;
3. Transfer representatives;
4. Children's representatives;
5. Campsite representatives.

In the following sections of this unit we will investigate these categories in turn, examining the key roles and responsibilities of each.

Resort representatives

These are the types of reps that are familiar to most of us who have been on a holiday abroad or seen TV programmes about working in travel and tourism abroad. Resort representatives look after customers staying in a range of different types of accommodation – hotels, villas, apartments, forest lodges, campsites, timeshare accommodation, caravan parks, holiday centres, etc. – or are responsible for particular types of holidaymakers, e.g. young people on 18-30s type holidays or customers over 50.

Whatever their particular job situation, the responsibilities of resort reps are very varied and include:

- Conducting welcome meetings;
- Visiting properties to meet customers;
- Accompanying holidaymakers on transfers between airport and accommodation;
- Providing and maintaining local information boards for holidaymakers;
- Ensuring health and safety requirements;

- Running entertainments and events for customers;
- Selling and organising excursions;
- Calculating payments, currency conversions and commissions;
- Carrying out routine administration;
- Liaising with hotel owners and managers;
- Solving problems for guests;
- Handling complaints;
- Dealing with non-routine incidents, illness and emergencies.

A resort representative has three key roles:

1. To represent the company – holiday reps are the public face of the holiday company. Customers on a Cosmos holiday, for example, will not meet the senior managers or directors based in the UK, but they will have regular contact with their rep, expecting him or her to provide information and be able to handle any problems or enquiries speedily and efficiently. How good reps are at their jobs can have a significant impact on holidaymakers' enjoyment of their holiday and the overall image of the company;

2. To provide excellent customer service – it goes without saying that holiday reps must deliver very high standards of customer service if they are going to satisfy their customers' needs. They must be available at all reasonable times to inform and entertain their customers, deal with complaints and handle sometimes difficult situations with tact and diplomacy;

3. To generate revenue for the tour operator – travel and tourism is a commercial operation, so reps are expected to sell extras to holidaymakers while in the resort, for example day and evening excursions, accommodation and travel upgrades, car hire and activities, for which they normally earn a commission.

These three key roles and responsibilities are summed up well in the following case study on the roles and responsibilities of Thomas Cook Overseas Representatives.

Thomas Cook Overseas Representatives

Introduction

Thomas Cook UK and Ireland is one of the UK's biggest travel companies, employing around 11,000 people in more than 700 locations across the world. The company's principal operations include 570 high street shops selling travel and foreign exchange, 121 separate bureaux de change, seven Thomas Cook travel warehouses, three call centres, Thomas Cook TV and thomascook.com, one of the most popular UK travel websites. In addition, Thomas Cook has more than ten tour operating brands including Thomas Cook, JMC, Sunset, Thomas Cook Signature, Club 18-30, Flexibletrips.com, Neilson, Latitude, Sunworld Holidays and Style Holidays. The company also operates Thomas Cook Airlines, the UK's second largest leisure airline.

Working overseas

Thomas Cook's Overseas Representatives are the public face of the company, always on hand to help. One minute a rep might be recommending a nice quiet spot to sunbathe, the next could be dealing with a guest to solve their issue or complaint. The company stresses that the variety and unpredictability of the job will call for some very special qualities. So while the company doesn't insist on specific qualifications or experience, reps do need bags of personality, a knack for dealing with people and the ability to stay calm under pressure and still keep smiling.

Key responsibilities and roles

- To professionally and efficiently accompany customers to and from the airport;
- To deliver 'introductions' to customers after their arrival, with the objective of providing customers with practical and interesting information in accordance with the company's guidelines;
- To deliver exceptional customer service in order to achieve the customer service targets given by the destination management;
- To actively sell Thomas Cook events, car hire and ad hoc events in order to achieve the income targets given by the destination management;
- To actively monitor health, safety and quality standards;
- To accurately complete weekly/fortnightly paperwork in accordance with the company guidelines and the resort deadlines;
- To establish a friendly, respectful relationship with all hotel staff, suppliers and airport officials;
- To guide both day and night events as required;
- To take an active role in any in-house entertainment/activity where possible;
- To conduct police and clinic visits as required.

Key skills required

- Good communication skills and the ability to hold conversations with customers;
- The ability to work either as part of a team or independently;
- The ability to listen and respond sympathetically to customers' requests/needs;
- An enthusiastic, positive personality – must like working with people;
- The initiative to escalate problems and incidents to the destination management;
- The ability to resolve problems.

Case Study Questions

1. What specific personal qualities do Thomas Cook management look for when recruiting holiday representatives?
2. Describe the key roles and responsibilities of a Thomas Cook Overseas Representative.
3. Find a vacancy for a holiday representative's job with Thomas Cook (or another tour operator) and write a short report on how you feel you meet the key requirements of the post and in which areas you would need further development and training before taking the job.
4. Which aspects of being a Thomas Cook Overseas Representative appeal most to you and which responsibilities would you feel least comfortable with?

This case study is designed to provide evidence for P1.

Weblink

Check out this website to help answer the questions and for more information on holiday representative job opportunities with Thomas Cook. www.thomascookjobs.co.uk

Property representatives

Property representatives work in a variety of different locations and meet the needs of many different types of customers, as the following sections of this unit explain.

Hotel representatives

The work of most overseas holiday reps working for the big, mass-market tour operators is hotel or apartment-based. The large numbers of holidaymakers in a hotel or apartment complex means that it makes sense for a rep to spend most of his or her time in a single location or a group of properties that are close together, thereby keeping in regular contact with holidaymakers. This also cuts

down travelling time between properties, which may be by public transport, moped, car, bicycle or walking, depending on the circumstances. Applicants for these jobs usually need to be over 20 or 21 years of age, are provided with accommodation and a company uniform, and receive training before starting the job and while working in-resort.

Villa representatives

Villas tend to be more spread out than hotels or apartments, so reps have to spend more time travelling between properties and may not see villa-based customers quite as often during their holiday. They are likely to be given some form of transport for their work, either a car or moped. Roles and

Cosmos overseas representatives

in all the activities on offer to the young holidaymakers, so need boundless energy, enthusiasm and stamina. These include trips to clubs, pubs and bars, plus beach and pool games and activities. Such a volatile mix of alcohol, activities and hot sun can sometimes lead to problems, so reps often have to 'think on their feet' and handle awkward situations in a professional manner. Although sometimes difficult, reps working on young people's holidays must remain professional at all times and not be tempted to get too involved with their clients. For people with the right attitude and skills, these jobs give young reps the chance to visit the 'hot spots' of Europe, such as Ayia Napa, Faliraki and Kavos.

responsibilities are very similar to those of hotel/ apartment reps, although information about what to do in the resort is likely to be given on a one-to-one or small group basis rather than by using the type of information board used in a hotel or apartment complex. Villa reps working for the big holiday companies are employed full-time for the season, but smaller tour operators offering villa holidays sometimes use the services of a freelance rep based in the resort, i.e. somebody who is self-employed and looks after the customers of a number of different holiday companies.

Reps for young people's holidays

Holidays for young people often involve partying until the small hours, meeting lots of new people and having a good time in the resort. Reps working for holiday companies that offer young people's holidays, for example Club 18-30 (part of the Thomas Cook Group) and 2wentys (now owned by TUI Travel plc), look for very outgoing personalities in the people they employ. Reps are expected to take part

Activity 14.1

Carry out some research into holiday reps' jobs with companies that offer holidays specifically for young people and make a list of the key roles and responsibilities of the jobs, plus the skills, qualities and experience needed to do the job well.

This activity is designed to provide evidence for P1.

Reps for seniors holidays

Holidays for the over 50s and 'seniors' in general tend to be much more sedate, although there is a growing trend for older people to be far more active in later life. Recent research commissioned by Saga, Britain's leading travel company for the over 50s, indicated that the top ten most popular activities that over 50s would like to try include learning to fly, rally car driving, white water rafting, surfing and even sky diving! Holiday reps working with senior holidaymakers need to understand the particular needs of older people on holiday, which may include more time needed when travelling on excursions, help with access to facilities and empathy with their particular circumstances. For this reason, many tour operators recruit older and more mature people to fill these posts, making it easier for the holidaymakers to relate to their reps.

Weblink
Check out this website for more information on Saga Holidays and the job opportunities they offer. www.saga.co.uk

Reps for family holidays

Holidays for families are the backbone of the package holiday market – they offer good value for money at an all-inclusive price in a safe and secure environment. Reps help families to settle in to what are likely to be unfamiliar surroundings in the resort accommodation and point out activities and attractions that are geared particularly to families. They may be asked to help families who have special dietary or other requirements, by liaising with hotel management. Families with young children tend not to go on late night excursions, so reps should point out the day trips that are likely to appeal most to this segment of the market. Many tour operators offer clubs and activities for children, to keep them entertained and give their parents a rest. These are usually divided by age groups and full details are normally given out at the welcome meeting at the start of the holiday. Reps play an important part in making the sometimes stressful activity of taking children on holiday as carefree and enjoyable as possible.

Ski representatives

Ski tour operators offer a range of overseas appointments throughout the season, most of which involve close contact with customers. Positions include chalet hosts, bar managers, chefs, receptionists, chalet managers and resort managers. Working as a chalet host is a common first appointment in a ski resort, giving a good grounding for career progression within a particular company or the industry generally. Chalet hosts employed by Inghams, a specialist ski tour operator, have the following responsibilities:

1. Running a catered chalet;
2. Catering and cleaning to a very high standard;
3. Looking after guests;
4. Menu planning;
5. Budgeting and basic administration.

The company's chalets vary in size from those accommodating up to 8 people, which may be managed by a single chalet host, to larger chalets suitable for friends and couples to run together. Inghams look for individuals who are outgoing and cheerful, with a sense of humour and a basic love of cooking. The specific requirements for the post of chalet host are:

- A cooking diploma or proven experience of catering;
- Basic hygiene knowledge;
- Minimum age of 19 years;
- Previous experience within the hospitality industry;
- Excellent customer service skills.

Ski reps who do well in their winter season jobs may be offered summer season positions in different resorts or a job in the UK company headquarters.

A chalet hostess in the Alps (courtesy of Ski Verbier)

Transfer representatives

If a tour operator has a very large number of passengers arriving regularly at a particular airport or airports, they may employ a transfer rep specifically to organise client transfers between the airport and their accommodation, thereby releasing the resort reps to carry out their normal duties. In most cases, however, resort reps carry out airport transfers on a rota basis. The role of the transfer rep is to meet and greet customers as they arrive at the airport and transfer them safely and speedily to their holiday accommodation. This is normally by coach, but could be by taxi or even a hired car. At the end of their holiday, the process is reversed and the transfer rep supervises the collection of passengers from their accommodation and transfers them to the airport to catch their flight home. Specific responsibilities of the transfer rep include:

- Meeting and greeting customers at the airport;
- Checking the passengers against a manifest (a list of passengers' names);
- Escorting the customers to the coach;
- Giving a welcoming speech on the coach;
- Checking the holidaymakers into their accommodation;
- At the end of their holiday, collecting guests from their accommodation;
- Transferring the customers to the airport;
- Directing guests to the check-in desks;
- Waiting at check-in until all guests have departed safely.

Transfer reps are the very first representative of the holiday company that the customer meets, so they play a very important part in making sure that customers get their holidays off to a good start. Sometimes, however, transfer reps have to deal with problems, such as lost luggage, delayed flights, long queues at check-in and passengers arriving late for their return flight. These situations can be very stressful and call for a great deal of patience, tact and diplomacy on the part of the transfer rep.

Children's representatives

Becoming a children's rep is a good way to start a career as a representative since the starting age is often lower (over 18 years) than for a resort rep. If you enjoy the life as a children's rep and do well in your job, you may decide to stay on in the travel and tourism industry by applying for a resort rep's position when you are older. Jobs as a children's rep are offered by the major holiday companies and campsite operators, some of which ask for an NNEB, BTEC or NVQ level 3 in Childcare, a Diploma in Nursery Nursing or an equivalent UK qualification from applicants.

The main role of a children's rep is to carry out a varied programme of activities for children, which provides them with a valuable social experience while on holiday. Children's reps need to create a child-friendly environment that is safe, clean and effectively managed so as to ensure maximum enjoyment for all children. Specific responsibilities include:

- Providing a variety of stimulating activities for children in different age ranges;
- Maintaining and promoting an informative and attractive notice board of events;
- Attending welcome meetings to explain the services available for children;
- Managing groups of children during activities and events;
- Maintaining appropriate health, safety and security measures;
- Completing report forms and carrying out basic accounting in line with company procedures;
- Controlling and managing stock effectively;
- Liaising with and helping other reps as and when required;
- Offering a baby-sitting service.

Successful candidates for children's rep jobs are screened via an enhanced disclosure check from the Criminal Records' Bureau (CRB) to satisfy all concerned that there are no good reasons why they should not carry out the role.

A children's rep working for Neilson Holidays

Activity 14.2

Compare the roles and responsibilities of a transfer representative with those of a children's representative on a campsite.

This activity is designed to produce evidence for P1 and M1.

Campsite representatives

Campsite reps (or couriers) work overseas or in the UK and are responsible for looking after customers during their holiday in a tent or mobile home. Major companies that recruit couriers for overseas work include Keycamp and Eurocamp (both part of Holidaybreak plc) and Canvas Holidays. Most jobs are from May to September, so they appeal particularly to students; the normal minimum age for recruitment is 18 years of age. Couriers spend a lot of time cleaning and preparing tents and mobile homes for new guests, plus making their stay as enjoyable as possible when they arrive, as the example from Canvas Holidays in Figure 14.2 explains.

Approachable, well mannered, friendly and helpful are just a few of the qualities you will need as a Campsite Courier or Courier Couple and remember, your main focus will be ensuring that our customers return home having had 'the best holiday they have ever had.'

So how are you going to achieve this? Your duties will mainly involve cleaning customer accommodation for their arrival, welcoming them onto the campsite and ensuring that all the customer's needs are attended to during their stay.

You will need to have initiative and be a quick thinker, able to resolve any problems that may occur on site efficiently and effectively.

As a Courier or Courier Couple you may, dependent on the dates available to work, also be involved in montage (putting up tents) and demontage (taking down tents) at the beginning and end of the season.

Every year we welcome staff of all ages to our overseas team. We have designated 'Couple Sites' or 'Single Courier Sites.' There is also the chance to progress to a senior position within the company.

Figure 14.2– Working as a Campsite Courier for Canvas Holidays

There are a number of different jobs available as campsite couriers, for example:

● Courier – the most common position, ensuring customers enjoy their holiday to the full (as described in Figure 14.2);

- Senior courier – required to organise the daily workload of a small team of couriers and children's couriers, as well as being able to carry out full courier duties as required. Positions tend to be for the full season only;

- Mature courier – some companies welcome mature couple and single applicants as couriers. Mature couriers provide invaluable benefits to customers, since many of them have considerable experience of camping and travelling in Europe. Mature couriers can choose to live in company tents or their own caravan or motorhome;

- Site manager – people with proven supervisory experience are recruited to lead the largest teams for the major camping tour operators. They are expected to set and maintain excellent standards of service and behaviour amongst staff;

- Team leader – responsible for managing the work of a team of couriers, with responsibility for customer service and accommodation standards;

- Children's courier – responsible for organising and delivering a regular programme of events for children on site, as well as being available for general courier duties as required.

In addition to these posts, the larger companies offer jobs at the beginning and end of each season in montage (erecting tents) and demontage (dismantling tents), including team leaders, assistants and drivers.

Weblink

Check out these websites for more information on campsite rep job opportunities.
www.keycamp.co.uk; www.eurocamp.co.uk; www.canvasholidays.co.uk

Activity 14.3

Carry out some research into holiday reps' jobs with companies that offer camping holidays in Europe and make a list of the key roles and responsibilities of the jobs, plus the skills, qualities and experience needed to do the job well. Present your findings as a series of fact sheets on the jobs found.

This activity is designed to provide evidence for P1.

Activity 14.4

Analyse how the roles and responsibilities of holiday representatives can contribute to the overall holiday experience for their customers.

This activity is designed to provide evidence for D1.

A campsite courier with Keycamp Holidays

Understand the legal responsibilities of a holiday representative

Customers are becoming more conscious of the law and what happens if a company doesn't carry out its legal responsibilities. People are much more willing to complain about products and services, including holidays, and are prepared to fight for their rights, including taking court action if necessary, as the following recent headline from the Travemole website describes:

> ## Thomson and Thomas Cook in massive compensation payout
>
> *A court this week officially settled a compensation claim by hundreds of holidaymakers against Thomson, Thomas Cook and other UK operators. The 790 holidaymakers won a total of more than £2.5 million in compensation after falling ill at a Spanish hotel.*

Travel and tourism companies have to follow their legal responsibilities to the letter, whether this is to do with the quality of products and services they sell, issues to do with employing staff, health and safety matters, and consumer rights when things go wrong.

Overseas representatives play a very important part in carrying out tour operators' legal responsibilities, whether at the airport, on transfers, in resort or on excursions.

Legal responsibilities

Tour operators, and the staff they employ, must work within the legal framework when supplying holidays and other travel products to customers. All staff, including holiday reps working overseas, have a general 'duty of care' to everybody they come into contact with as part of their work, such as customers, colleagues, contractors and suppliers. Over and above this duty of care, the work of holiday reps is concerned with a number of important pieces of legislation, including:

- The Package Travel Regulations;
- Supply of Goods and Services Act;
- Health and Safety at Work Act;
- Trade Descriptions Act;
- Disability Discrimination Act.

Package Travel Regulations

The Package Travel Regulations came into operation on 1st January 1993 in the then 12 Member States of the European Union. The main aim of the Regulations is to give people buying package holidays more protection and access to compensation when things go wrong, while at the same time harmonising the rules covering packages operated throughout European Union countries. Up to the introduction of the Regulations, tour operators had been able to disclaim responsibility when holiday arrangements went wrong, for example overbooking at a hotel or the failure of a coach transfer to arrive, on the grounds that they had no control over these unfortunate events. Under the terms of the Package Travel Regulations, tour organisers must accept legal responsibility for all the services they offer to travellers. Exceptions would be made in circumstances which could neither have been foreseen nor overcome, although in such circumstances, organisers must give all necessary assistance to consumers.

The Package Travel Regulations place a number of duties and responsibilities on tour operators, for example:

- Providing information to customers on who is responsible for the package they have booked. That person or organisation is then liable in the event of failure to deliver any elements of the package;
- Providing clear contract terms;
- Giving emergency telephone numbers;

- Providing proof of the organiser's security against insolvency and information on any available insurance policies;
- Giving immediate notification with explanation of any increase in prices permitted within the terms of the contract;
- Providing a variety of compensation options if agreed services are not supplied;
- Producing accurate promotional material including brochures.

Holiday representatives are not expected to know every detail of the Package Travel Regulations, but must be aware of their existence and why they have been put in place. The sorts of circumstances when the Regulations could come into force include overbooking of accommodation, leading to some customers' rooms being unavailable, and serious flight delays.

Activity 14.5

Identify and explain the legal responsibilities of a holiday representative in the following holiday situation.

You are a Resort Representative on the island of Malta. The Brown family from Rochdale have complained that the hire car they booked in advance for their holiday was not available when they went to pick it up from the airport. The car hire company insisted that they had never received a booking for the Smiths from your holiday company and refused to hire them a vehicle.

This activity is designed to provide evidence for P2.

Supply of Goods and Services Act

This legislation states that any contract for a holiday should be carried out using 'reasonable care and skill'. The tour operator and travel agent should ensure that the booking is carried out correctly and that the holiday itself should be of a generally satisfactory standard, complying with any descriptions made. Tour operators must take great care when selecting accommodation, transport and any services they provide as part of their package holidays.

Health and Safety at Work Act

This piece of legislation is mainly concerned with employers' responsibilities to their staff while in the workplace. The 'workplace' for overseas representatives is not easy to define! It could be a hotel lobby, theme park, overseas resort office or even a nightclub! Whatever the location, tour operators must make sure that all work systems and practices are safe for their staff. They must provide adequate information and training for employees on relevant health and safety matters, such as the safe use of chemicals, using equipment, handling stock and escorting customers. Overseas reps are responsible for completing necessary documentation in relation to health and safety, such as the type of accident/incident form shown in Figure 14.3.

Health and safety issues that affect holidaymakers are discussed in detail in the third section of this unit (see page 121).

Trade Descriptions Act

This Act protects consumers against false descriptions made knowingly or recklessly by anybody selling products and services, including holidays and other travel products. Any description of, for example, a hotel or resort must be truthful at the time it was written (if circumstances change, then the company must inform the customer of the nature of the changes). The Act places a duty on owners and operators of travel and tourism facilities to produce brochures, websites and other promotional materials that are not intended to deceive customers.

Activity 14.6

Identify and explain the legal responsibilities of a holiday representative in the following holiday situation.

You are a Resort Representative in Palma Nova, Majorca. A young couple have complained to you that the brochure they used to book their holiday mentioned there being a disco in their hotel every Friday evening, but this was not the case.

This activity is designed to provide evidence for P2.

Accident/Incident Report Form

Form completed by ....

Property/location..

Date form completed..

Nature of the accident	Date and time .... Location .... Was a photograph taken? Yes/No
Full description of the incident	.... Was medical treatment needed? Yes/No
The Injured party	Name... Holiday ref: .... Home address ....Tel. No: ....
Witnesses	Name .... Address .... Name .... Address ....

Figure 14.3 – Example of an accident/incident report form

Disability Discrimination Act

Meeting the needs of disabled people not only makes good business sense, but it is also the law of the land. The Disability Discrimination Act (DDA) was designed to protect disabled people from discrimination in employment and to increase access to goods, facilities and services. The Act defines 'disability' as:

'A physical or mental impairment which has a substantial and long term adverse effect on a person's ability to carry out normal day-to-day activities.'

Since October 1999, service providers have had to make 'reasonable adjustments' to accommodate disabled people. From October 1st 2004, the Act required all organisations to make alterations to the built environment, e.g. access to buildings and the ability to move freely inside buildings. Reps must be fully aware of the scope of the DDA and to provide assistance to customers in line with the Act.

Booking conditions and contracts

Tour operators' booking terms and conditions are explained in their brochures and customers are deemed to have accepted these, and enter into a contract with the tour operator, when they sign their holiday booking form. The circumstances when customers can claim refunds and compensation are included in the booking conditions and reflect the need to comply with the Package Travel Regulations described earlier in this unit. Payments can be made when, for example, holidaymakers are forced to take a lower standard of accommodation than they had booked as a result of overbooking by the hotel.

Activity 14.7

Study the booking conditions found in a range of holiday brochures and summarise the responsibilities of tour operators to their customers and vice versa.

This activity is designed to provide evidence for P2.

Overseas resort office

The resort office is the hub of a tour operator's overseas operations. Depending on the size of the tour operator, the office will house administration and/or management staff who are responsible for the smooth running of all aspects of the overseas operations, including:

- Preparing transfer lists of passengers (manifests);
- Co-ordinating accommodation reservations;
- Dealing with medical cases;
- Accounting for payments, receipts, etc;
- Handling complaints from customers;
- Organising promotional materials for reps, e.g. flyers for excursions;
- Liaising with local suppliers and the UK head office;
- Ensuring that all paperwork is completed accurately and within deadlines.

Figure 14.4 shows the duties expected of an Operations Assistant in a Cosmos overseas resort office.

OPERATIONS ASSISTANT

As an Operations Assistant you will be involved in all aspects of running a busy resort office, including handling hotel reservations, producing transfer lists, handling incoming calls to the resort office and dealing pro-actively with all issues. You will be computer literate and ideally familiar with using Word and Excel. You will also have a strong attention to detail and be prepared to work flexible hours. As with our Overseas Consultants positions, you will need to be confident with an outgoing personality, show commitment and most importantly have common sense.

Figure 14.4 – Duties of a Cosmos Operations Assistant in a resort office

Understand the importance of health and safety in relation to the role of the holiday representative

Overseas holiday representatives play a crucial role in ensuring that customers not only have an enjoyable holiday, but also one that is as safe as possible. We have already seen that under the terms of the Package Travel Regulations, and other legislation, tour operators have a legal duty to ensure that the holidays and other services they offer to customers meet all current health and safety regulations. It is no longer acceptable for a tour operator to say that it is not responsible for parts of its programmes that are delivered by other companies.

Health and safety risks and hazards

Most overseas holidays enjoyed by British people pass without any health or safety problems at all, but tour operators must have procedures in place to deal with issues when things go wrong. A 'hazard' is anything that can cause harm, while a 'risk' is the likelihood, high or low, that somebody could be harmed by the hazard, together with an indication of how serious the harm could be. For example, riding a moped while in a holiday resort is a hazardous activity, but the risk that it will cause you harm can be reduced by taking a number of steps, e.g. by being briefed in advance about safety procedures and wearing the correct helmet and other equipment.

Hazards are all around us, whether we are on holiday or just going about our everyday lives. In holiday situations, hazards may be found in:

- Accommodation – for example, a faulty gas or electric fire in an apartment or a dangerous balcony;
- Facilities for holidaymakers – for example, poorly-maintained swimming pools, children's playgrounds and lifts;
- Food outlets – for example, dirty kitchens and food preparation areas;
- Excursions and activities – for example, a weak bridge over a gorge or a coach without seat belts.

Activity 14.8

Design a chart that lists the hazards that could be found on an excursion that involves exploring sand dunes in 4 x 4 jeeps in the morning and a boat party in the afternoon/evening, plus all the measures that should be taken to minimise risks.

This activity is designed to provide evidence for P3.

Minimising risks

A great deal can be done to minimise the risks associated with a holiday abroad, through tour operators providing relevant information, carrying out regular checks in resort, reporting incidents correctly and following industry guidelines on good practice.

Providing information

Many holiday companies provide health and safety information before customers travel to a resort (see Figure 14.5), while overseas reps use a number of opportunities to give health and safety advice, including:

- At welcome meetings;
- During transfer commentaries;
- Via noticeboards and information books;
- En-route to excursions and activities.

Safety Standards

Hoteliers and suppliers should meet local and national safety standards, however these vary widely across the programme and rarely match those standards that we enjoy in the UK, only a minority of hotels and apartments meet European Commission recommendations on fire safety. We nevertheless seek to raise standards in all of our destinations. You will receive a Safety First leaflet on arrival in resort, please take a few minutes of your time to familiarise yourself with the information that it contains.

Health and Hygiene

We promote good hygiene practices within hotels, but the hygiene standards in some foreign countries, particularly developing destinations, are generally much lower than in the UK. Care should be taken to minimise the risk of holiday sickness, especially among pregnant women, infants and the elderly. Your GP can provide you with up-to-date health advice and we recommend that you consult your doctor well in advance before travelling.

Swimming Pool and Beach Safety

It is extremely unlikely that the pool in your holiday accommodation will have a lifeguard. It is therefore important to remember, especially when travelling with children, to take a few minutes to familiarise yourself and your party with the pool area on arrival. Children must always be accompanied by an adult in the pool, including children's pools and surrounding areas, and at all other times. Familiarise yourself with any flag warning systems that may be in operation on local beaches, and take into account local conditions.

Children's Safety

Naturally the safety of our younger holidaymakers is also of paramount importance. We take advice from leading UK child safety organisations and accident prevention agencies, to ensure that standards are as high as possible. Parents should check that they are happy with hotel operated clubs and children's facilities, including playgrounds

Excursion Safety

We work with excursion suppliers to ensure that they operate to appropriate safety standards. Whilst every care is taken with those activities that we recommend, should you independently choose to use an alternative supplier we advise that you should satisfy yourself that your insurance and the insurance, legal cover and safety standards of the company you are choosing to use is adequate.

Figure 14.5 – Advice on health and safety from Thomson Holidays

Health and safety checks

Before signing contracts with any of its suppliers before the start of a holiday season, for example hoteliers and coach operators, tour companies inspect premises and vehicles to make sure they comply with health and safety guidelines. Once the contracts have been signed and the season is underway, it is the responsibility of reps to carry out regular checks to make sure that health and safety standards are being maintained. This involves systematic inspections of a number of items, including:

- Fire alarms and evacuation signs and procedures;
- Swimming pool safety equipment and notices;
- Electrical, gas and water systems;
- The safety of balconies in rooms;
- Warning flags on beaches;
- Hygiene standards in accommodation, eating areas, public areas and toilets;
- Safety equipment used for activities, including children's clubs.

An example of a health and safety report form that reps have to complete is shown in Figure 14.6.

The Federation of Tour Operators (FTO) provides its members, which include all the leading UK holiday companies, with practical help and information on managing health and safety in resort areas. To ensure consistency in regulations and standards of health, hygiene and safety between destinations, the FTO has appointed a health and safety co-ordinator and developed a code of practice. This publication contains advice on a range of issues, including:

- Fire safety;
- Food safety;
- Pool safety;
- General safety;
- Beach safety;
- Legionella (legionnaire's disease) management;
- Children's clubs;
- Incident management.

Health and Safety Report

Form completed by ....

Property...

Date form completed ....

Date faxed to Area Office ....

Description of defect	Reported to	Action to be taken	Target date for completion
Loose wiring in guest bedroom	*Hotel manager*	*Repairs to wiring*	*21 April 09*

Signed ....(Representative)

Signed ....(Hotel Management)

Figure 14.6 – A health and safety report form

The Federation has also developed a health and safety training video to complement the code of practice.

Weblink

Check out this website for more information on the FTO health and safety guidelines. www.fto.co.uk

Activity 14.9

Under the direction of your tutor, carry out a health and safety inspection, and complete a health and safety report form. This could take place in your college/school, a nearby tourist facility or while investigating accommodation or an attraction as part of a study tour in the UK or overseas.

This activity is designed to provide evidence for P3.

Water Park Risk Assessment

Location .... Carried out by ....

Date .... Checked by ....

Location	Hazard	Risk	Control measures
Travel to park	Safety of coach/minibus	Low	• Visual inspection • Check seatbelts • Check emergency doors
Swimming pool	Injury caused by trips and slips Possibility of drowning	Medium	• Verbal warning to customers • Inspection of safety aids • Monitoring behaviour
Flumes and slides	Injury caused by falls and slips Possibility of drowning	Medium	• Verbal warning to customers • Inspection of safety aids • Monitoring behaviour
Across the park	Injury from traffic	Low	• Verbal warning to customers • Inspection of speed restriction measures • Supervision of customers
Across the park	Possibility of loss, abduction or assault of children	Low	• Verbal warning to customers • Supervision of children • Checks on procedures

Figure 14.7 – A risk assessment form

Risk assessments

A risk assessment is a systematic investigation of the potential hazards in a given situation. Holiday reps may be required to carry out risk assessments when planning an excursion, for example a trip to a water park as part of an activity for children's club members. Reps complete a form that lists potential hazards and the action that needs to be taken to minimise risks. An example of a risk assessment form is given in Figure 14.7.

Reporting accidents

Reps are trained to report all serious accidents and incidents involving holidaymakers in the resort, by completing an accident/incident report form (see Figure 14.3 on page 119) or logging the details in an accident book. The reports must be as detailed as possible, since they may be needed for future claims against the tour operator by customers.

Be able to apply social, customer service and selling skills when dealing with transfers, welcome meetings and other situations

A holiday rep's main role is to provide excellent customer service to his or her customers, so being able to demonstrate effective social, customer service and selling skills in a range of different situations is an essential part of the job.

Social skills

So far in this unit we've seen that the role of holiday representatives revolves around dealing with people in a pleasant and professional manner. Social skills play a big part in a rep's role and are extremely important in:

- Creating rapport – with customers, work-colleagues, suppliers, contractors, etc. in a variety of different situations;

- Providing a welcome – to customers, from the time they arrive in the resort to their departure flight home;

- Empathising – reps need to be able to understand issues from the customers' point of view;

- Providing a friendly and helpful service – should be the prime motivation for taking a job as a rep;

- Using appropriate language – social and communication skills will vary depending on the type of customer, e.g. language used when talking with young people on holiday is likely to be different from that used to deal with older customers or those whose first language isn't English.

Some people naturally have a more sociable nature, but it's important to remember that social skills can be learned and improved through training, practice and experience.

Activity 14.10

Working in a small group, discuss how you would handle the following situation in order to provide excellent customer service.

You are working as a transfer rep at Athens airport and are expecting 145 passengers to arrive on a flight from Luton. Their take-off from the UK was delayed by 4 hours due to technical problems with the aircraft. You will be accompanying 45 of the passengers on a transfer coach to their accommodation when they arrive.

This activity is designed to provide evidence for P3.

Customer service skills

Elsewhere on your course you have learned about the importance of developing and delivering excellent customer service skills in the workplace – identifying and meeting the needs of customers is the number one goal for travel and tourism companies that want to succeed in business. The effects of not providing acceptable levels of customer service can be very damaging to the company concerned, resulting in fewer sales, lost revenue and a poor image. Reps who are found to have poorly-developed customer service skills can be helped with extra training, but if this fails to improve matters they may well be advised to consider a career in a different aspect of travel and tourism.

Product knowledge

Product knowledge is knowing all the facts and features of products being sold. In the case of holiday representatives, their product knowledge must extend to:

- Details of the holidays that their customers have booked;
- Facts about the resort and surrounding area;
- Detailed information about the excursions and other 'extras' they sell;
- Information about medical and emergency facilities in the resort.

Having good product knowledge not only helps reps to provide excellent customer service to their holidaymakers, but can also lead to increased income via the commission earned on sales of excursions, car hire, merchandise and other products.

Handling complaints

Although the great majority of holidaymakers have a trouble-free holiday, there are occasions when reps have to deal with complaints from clients. This may result from a number of causes, including overbooking, flight delays, accommodation of a poor standard, noise or poor quality food.

The key actions to take when handling complaints are:

- Listen attentively so that you get the whole story first time;
- Thank the customer for bringing the problem to your attention;
- Apologise in general terms for the inconvenience but do not grovel;
- Provide support for the customer by saying that the complaint will be fully investigated and matters put right as soon as possible;
- Sympathise with the customer and try to see the situation from their point of view;
- Don't justify the circumstances that led up to the complaint and go on the defensive;
- Ask questions if you are not clear on any points of the customer's complaint;
- Find a solution to the problem;
- Agree the solution with the customer;
- Follow through to make sure that what you promised has been done;
- In future, try and anticipate complaints before they happen!

One step on from somebody who has a justifiable complaint is the customer who is intent on 'causing a scene'. Just like handling complaints, there are tried and tested ways of dealing with these individuals:

1. Try not to let them get you down or get under your skin. The fact that they wish to cause a fuss may be a sign of their own insecurity;

2. Never argue with them – it can often get the member of staff into deeper trouble;

3. Never be rude to the customer, however rude they are being to you!

4. Try not to take any remarks personally – you may have had nothing to do with the alleged incident but are simply the nearest member of staff;

5. Let the customer do the talking and listen to what they have to say.

If a situation appears to be getting out of hand, it is wise to seek help from another rep or senior member of the overseas team.

Activity 14.11

Working with other members of your group, role play the following situations that reps sometimes encounter:

1. A customer complaining about the poor quality food in her hotel;
2. The leader of a school group complaining about the time his pupils have to queue to use the hotel's games room;
3. A couple complaining to the transfer rep when they arrive in their resort about the long delay in their outward flight from Manchester.

You should take it in turns to play the person complaining and the rep dealing with the complaint. Members of the group should make notes on how well the 'rep' handles the complaint, in line with the key points discussed above.

This activity is designed to provide evidence for M3 and D2.

Image

Tour operators spend a great deal of money developing their image or 'brand', which is used on all advertising, promotional work, aircraft, stationery, etc. Reps play an important part in reinforcing the company's image, not just with the uniform that they wear, but in the way they deal with customers. If treated well by reps while on holiday, customers come away with a positive impression of the tour operator and will tell their friends about the good time that they had, leading to extra business for the company.

Dress code and behaviour

Nearly all holiday companies provide uniforms for their holiday reps. Uniforms help to create a positive first impression with customers and make staff easily identifiable if customers need help or advice. The wearing of a uniform also presents a consistent image to the public and helps to build customer loyalty. However, it is important to remember that the word 'uniform' does not necessarily mean a very formal

Uniforms create a good impression with holidaymakers (courtesy of Cosmos)

dress code. Holiday reps working on campsites or as children's reps, for example, wear a company 'uniform', but it often consists of a polo shirt, shorts and trainers. The important point about a uniform is that it should be appropriate and functional, i.e. suited to the nature and demands of the job. Overseas staff should be informed at interview about the dress code for the job and what type of uniform is supplied.

Training of representatives before they start work in the resort covers a number of sensitive issues concerning behaviour in the workplace. Reps are reminded about using appropriate language at all times with clients and other members of staff, including not swearing or using slang. Tour operators have different policies on staff smoking and drinking while on duty. The overriding concern of all companies is that reps must not be under the influence of alcohol while at work. With many companies, this is an offence for which staff can be instantly dismissed. Holiday reps must also comply with the tour operator's policies on relationships with colleagues and customers. As with drinking while on duty, inappropriate relationships with clients and colleagues are to be avoided.

Personal appearance

All reps must report for work in a presentable fashion, well groomed and with a smart uniform. Personal appearance can be a sensitive area, particularly when supervisors and managers have to remind staff about the importance of arriving at work in a clean, hygienic and presentable fashion. All staff working in travel and tourism, but especially reps whose work brings them into close contact with customers, must:

- Be generally clean;
- Have hair that is clean and tidy;
- Have fresh breath.

Customers will not tolerate staff with poor body odour or bad breath and may well take their custom elsewhere. It is important to remember that the staff are the outward image of an organisation.

For example, if you are greeted at an airport by a representative who smells of stale cigarettes or whose hair is unkempt, your first impressions of the company and your holiday are likely to be negative. If, on the other hand, the rep is smartly presented, with a pleasant smile and tidy hair, you are much more likely to be impressed with the tour company from the outset.

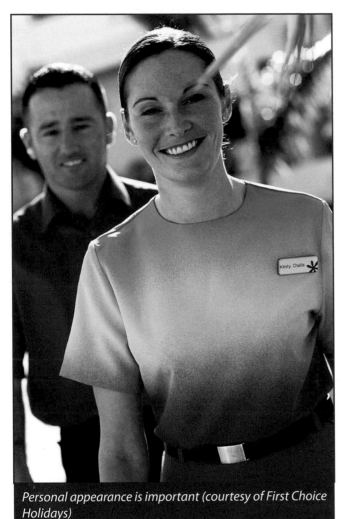

Personal appearance is important (courtesy of First Choice Holidays)

Communication skills

Communication is an essential part of a holiday representative's job, whether dealing with customers, hoteliers, work colleagues, contractors or suppliers. For most of the time, communicating with these people is a straightforward and pleasant affair, but there are occasions when reps have to use their communication skills to deal with difficult and awkward situations.

Informal and formal communications

It's fair to say that reps have to talk a lot while doing their jobs, so good verbal communication skills are essential. Verbal communication can be formal or informal. Examples of formal communication involving reps include:

- Conducting a welcome meeting for new arrivals in a resort;
- Telling customers about health and safety procedures in a hotel;
- Making a speech to thank your work colleagues at the end of the season;
- Complaining to a supplier that some equipment is faulty;
- Providing a commentary on a coach excursion.

Reps communicate informally when they are talking to customers and colleagues in a more relaxed manner, perhaps while on an excursion or in a hotel lobby.

Non-verbal communication

Non-verbal communication or 'body language' is the process by which we send and receive signals and messages without the use of the spoken word. When at work, reps are always in the public eye, not just in formal situations such as while hosting a welcome meeting, but every minute while on duty. This means that they have to conduct themselves appropriately and professionally at all times, by projecting a positive and welcoming image, making eye contact while talking, maintaining a good posture and keeping any irritating habits or mannerisms to a minimum!

Communicating with groups and individuals

Reps come into contact with all sorts of customers while at work, e.g. groups, individuals, adults, children, youths, people whose first language isn't English, mixed age groups, people with special needs, etc. Reps must be able to assess customers' needs quickly and provide appropriate information, help, advice and guidance.

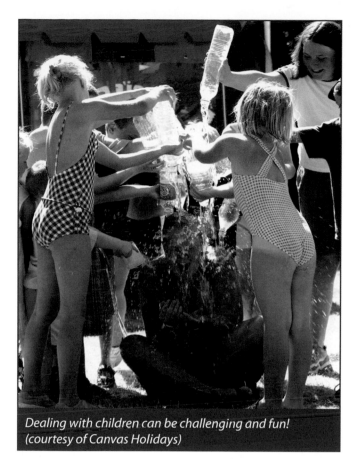

Dealing with children can be challenging and fun!
(courtesy of Canvas Holidays)

- Making yourself available afterwards if people want further clarification on a one-to-one basis.

Dealing with groups of clients is an important part of the work of a holiday representative, for example when organising transfers, conducting excursions or on guiding duties. Developing group handling skills will ensure that you can:

- Ensure the safety and welfare of groups of clients;
- Handle mixed groups, e.g. by age, gender, language;
- Handle difficult groups, e.g. rowdy, under the influence of alcohol or complaining;
- Deal with medical and emergency situations.

> ## Activity 14.12
>
> To improve your group handling skills, take turns at playing the role of a tour guide by taking the rest of your group on a tour of your college/school or the local area. When the tour has finished, the 'customers' should discuss the strengths and weaknesses of each guide, concentrating on communication with the group as a whole as well as with individual group members. You may also like to role play the situation of a group of rowdy holidaymakers to practise some different group handling skills!
>
> *This activity is designed to provide evidence for P5.*

Dealing with groups can be an altogether more challenging task than communicating with an individual customer. Handling group situations calls for good organisational and communication skills, so that every member of the group turns up in the right place at the right time! Although the group you are dealing with may be very large, it is important to make every effort to treat the members of the group as individuals by, for example, addressing people by name and taking time to talk to them on a one-to-one basis, particularly those that you feel may need a little more attention or support.

There are certain ground rules that you need to adopt when communicating information to a group of customers, including:

- Making sure that members of the group can see, hear and understand you;
- Communicating effectively using simple language in a clear, confident tone of voice;
- Making sure that everybody has understood what you have said by allowing time for questions;

Written and visual communication

Many of the responsibilities of holiday reps are concerned with gathering local information and communicating this information in written and visual form to customers, for example:

- Giving holidaymakers leaflets about local facilities and attractions at the welcome meeting;
- Passing on information during transfers to and from the airport;
- Compiling information books and folders for guests to use while in-resort;
- Maintaining informative and attractive notice boards with information on resort attractions, events and activities;
- Making posters to advertise events.

Sources of local information include tourist offices, guidebooks, the internet, local hoteliers, attractions and restaurateurs, as well as other overseas staff. As well as investigating what local attractions, facilities and events a resort has to offer holidaymakers, reps also need to know about local laws and customs, such as religious codes and festivals.

Notice boards are an excellent way for customers to keep up to date with what's happening in their resort and for reps to provide important information, as well as promoting and selling excursions and other travel services. The board needs to be located in a central position where holidaymakers regularly congregate, for example in a hotel foyer or by the welcome tent or mobile home on a campsite. Notice boards differ from one company to another, but minimum requirements are:

- Photographs, regular visiting times and details of how to contact the reps;
- Emergency contact details;
- Details of excursions and events;
- Details of return flights and any changes to travel arrangements;
- Facilities available in any children's clubs.

At the beginning of the season, reps usually prepare an information book or file for use by guests. This includes a great deal of useful local information such as an overview of the resort, public transport information, details of attractions, where to eat, doctor and dentist contact information, details of excursions, car and moped hire, foreign exchange, etc.

Notice boards and information books must look professional and business-like. When designing them, reps must make sure that:

- There are no spelling or grammar mistakes;
- All the information is current and not out of date;
- Where possible, information is typed or word processed;
- There is good use of colour to attract attention;
- There is not too much information on the notice board.

You saw earlier in this unit that reps have to

Activity 14.13

Working as part of a team, choose a popular overseas holiday destination and gather together information on its attractions, facilities and events. Use the information you collect to make a notice board that could be used by British people on holiday in the resort. Use a range of information sources, such as brochures, guidebooks, tourist offices and the internet, to gather your information. Many of the major tour operators' websites have destination guides.

This activity is designed to provide evidence for P5.

complete quite a lot of paperwork as part of their job, e.g. health and safety reports, customer complaint forms, risk assessments, etc. Tour operators provide guidance on how these should be completed during rep training and while in the resort. Reps must ensure that all written documents are completed accurately and written in a clearly understood manner.

Selling skills

Selling is an important part of a rep's job, earning the tour operator extra revenue and the member of staff extra income (commission) on sales. Selling skills and techniques are covered in the rep's training before starting work in resort. As with other aspects of travel and tourism, selling in overseas resorts follows the traditional sales process shown in Figure 14.8.

Taking the example of selling excursions at a welcome meeting, the different stages of the sales process could be as follows:

1. Building rapport – e.g. creating a professional and welcoming image, using people's names as appropriate, telling jokes, etc;
2. Establishing customer needs and expectations – holidaymakers are all looking for something different, so asking questions helps at this stage;
3. Features and benefits – e.g. spending time explaining the advantages of different excursions and the features of each;
4. Overcoming objections – e.g. explaining that there

| Stage 1 |
| Building rapport |

| Stage 2 |
| Establishing customer needs and expectations |

| Stage 3 |
| Features and benefits |

| Stage 4 |
| Overcoming objections |

| Stage 5 |
| Closing the sale |

| Stage 6 |
| Completing documentation |

| Stage 7 |
| After-sales service |

Figure 14.8 – The sales process in travel and tourism

When selling excursions and other products, reps must:

1. Listen carefully to customers' needs;
2. Speak in a clear tone and at an appropriate pace;
3. Have excellent product knowledge;
4. Use visual aids as appropriate;
5. Project a positive image;
6. Use appropriate body language;
7. Answer questions fully and frankly;
8. Recognise buying signals to close a sale.

Unit 4 in Travel & Tourism for BTEC National Book 1 (2nd edition) has more detailed information on selling in travel and tourism.

Activity 14.14

Take it in turns to play the role of a holiday representative selling an excursion to an evening banquet in a nearby Spanish castle at a welcome meeting in Torremolinos.

This activity is designed to provide evidence for P4.

Transfers

We saw at the beginning of this unit that transfers between airport and accommodation are an important part of a rep's job, carried out on a rota basis amongst staff in the resort. After welcoming the holidaymakers, the rep on duty escorts the customers to their waiting coach and makes sure that they are all safely on board before setting off for the accommodation. On the journey to the accommodation, the rep will use the microphone on the coach to talk to the passengers. On a typical transfer trip the rep will:

● Welcome the customers on behalf of the tour company;

● Introduce himself/herself and the coach driver;

● Give the local time and indicate how long the transfer should take;

● Point out the emergency exits and other safety features on the coach;

● Explain that a number of different stops will be made to various accommodation bases;

are wheelchairs available at a cave complex if an elderly customer says she could not walk very far;

5. Closing the sale – this is concerned with persuading customers to make a commitment by, for example, putting their name on a list, paying a deposit, etc;

6. Completing documentation – e.g. completing and issuing tickets for the excursion;

7. After-sales service – e.g. asking customers how they enjoyed their excursion after the event.

- Give an overview of the local area and resort facilities;
- Give the time and location of the welcome meeting;
- Distribute welcome packs;
- Provide information about the weather, safety of drinking water, banking facilities, etc;
- Give details of check-in procedures at the accommodation.

Reps should give customers the opportunity to ask any questions they may have or to clarify any points they are not sure about.

Although daunting at first, most holiday reps need to be able to use a microphone, usually on a tour bus or at a welcome meeting, to communicate with large groups of clients. Many tour operators include developing this skill in their reps' pre-resort training, where staff role play the sort of situations they are likely to find themselves in when abroad. The same general rules that are followed when communicating using your natural voice also hold good when using a microphone, for example making sure that you can be heard by everybody, speaking slowly in a clear tone and giving people time to ask questions or clarify points.

Activity 14.15

Assume that you are a resort rep working for Thomson Holidays. Plan and role play a coach transfer between Palma Airport and the Hotel Don Paco in Magaluf. The rest of your group should critically evaluate your performance based on the information on communication techniques already covered in this unit.

This activity is designed to provide evidence for P4.

Welcome meetings

Welcome meetings are normally held the morning after the holidaymakers arrive in the resort, to allow them time to get over the journey and settle into their accommodation. Refreshments are normally served at the meeting, which should be conducted in a friendly and welcoming manner by the rep.

At the welcome meeting, the rep will cover a number of items, including:

- An introduction to the rep, the resort and accommodation on behalf of the tour company and the hotel management;
- Rep's availability and the location of the notice board;
- Details of local attractions in the resort;
- 'Housekeeping' items such as the times of meals and pool opening in the accommodation, use and cost of telephones, baby changing facilities, availability and cost of safes, etc;
- Information on facilities in the resort, including the location of banks, shops, medical facilities, car hire, beaches, public transport, etc;
- Details of the type and cost of excursions offered by the tour company, and how they can be booked;
- Any questions or concerns from the holidaymakers.

Other situations and documentation

In addition to supervising transfers and arranging welcome meetings, holiday reps have to deal with a wide range of other situations, for example over bookings at accommodation, complaints about standards in hotels, misleading brochure descriptions, illnesses, crimes and accidents. As discussed previously, they are also responsible for completing a variety of forms relating to health and safety, accounting and customer service (see Figure 14.9).

Activity 14.16

Still assuming that you are working as a resort rep for Thomson Holidays, plan and deliver a welcome meeting for the Magaluf holidaymakers who were on the coach transfer in the previous activity in this unit. The rest of your group should critically evaluate your performance based on the information on communication techniques already covered in this unit.

This activity is designed to provide evidence for P3.

Customer Service Report Form

Tour operator .... Resort...

Customer name .... Booking reference ....

Accommodation ....…... UK departure date ....

Room number .... Date of complaint ....

Rep's name ....

Customer's home address ....

.... Postcode ....

Telephone number .... Mobile ....

Details of the complaint or issue (to be completed by customer or rep)
....
....
....
....
Summary of actions taken to resolve the issue
....
....
....
....

Signed (customer)..…Signed (rep) ....

Date ....…..

Copy sent to hotel   Yes/No
Copy sent to resort office   Yes/No
Copy sent to UK head office   Yes/No

Figure 14.9 – Customer service report form

Unit summary

In this unit you have examined many aspects of the work of overseas holiday representatives. You have found that there are actually many different types of holiday representatives, from campsite couriers to transfer reps. All need the same qualities to succeed – a pleasant and welcoming manner, excellent presentation and communication skills, a willingness to help others, bags of initiative and enthusiasm, plus good organisational skills. The unit has examined legal aspects of the rep's role and found that ensuring a safe and secure environment for holidaymakers is a very important part of the job, involving carrying out health and safety inspections and completing the necessary paperwork and reports. You have leaned about, and practised, a range of social, customer service and selling skills when dealing with a variety of situations, including transfers and welcome meetings. Throughout the unit you have been shown many industry examples, while the case study on Overseas Representatives at Thomas Cook highlights key roles and responsibilities of holiday reps.

If you have worked methodically, by the end of this unit you should:

- Know the roles and responsibilities of different categories of holiday representatives;
- Understand the legal responsibilities of a holiday representative;
- Understand the importance of health and safety in relation to the role of the holiday representative;
- Be able to apply social, customer service and selling skills when dealing with transfers, welcome meetings and other situations.

You are now in a position to complete the assignment for the unit, under the direction of your tutor. Before you tackle the assignment you may like to have a go at the following questions to help build your knowledge of the roles and responsibilities of holiday reps.

Test your knowledge

1. What are the three key roles of a resort representative?
2. List five responsibilities of resort reps.
3. Describe three of the different courier jobs available on campsites.
4. What are the specific requirements for the post of chalet host in a ski resort?
5. Explain how a rep would go about meeting the needs of young people on holiday and holidaymakers aged over 50.
6. Name three companies that offer jobs as campsite couriers.
7. What qualities does a children's rep need to succeed in his or her job?
8. Name four different types of holiday representatives.
9. Explain how a rep's job is influenced by the requirements of the Package Travel Regulations.
10. List five items that are normally inspected by reps on a health and safety check of a hotel or apartment complex.
11. What is a 'risk assessment' and when might a rep have to carry one out?
12. What are the key points to bear in mind when communicating with a group?
13. What duties does a rep carry out on a typical transfer between airport and accommodation?
14. What aspects of personal presentation are particularly important to reps while on duty?
15. What are the key points to follow when dealing with complaints from customers?

Answers to these questions can be found on the Book 2 Tutor's CD-ROM that accompanies this book (ISBN 9780955019050). Full details can be found at www.tandtpublishing.co.uk

Roles and Responsibilities of Holiday Representatives

Introduction

This assignment is made up of a number of tasks which, when successfully completed, are designed to give you sufficient evidence to meet the Pass (P), Merit (M) and Distinction (D) grading criteria for the unit. If you have carried out the activities and read the case studies throughout this unit, you will already have done a lot of work towards completing the tasks for this assignment.

Scenario

Since completing your BTEC course you have worked in a Birmingham hotel for 15 months on reception duties. You feel that the time is right to make a career move and you have applied for a job as an overseas resort representative with one of the major holiday companies. You put in an excellent application and have been invited to an interview and selection day at the company's head office. During the day, you are asked to complete a number of tasks to assess your suitability for the job. The first two tasks involve making a presentation and writing a short report, while tasks 3 and 4 are role plays involving other applicants for representative jobs.

TASK 1

For this task you must make a presentation to the selection panel and the rest of the applicants in which you must:

(a) **Describe** the roles and responsibilities for three different categories of holiday representatives. This must include one type of resort representative, i.e. property, over 50s or 18-30s, plus two others selected from ski, transfer, children's and campsite representative.

This task is designed to provide evidence for P1.

To be considered for a Merit grade for this task, you must also:

(b) **Compare** the roles and responsibilities of two different categories of holiday representatives, for example a property rep and a campsite rep. You cannot choose two different types of resort reps, such as an 18-30s and a property representative.

This task is designed to provide evidence for M1.

To be considered for a Distinction grade for this task, you must also:

(c) **Analyse** how the roles and responsibilities of the holiday representative can contribute to the overall holiday experience for the customer.

This task is designed to provide evidence for D1.

TASK 2

The first part of this task asks you to write a short report that could be read by your resort manager. In the report you must:

(a) **Identify** and **explain** the legal responsibilities of holiday representatives in the following holiday situations:

1. You are a Campsite Representative working on a campsite in the south of France. A couple complain to you that their young child has fallen off the slide in the campsite and cut his arm on a rusty nail that was sticking out from one of the benches.

2. You are a Resort Representative working for a major tour operator in Magaluf on the island of Majorca. A young couple have complained that, although the tour operator's brochure states that there are two pools in their hotel, there is, in fact, only one.

3. You are a Villa Representative on the Greek island of Corfu. The Smith family from Rochdale have complained that the hire car they booked in advance for their holiday was not available when they went to pick it up from Corfu Airport. The car hire company insisted that they had never received a booking for the Smiths from your holiday company and refused to hire them a vehicle.

4. You are a Resort Representative in Benidorm and have received a complaint from two customers about the standard of the food in their hotel. They say that hot food is often served only luke warm and that the 'gourmet nights' described in the holiday company's brochure and on its website, have never taken place.

For each situation, you must describe the procedures that the reps should go through to try to resolve the issues and identify the relevant laws or regulations that are associated with each case.

This task is designed to produce evidence for P2.

For this part of the task, you must make a presentation that:

(b) **Describes** the role played by holiday representatives in creating a safe and healthy holiday environment. You must identify typical risks and hazards in the holiday environment and the ways in which reps can minimise these risks. This must include safety in the accommodation, while using facilities, on transfers, on excursions and organised activities, and in the resort itself.

This task is designed to produce evidence for P3.

TASK 3

The selection panel would like you to role play this task, in which you must:

(a) **Use** social, customer service and selling skills to plan and deliver an arrival transfer speech, and plan and deliver a welcome meeting, completing appropriate documentation, e.g. tickets and receipts. The welcome meeting must be supported by visual aids and appropriate body language should be demonstrated. You must also deal with queries from the audience. The welcome meeting must incorporate the selling of excursions and you must demonstrate effective selling skills throughout.

This task is designed to produce evidence for P4.

To be considered for a Merit grade for this task, you must also:

(b) **Demonstrate** effective social, customer service and selling skills when delivering your transfer speech and welcome meeting.

This task is designed to produce evidence for M2.

TASK 4

(a) The members of the selection panel have given you the following two customer service situations to deal with in role plays. You must **use** social and customer service skills to deal with the customers, completing appropriate documentation, i.e. a customer report form:

1. You are a Resort Rep in the Algarve and have been informed by some customers, Mr and Mrs Khan from Oldham, that their villa has been burgled and that they have lost all their possessions, including their passport, money, credit cards, keys for their hire car and flight tickets home. They are both very upset and are looking to you to help them sort out their problems.

2. Working as a Campsite Courier in Switzerland, the Green family from Norwich have contacted you to complain about the dirty state that they found their mobile home in when they arrived this afternoon for their 10-day holiday. They are also very unhappy about the fact that the campsite does not have a children's pool, as described in the holiday company's brochure, and there are no bicycles for hire (again, as described in the brochure).

This task is designed to produce evidence for P5.

To be considered for a Merit grade for this task, you must:

(b) **Deal effectively** with customers in the different situations and accurately complete all relevant documentation.

This task is designed to produce evidence for M3.

To be considered for a Distinction grade for this task, you must:

(c) **Consistently project** a confident, professional image when dealing with the customers in the different situations.

This task is designed to produce evidence for D2.

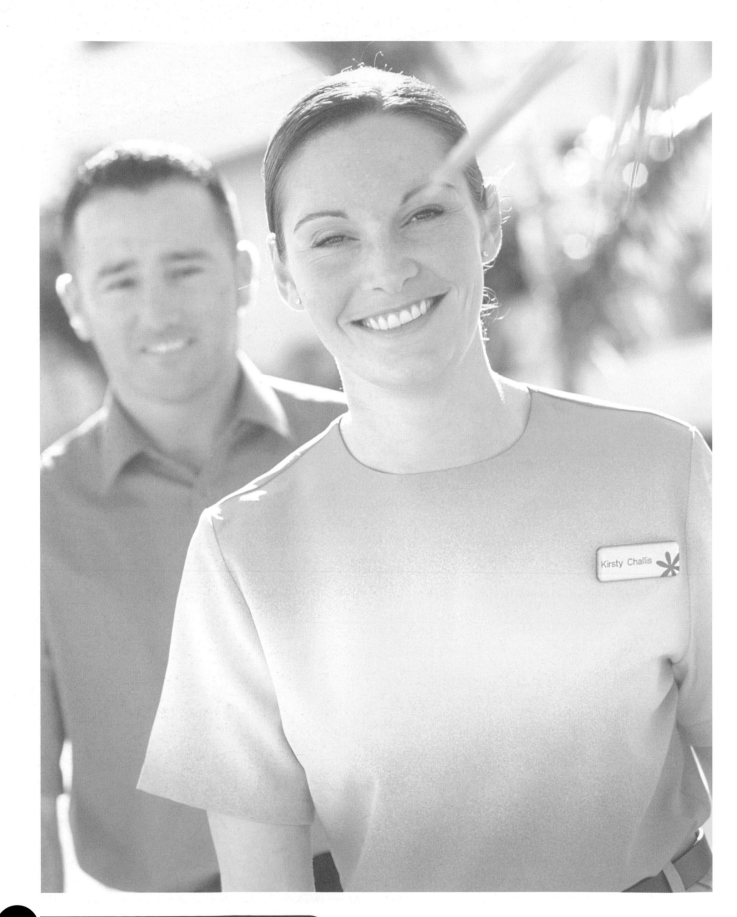

UNIT 15

Passenger Transport Issues for the Travel and Tourism Industry

INTRODUCTION TO THE UNIT

The UK passenger transport industry provides leisure and business travellers with the means of reaching their destinations and is the hub around which the whole of the travel and tourism industry revolves. Passenger transport is a very dynamic sector, making use of new technologies to supply faster, more convenient, better value, more accessible and safer means of travel to and within the UK. Having an effective passenger transport network is vital if the UK is to maintain its share of tourism in a fiercely-competitive global market.

This unit gives you the opportunity to examine the UK passenger transport industry, the different features of transport and the role of transport regulators. You will also explore the developments and factors affecting passenger transport in the UK, including high-speed rail, personal mobility and fuel prices. The relationships between UK passenger transport networks and the travel and tourism industry are explored in detail, covering areas such as contracting and agency agreements. Finally, the unit will help you understand how passenger transport provision affects the popularity and appeal of a specific UK tourist destination.

WHAT YOU WILL STUDY

When you have completed this unit you should:

1. **Know about passenger transport operations within the UK;**
2. **Understand the developments and factors affecting and influencing passenger transport in the UK;**
3. **Understand the relationships between UK passenger transport networks and the travel and tourism industry;**
4. **Understand how passenger transport provision affects the popularity and appeal of a specific UK tourist destination.**

You will be guided through the main topics in this unit with the help of the latest developments, statistics, industry examples and case studies. You should also check out the weblinks throughout the unit for extra information on particular organisations or topic areas and use the activities throughout the unit to help you learn more.

ASSESSMENT FOR THIS UNIT

This unit is internally assessed, meaning that you will be given an assignment (or series of assignments) to complete by your tutor(s) to show that you have fully understood the content of the unit. A grading scale of pass, merit or distinction is used when staff mark your assignment(s), with higher grades awarded to students who show greater depth in analysis, evaluation and justification in their assignments. An assignment for this unit, which covers all the grading criteria, can be found on page 169. Don't forget to visit www.tandtONLine.co.uk for all the latest industry news, developments, statistics and hot links to websites in this unit to help you with your assignments.

Icebreaker

This unit investigates passenger transport in the UK and its relationship with the UK travel and tourism industry. Working by yourself, or in small groups under the direction of your tutor, see how you get on with the following tasks to help you make a start on this unit:

- Name three airlines that offer domestic services within the UK;

- Thinking of a tourist area that is close to where you live, make a list of all the transport services you could use to reach the area, and travel around once there, and the names of the companies that provide them;

- Make a list of the factors that would be important to you when deciding which type of transport to use when travelling to a seaside resort for a short break;

- Think of some ways in which developments in technology are changing passenger transport services in the UK;

- Name an organisation that is responsible for regulating transport in the UK;

- Think about how the government helps passenger transport companies;

- Name one coach company that offers inter-city travel throughout the UK and a rail company operating in your local area.

When you've finished, show your answers to your tutor and compare your answers with what other students in your class have written.

SECTION 1   Know about passenger transport operations within the UK

By its very nature, the travel and tourism industry involves travelling to, from and around destinations in the UK. Transport, therefore, is a vital component of travel and tourism. Transport for tourism covers a variety of water, air and land-based services, including travel by coach, train, private car, taxi, hired car, bicycle, aircraft, cruise ship, water taxi, ferry and canal craft. It also includes the infrastructure that supports the means of travel, such as roads, motorway service areas, ferry terminals, airports and railway stations.

UK passenger transport provision

In the following sections of this unit we investigate a range of air, land and water-based services, starting with air transport.

Air transport

Air transport is a major UK industry, currently carrying 200 million passengers per year. The government expects this number to double by 2020 and has outlined its plans for airport expansion to deal with this growth in the Future of Air Transport White Paper published in December 2003. The document includes the following key facts on the scale and importance of air transport in the UK:

- Passenger numbers – 32 million at UK airports in 1970, 189 million in 2002, and between 350 – 460 million forecast for 2020;

- Fifty per cent of the UK population flew at least once in 2001;

- Air transport movements at UK airports – 607,000 in 1970, over 2 million in 2002;

- 70 per cent of all visits made to the UK in 2002 by

overseas residents were made by air, compared with 60 per cent in 1980;

- 40 percent of all passengers between Europe and North America fly to/from the UK;
- 20 per cent of international passengers start or finish their journey at UK airports;
- In 2002 there were 48 UK airlines operating a total fleet of 903 aircraft.

The White Paper also stresses the economic importance of air transport with the following facts:

- In 2001 air transport contributed £13 billion to the UK economy (2 per cent of total GDP);
- The aviation industry exported £7 billion of services in 2002;
- The UK air transport sector directly employs about 200,000 people;
- An estimated 600,000 jobs in the UK depend indirectly on the air transport industry, e.g. jobs in the energy sector generated by purchases of airline fuel, in the aerospace sector by airline purchases of equipment, in travel agencies and tour operators.

Air transport services

For statistical purposes, the International Air Transport Association (IATA) classifies air travel services into one of three categories, as follows:

- Domestic;
- International scheduled;
- International chartered;

Domestic services refer to air travel within a country, while international represents travel between different countries. Scheduled services are those that operate to a published timetable, on defined routes and under government licence. These services run regardless of the number of passengers and are used primarily by business travellers who are prepared to pay a premium for the extra convenience and flexibility offered. Many governments still fund their national airlines, for example Air France, although

there is a general move away from state ownership towards private sector operation. One notable success story of recent years has been the rapid growth in one particular sector of the airline business, namely budget, low-cost or 'no frills' airlines, which sell direct to the public and offer scheduled services on domestic and international routes at low prices.

Chartered air services are linked to the package holiday industry, where tour operators contract with an airline for a specific route for a season. Some of the major tour operators own their own airlines. Sales of charter flights have been declining in recent years, while passenger numbers carried by low-cost airlines have been growing rapidly. Figures from the CAA indicate that, in 2004, the proportion of passengers at UK airports using charter flights was just 15.1 per cent of all flights, the lowest level for 20 years and a decrease of 1.3 million passengers on 2003. Well-known charter airlines include Monarch, Thomas Cook and Thomsonfly.

Activity 15.1

Carry out some research into a UK airline and compile a fact sheet on the company that includes details of its UK route network, facilities offered on board, services for passengers with special needs and different levels of service offered.

This activity is designed to provide evidence for P1.

Airports and airport infrastructure

Most airports in the UK serve local demand, generally from within their own region. However, larger airports such as Manchester, Birmingham and a number of those in the south east of England also attract passengers from a wider area. These airports provide services to more destinations, some of which would not be viable from smaller airports, and also offer more frequent services.

The major London airports (Heathrow, Gatwick, Stansted) play a dual role. Around 80 per cent of their passenger traffic has an origin or destination

Glasgow airport (courtesy BAA/Glasgow Airport)

in London, the south east or the east of England. Theses regions have a very high level of demand for air travel, amounting to nearly half of total UK demand. This enables airlines to offer a very wide range of destinations from the London airports, with frequent services and one or more competing airlines on most routes. As a result, Heathrow, Gatwick and increasingly Stansted fulfil a national as well as regional role. Many travellers from other parts of the UK fly to one of these London airports in order to catch connecting flights and passengers from Wales, the midlands and parts of the south west of England travel by road or rail to the major London airports. The demand for passenger air travel is growing fastest outside the south east of England and this trend is expected to continue. As a result, airlines should be able to offer direct services to more destinations from a wider range of airports. The recent growth in popularity of the low-cost airlines has stimulated demand for air travel across the country, but has been a particularly important factor in the development of many regional airports, such as Bournemouth, Exeter and Liverpool.

As well as scheduled and charter services, air transport also includes helicopter flights and transfers, private jet hire and even flights in balloons!

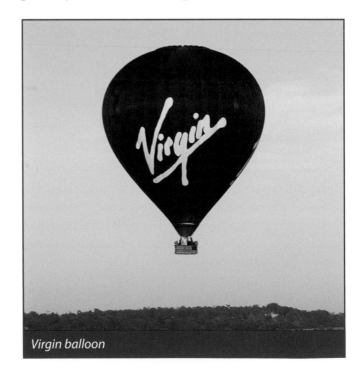

Virgin balloon

Rail transport

For one hundred years since its introduction in the mid-19th century, rail transport was the most popular mode of travel for business and leisure in the UK. However, the rise in car ownership and development of air travel in the 20th century have had a marked impact on the demand for rail travel, which in 2004 accounted for just 13 per cent of all tourist travel in the UK. Train travel is, however, increasing in popularity as the government invests more than £60 billion over the next 10 years to develop a bigger, better and safer rail system. Figures from the Association of Train Operating Companies (ATOC) indicate that around 1.15 billion passenger journeys were made on the UK rail network in 2006 – more than in any year since 1959. Over the past decade, passenger journeys have risen by 43.6 per cent in all.

Rail travel is increasing in popularity (courtesy ATOC/Hull Trains)

As well as the network rail services there are a number of 'niche' rail services developed specifically for tourists. These include the many restored steam railways in the UK, such as the Vale of Rheidol Railway in Wales, and luxury rail services such as the Orient Express.

Structure of the UK rail industry

The government, through the Department for Transport (DfT), sets the overall UK railway policy. The DfT works with the following bodies in achieving its aims:

1. The Office of Rail Regulation (ORR) – is independent of government and its function is to provide economic regulation of the monopoly and dominant elements of the rail industry. This includes determining the level, structure and profile of charges levied by Network Rail (which operates the infrastructure) and regulating its stewardship of the national rail network. The ORR is also responsible for all aspects of health and safety on the railways, a role previously carried out by the Health and Safety Executive (HSE);
2. Passenger Focus – the independent national rail consumer 'watchdog'. Its aim is to get the best deal for passengers travelling by rail in the UK;

3. Network Rail – is the operator of Britain's railway infrastructure, which includes 21,000 miles of track, 1,000 signal boxes, 40,000 bridges and tunnels, 9,000 level crossings and more than 2,500 stations. It operates the main passenger terminals, such as Edinburgh Waverley, London Waterloo and King's Cross. All other stations are leased to the main train operating company using the station. Network Rail's task is to deliver a reliable and safe rail network;
4. Train operating companies (TOCs) – are private companies that run the passenger train services in the UK. Currently, there are 26 TOCs, including Arriva Trains Wales, Hull Trains and Gatwick Express.
5. The government also maintains strong relationships with Transport Scotland and the Welsh Assembly Government, which both have devolved rail responsibilities. It also co-operates with a wide range of local and regional bodies, such as regional assemblies, regional development agencies, Transport for London and passenger transport executives around the country.

All the TOCs are members of the Association of Train Operating Companies (ATOC), which was set up by the train operators formed during the privatisation of the railways under the Railways Act of 1993. As well as being the official voice of the rail passenger industry, ATOC provides its members with a range of services that enable them to comply with conditions laid on them in their franchise agreements and operating licences.

Weblink
Check out this website for more information on the train operating companies (TOCs) and the work of ATOC.
www.atoc.org

Activity 15.2

Carry out some research into two of the train operating companies (TOCs) and find out what facilities and services they provide for their rail passengers, including regularity of services, costs of typical journeys, concessionary fares, customer service facilities, comfort and accessibility.

This activity is designed to provide evidence for P1.

Road transport

Road transport for tourism includes travel by private car, bus and coach, taxi, hired car, bicycle and even rickshaw! An increasing proportion of journeys in the UK are taken by car – up from 79 per cent of the total distance travelled in 1980 to 85 per cent in 2002. Travel by private car accounts for more than 70 per cent of all tourist trips taken in Britain. Cars offer a degree of flexibility, freedom, comfort and convenience that other forms of transport find hard to match. The shift towards car journeys has provided huge benefits for many people, opening up new opportunities at work and during leisure time. Part of the reason for the increase in car use in Britain is that cars are more affordable as people become better off. Improvements in production techniques and improved fuel efficiency have contributed to a fall in the relative cost of motoring and so have brought cars within reach of a far wider range of the population.

People choose their car for many tourist trips because it allows them to travel direct from one place to another in comfort. Cars can also get to places that are not always accessible by public transport services. Cars do, however, has considerable impacts on the environment and communities, leading to problems of pollution, physical erosion, loss of land to car parks and congestion in many popular tourist destinations, especially historic cities, coastal resorts and National Parks, where vehicles often spoil the very ambience that attracted the tourists in the first place. Central and local governments are attempting to minimise the impact of vehicles by introducing a variety of techniques, including public transport initiatives, road pricing and pedestrianisation. The government expects to see further growth in car ownership and use over the next 30 years. The car provides many benefits, but the challenge for the government is to ensure that people have other options, including good quality public transport and the opportunity to walk or cycle.

Travel by coach is an altogether more environmentally friendly form of tourist travel than the car, transporting large numbers of tourists on scheduled services, on transfer journeys or forming the transport element of a package holiday, for example a coach holiday in the Scottish Highlands. National Express is the largest, scheduled coach service provider in Europe, with a network of services linking 1200 destinations throughout the UK and carrying 16 million passengers every year.

Weblink
Check out this website for more information on the National Express network and services.
www.nationalexpress.com

Activity 15.3

Research and compile a fact sheet on train and coach travel services between your nearest city and London (or Belfast if you live in Northern Ireland). Include details of fares on offer, frequency of services, facilities provided at the departure point and on board, duration of a typical journey, etc.

This activity is designed to provide evidence for P1.

Stagecoach

Stagecoach

Introduction

With its headquarters in Perth, Scotland, Stagecoach Group plc is a leading international transport group, operating bus, train, tram and express coach services in the UK, USA and Canada. The Group's profit in 2007 was £161.3 million, up from £133 million in 2006. Stagecoach employs 30,000 staff, operates 13,000 vehicles and provides services to more than 2.5 million passengers every day.

Stagecoach divisions

The Group's operations are divided into three divisions:

1. UK Bus;
2. North America;
3. UK Rail.

UK Bus operations

Stagecoach owns 19 regional companies running more than 7,000 vehicles and covering around 100 towns and cities in the UK, including Liverpool, Manchester, Newcastle, Hull, Sheffield, Oxford and Cambridge. The company has a 14 per cent share of the UK bus market and carries approximately 2 million passengers every day. Stagecoach also operates megabus.com, an online, inter-city coach service based on the low-cost airlines model. More than 2.6 million passengers have travelled with megabus since the first trial route was launched in August 2003 and it has a national network covering nearly 40 locations.

North American operations

Stagecoach is a major provider of transport services in North America, employing around 4,900 people and operating a fleet of 3,000 vehicles. Its businesses are focused on commuter services, but also include tour and charter, sightseeing and school bus operations. In Canada, the company owns four transport companies, which together operate around 500 vehicles in the Provinces of Quebec and Ontario.

UK Rail operations

Stagecoach has three wholly-owned UK rail franchises – South West Trains (the largest franchise in the UK), Island Line on the Isle of Wight and East Midlands Trains (East Midlands and South Yorkshire). It also has a joint venture with the Virgin Rail Group, which operates the West Coast Main Line franchise. Altogether, Stagecoach has a 25 per cent share of the UK rail market. It also operates the Sheffield Supertram system, comprising three light-rail routes across the city and into the suburbs, and the Manchester Metrolink light rail network in the city.

Partnerships

Stagecoach works in partnership with a range of stakeholders at local and national levels to improve the quality of bus and coach provision. These include:

- Investors and the financial community – essential to the long-term investment in the Group's operations;
- Customers – the Group carries out extensive market research to help improve its services to the travelling public;
- Customer interest groups – the Group's businesses have a regular and ongoing dialogue with bus and rail user groups;
- Government – senior executives liaise with national and local governments on all matters relating to passenger transport operations;
- Transport authorities – Stagecoach works closely with local authorities and Passenger Transport Executives (PTEs) in the planning and delivery of bus, coach and rail services;
- Government advisory bodies and lobbying groups – the Group has constructive meetings with organisations such as the Commission for Integrated Transport, which provides advice to the UK government, and campaigning groups such as Transport 2000;
- Staff – in addition to one-to-one dialogue with its employees, Stagecoach works in partnership with trade unions on a range of issues, such as pensions, health and safety, training and pay rates;
- Suppliers – Stagecoach relies on a range of suppliers to provide products and services related to its bus, coach and rail operations.

Case Study Questions

1. Describe Stagecoach's passenger transport operations within the UK.
2. What are the benefits and challenges associated with having transport operations in different parts of the world?
3. The Group's annual report mentions 'corporate social responsibility'. What exactly is this and what activities does Stagecoach get involved with in this area?
4. What does Stagecoach do to help protect the environment?
5. How can companies such as Stagecoach help the government achieve its aim of reducing car use amongst the public?

This case study is designed to provide evidence for P1.

Weblink

Check out this website to help answer the questions in this case study and for more information on the Stagecoach Group.
www.stagecoachgroup.com

Sheffield Supertram is operated by Stagecoach

The main ferry operators in UK waters are:

- Short-sea Channel routes – P & O Ferries, Speed Ferries, Sea France and Norfolk Line;
- Western Channel – P & O Ferries, Brittany Ferries, Condor Ferries, Wightlink;
- North Sea – P & O Ferries, DFDS Seaways, Fjord Line, Superfast Ferries and Stena Line;
- Irish Sea – Stena Line, Irish Ferries and Isle of Man Steam Packet;
- Scottish Islands – North Link Ferries and Caledonian MacBrayne.

Activity 15.4

Choose three of the ferry operators named above and find information on the services they operate, facilities provided on board and at terminals, costs of a typical return journey and additional products they sell, e.g. mini cruises, short breaks, holidays, etc. Present your findings as fact sheets on each operator.

This activity is designed to provide evidence for P1.

Domestic ferries and water craft

In many parts of the world, ferries offer inexpensive and reliable services on short sea crossings. In places where there is strong competition between ferry operators, such as on the short sea crossings in the English Channel, there have been considerable advances in vessel technology, with the introduction of hydrofoils and jet-foils to compete with the fast, new generation of passenger ships. The opening of the Channel Tunnel in 1994 increased competition on cross-Channel services still further. In addition to operating the faster vessels, ferry companies have responded to this challenge by offering price reductions, enhanced levels of customer service and greater on-board shopping and entertainment facilities on their services.

Water taxis are commonplace in the Mediterranean, especially in the Greek Islands. Their potential is yet to be fully exploited in the UK, although there are river bus services offered on the Thames in London and in a small number of coastal locations, e.g. Falmouth in Cornwall and in the Scottish islands. Pleasure craft are not only found at sea but also on inland waterways, e.g. on canals and reservoirs.

Features of transport

There are many features of passenger transport operations that people take into account when choosing a service, as shown in Figure 15.1 and described in the following sections of this unit.

Cost

For many people, cost is the most important consideration when using transport services.

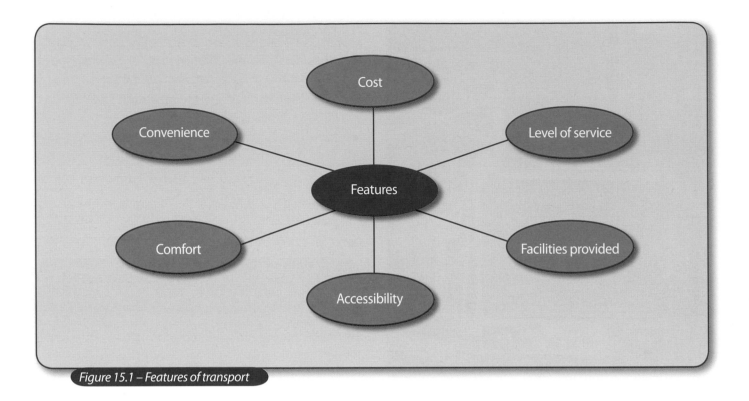

Figure 15.1 – Features of transport

People travelling on a tight budget will look for the cheapest fares possible, even if it means travelling through the night, leaving very early in the morning or arriving home from a journey very late at night. Transport operators of all kinds use variable pricing to maximise their revenue, i.e. they charge the highest prices at periods of peak demand and offer reduced off-peak rates to stimulate demand. They also offer concessionary fares to different groups of passengers, e.g. children, students, groups, over 50s, senior citizens, etc., which may be via a discount card of one sort or another. Most transport companies give discounts for tickets purchased in advance of a journey – the greater the time between booking and travel, the bigger the discount. This makes sense for the company since they receive revenue earlier than would otherwise have been the case, thereby helping their cash flow.

Level of service

All transport operators strive to provide a good standard of service to their passengers. Some offer different levels of service, which is reflected in the price paid by the customer, e.g. first or business class travel on an aircraft or train, a luxury cabin on a cruise ship or an upgraded lounge area on a ferry. Customers who are willing and able to pay extra benefit from more personal attention and extra services, such as complimentary drinks, express check-in or priority attention.

Facilities provided

Extra investment in transport services by the government and private sector companies is helping to improve facilities for the travelling public, both on board and at terminals. Customers' expectations are rising all the time and transport operators must respond by providing facilities that people want, whether it is 24/7 online booking, wireless internet technology at passenger terminals or extra comfort while travelling.

Accessibility

All transport operators try to provide access to their services and facilities for all sections of the community, especially people with disabilities. The Disability Discrimination Act (see page 157) places

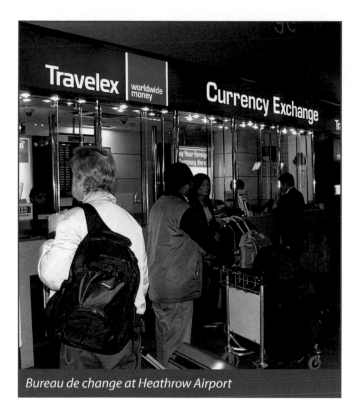
Bureau de change at Heathrow Airport

responsibilitics on passenger transport companies to provide facilities and services that are accessible to all.

FOCUS ON INDUSTRY

Rail travel for disabled people

Special arrangements can be made for disabled people to travel by train, including those who are:

- Permanent wheelchair users;
- In need of wheelchair assistance;
- Registered blind or partially-sighted;
- Disabled Persons' Railcard holders;
- Registered deaf;
- Registered disabled.

Foe many years new facilities have been designed with disabled people in mind, for example level or ramped access to stations, induction loops at ticket office windows for hearing aid users, wheelchair-accessible toilets on stations and on trains, improved signage and audible messages, and spaces for wheelchairs on trains.

Literature is also provided in alternative print formats for people with visual impairments. For those who need assistance during their journey, train companies can make arrangements to cover the entire journey, providing help with access to stations, wheelchair ramps for getting on and off trains or assistance in changing platforms. At stations with car parks there are designated parking spaces for disabled people close to the station entrance. Many of Britain's 2,500 railway stations have yet to be fully modernised and are, therefore, not completely accessible to wheelchair users or others who have difficulty in walking or using stairs.

Weblink

Check out this website for more details of facilities for disabled people on trains.
www.atoc.org

Comfort and convenience

Comfort levels on board transport services and in terminals is an important consideration for all passengers, but especially older travellers and those with special needs. Increased levels of investment in public transport services and facilities in the UK are delivering enhanced levels of comfort and

First class travel on Hull Trains (courtesy ATOC)

convenience across all modes of transport. Some passengers are willing to pay extra for a higher standard of service, such as first class travel by train.

Transport operators

Passenger transport is primarily a private sector industry in the UK. Train companies, coach operators, taxi firms, airlines and ferry companies are run on a commercial basis with the main aim of making a profit for their owners and/or shareholders – people who have invested in the company and expect a financial return on their investment.

Public sector organisations, such as the government and local councils, are responsible for setting the overall policy on passenger transport by, for example, arranging subsidies to operators to make sure that services run and regulating the industry so that services are safe and efficient. Much of the transport infrastructure is provided by public agencies, or by public/private sector partnership arrangements, including roads, bridges, terminals, etc. As demand for travel has grown, many transport terminals have developed into large, integrated complexes offering a range of catering, currency exchange, business, retail and entertainment facilities.

Not-for-profit organisations concerned with passenger transport include campaigning groups such as Transport 2000, Friends of the Earth and Sustrans, plus groups that represent the interests of the travelling public, for example Passenger Focus and the Air Transport Users Council.

Weblink
Check out these websites for more details of these not-for-profit transport organisations. www.bettertransport.org.uk; www.foe.co.uk; www.sustrans.org.uk; www.passengerfocus.org.uk; www.caa.co.uk/auc

Roles of regulatory organisations

There are legal obligations on all passenger transport operators to provide safe, secure and efficient travel for their paying passengers and staff – this applies to all types of air, road, rail and water transport. Regulatory organisations exist to make sure that passenger transport operators comply with all necessary rules and regulations concerning:

1. Health, safety and security;
2. Relevant laws;
3. Improvements to transport services and infrastructure;
4. Enhanced levels of service for passengers.

The regulatory bodies that operate in the UK include:

- Air transport – the Civil Aviation Authority (CAA) is the UK's independent aviation regulator, with all civil aviation regulatory functions – economic regulation, policy on airspace, regulation of safety and consumer protection for air travellers. The Health and Safety Executive (HSE) is responsible for all aspects of safety on the ground at airports and has some responsibility for aircraft safety while airborne, for which it works in partnership with the CAA;

- Road transport – the Department for Transport (DfT) takes the lead on all matters relating to road safety. Working with other agencies, such as the HSE, it offers advice and regulates operators. The Traffic Commissioners have responsibility for licensing buses and coaches (public service vehicles – PSV) and for issuing PSV driving licences;

- Rail transport – the Office of Rail Regulation (ORR) is a government agency that provides economic regulation of the monopoly and dominant elements of the rail industry. This includes determining level, structure and profile of charges levied by Network Rail and regulating its operation of the rail network. The ORR is also responsible for all aspects of health and safety on the railways, a role previously carried out by the Health and Safety Executive (HSE);

- Water transport – the Maritime and Coastguard Agency (MCA) is responsible for implementing the government's maritime safety policy throughout the UK, including checks on passenger ferries and cruise ships to make sure they meet UK and international safety rules.

Weblink

Check out these websites for more information on the work of the Civil Aviation Authority, Health and Safety Executive, Office of Rail Regulation, Department for Transport and the Maritime and Coastguard Agency.

www.caa.co.uk; www.hse.gov.uk;

www.rail-reg.gov.uk; www.dft.gov.uk;

www.mcga.gov.uk

Activity 15.5

Research and make notes on the roles and activities of the Civil Aviation Authority (CAA) and the Office for Rail Regulation (ORR) in relation to passenger transport regulation.

This activity is designed to provide evidence for P1.

SECTION 2 Understand the developments and factors affecting and influencing passenger transport in the UK

Using transport to travel for purposes of trade, religion, leisure and to fight in battles goes far back in history, from pre-Egyptian times and the beginning of the Greek civilisation. The Romans were great travellers, building an extensive road network across all parts of the Roman Empire. From the middle of the 17th century, young gentlemen of the aristocracy travelled to the capital cities of Europe as part of the 'Grand Tour', to broaden their education and experiences of life. Travel to spa towns became popular in the 17th and 18th centuries with visitors experiencing the healing power of their spa waters.

The development of rail transport from 1830 onwards was to have a far-reaching effect on travel for business and leisure purposes. Thomas Cook organised his first excursion by train on 5 July 1841, taking a group of 500 temperance association members from Leicester to Loughborough for a meeting. During the next three summers he arranged a succession of trips between Leicester, Nottingham, Derby and Birmingham. Rail travel in steam-driven locomotives also played a very significant role in the growth of seaside resorts around the UK coast.

Steam also played an important part in the development of long-distance travel by boat. In the 1880s, the Orient Line and North of Scotland Company, both later to be taken over by P & O, pioneered modern-style cruises and in 1904 P & O offered its first cruise holiday programme, arranged by Thomas Cook. The tour used the liner Rome, renaming her Vectis in her new role as a 'cruising yacht'.

The development of the car in the 20th century began to give people greater freedom to explore the coast and countryside, while the introduction of passenger services in jet aircraft after World War Two was to stimulate the rapid growth of the 'mass tourism' that exists around the world today. Vladimir Raitz of Horizon Holidays organised the first modern-day package holiday to Corsica in 1949.

This 'snapshot' of the historical development of passenger transport shows that just how much the industry has developed in a relatively short period of time. Clearly, passenger transport doesn't stand still! Today, the pace of change is even greater, driven by advances in technology, faster economic development and greater expectations from the travelling public.

Developments

The following sections of this unit investigate a variety of developments that affect passenger transport in the UK, including:

1. Toll roads;
2. Congestion charging;
3. High-speed rail services;
4. Developments in aircraft technology;
5. Developments in new technology and e-tourism;
6. Health, safety and security;
7. New routes and terminals.

Toll roads

Toll roads, where motorists have to pay an extra charge to travel on a section of road, are not as common in the UK as in some other European countries, although bridge tolls are well established in this country, e.g. the Severn Bridges, Dartford Crossing, Humber Bridge, etc. The M6 Toll is Britain's first privately-funded toll motorway, stretching for 27 miles from Cannock in Staffordshire to Coleshill, Warwickshire. Opened to traffic in December 2003, the M6 Toll

gives drivers the opportunity of avoiding a heavily-congested section of the M6 motorway, giving significant time savings at peak times. Research has shown savings of around 30 minutes in peak hours on a mid-week day to more than 70 minutes time saving on Fridays. Travellers who continue to use the existing M6 have also benefited from the new toll road, with reduced traffic volumes of up to 10 per cent. The M6 Toll was built by Midland Expressway, which will operate and manage it until 2054 when it will be handed back to the government. The M6 Toll benefits people travelling between the north and south of Britain for day trips and holidays.

Weblink
Check out this website for more details of the M6 Toll.
www.m6toll.co.uk

Toll charges were levied on the bridge linking the Isle of Skye to the Scottish mainland when it was built in 1995. This proved very unpopular with local people on the island, who were forced to pay a toll every time they left and returned to Skye. The tolls

The M6 Toll road at night

also had a negative impact on tourism, one of the island's most important industries. After many years of campaigning, the Skye bridge tolls were finally abolished in December 2004 and there are now no charges to cross the bridge.

Congestion charging

Charging motorists to enter a controlled area is a way of reducing traffic congestion and generating revenue to plough back into public transport services such as buses, trains and trams. The Mayor of London introduced a congestion charge in February 2003 to help reduce traffic congestion, which clogs up roads, threaten businesses and damages London's status as a thriving world city for British people and overseas visitors. Before the introduction of the congestion charge, London suffered the worst traffic congestion in the UK and amongst the worst in Europe. Drivers in central London spent 50 per cent of their time in queues.

London's congestion charge has led to reduced traffic levels and pollution, shorter journey times and better air quality. Since the scheme started, London has seen:

- Traffic entering the original charging zone reduced by 21 per cent;
- An increase in cycling within the zone of 43 per cent;
- Reductions in accidents and key traffic pollutants;
- Public transport successfully accommodating displaced car users;
- Numbers of shoppers now outperforming the rest of the UK and returning to a pattern of year-on-year growth;
- £123 million being raised in the financial year 2006-2007 to invest back into improving transport in London.

London's congestion charge has clearly benefited those who live and work in the city as well as the millions of tourists that visit every year.

London's congestion charge road logo (© Transport for London 2005)

High-speed rail services

Many European countries have developed very efficient high-speed rail services, notably France with its TGV services. Britain currently has just one high-speed rail service that links London to the Channel Tunnel and onward to the French rail network. It is known as High Speed 1 (HS1) and covers 109km in total. London and Continental Railways (LCR) completed the construction of HS1, the UK's first high-speed line, linking the Channel Tunnel in Kent via Ashford and Ebbsfleet International to the newly renovated St Pancras International, home to Eurostar services to Europe, on November 14th 2007. Constructed at a cost of £5.8 billion, HS1 is the first mainline railway built in Britain since the Great Central steamed into Marylebone in 1899.

High-speed rail services benefit tourism by allowing visitors to reach their destinations faster and in greater comfort. The UK's HS1 service encourages tourists from France and other continental countries to visit London and the rest of the UK, thereby increasing the economic impact of tourism. With HS1, the UK is now fully connected to the growing European high-speed rail network, which stretches across 3,750 km (2,330 miles) from The Netherlands and Germany to Italy, Spain and beyond.

Eurostar trains at St Pancras International (courtesy of London and Continental Railways)

Weblink

Check out this website for more details of Britain's first high-speed rail service.
www.highspeed1.com

Activity 15.6

Research and make notes on how high-speed rail developments (existing and planned) affect and influence passenger transport within the UK.

This activity is designed to provide evidence for P2.

Developments in aircraft technology

From the introduction of the Boeing 747 'jumbo jet' in 1970 to the first flight by an aircraft partly run on bio-fuel in 2008, the aviation industry has always been at the forefront of developments in new technology. In the UK, there has been a rapid growth in domestic air travel in recent years, due in no small part to the popularity of low-cost airlines like Ryanair, flybe, easyJet and bmibaby. Aircraft developments have enabled the low-cost carriers to offer cheap fares to more UK destinations for their passengers. This has led to the growth in demand for travel from regional airports, such as Exeter, Southampton, Norwich, Coventry and Liverpool. There is growing interest in using turbo-prop aircraft on domestic routes, given

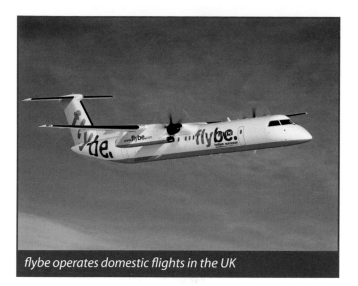
flybe operates domestic flights in the UK

that they are more fuel-efficient and less polluting than jets.

Developments in new technology and e-tourism

New technology affects passenger transport for tourism in a number of ways:

1. The means of transport itself – technology enables aircraft, trains, coaches, ferries, cruise liners, etc. to travel faster, more safely, more economically and with less harmful impacts on the environment;

2. The infrastructure that supports transport services – facilities such as ferry terminals, train stations and track, airport terminals, etc. benefit from new technology developments to provide a safe and efficient environment for passengers;

3. The sales and distribution of transport products – developments such as online booking and mobile 'phone technology have revolutionised the way passengers make their travel arrangements. Low-cost airlines have led the way in doing away with paper tickets and using e-tickets instead.

Health, safety and security

These are important issues for the transport sector, especially since the tragic events of September 11th 2001 and subsequent terrorist attacks around the world. Security at UK airports, railway stations, ferry terminals and cruise ports has increased noticeably. This sometimes results in delays for passengers, but most are happy to put up with a little inconvenience. Transport operators of all kinds must comply with stricter security guidelines when carrying out their business, which can sometimes lead to increased operating costs. Health scares and epidemics, such as foot and mouth disease, SARS and Asian bird 'flu, can also affect travel, with knock-on effects for transport providers.

New routes and terminals

We discussed earlier in this unit that the number of passengers travelling by air is predicted to double by 2020, while rail travel and cruising are steadily increasing in popularity. Transport operators respond to this increased demand by introducing new routes and working with the public sector to develop new terminals and transport infrastructure. There are often considerable objections from local people to developing new terminals. They are concerned about the impact on the environment and their quality of life. This is particularly the case with new airport developments, such as extra airport runways or new access roads.

FOCUS ON INDUSTRY

Terminal 5

Terminal 5 at Heathrow began operating for passengers on 27 March 2008, after being officially opened by the Queen on 14 March. The terminal has taken six years to build at a cost of £4.3 billion. It consists of a main terminal building and two smaller 'satellites', the second of which is due to open in 2010. Terminal 5 has been designed to give passengers an efficient and stress-free experience when checking-in and waiting for their departure. In addition to the buildings, the Terminal 5 development includes:

* A six-platform railway station;
* Extensions to the London Underground Piccadilly Line and Heathrow Express;

- A spur road linking Terminal 5 to the M25 motorway;
- A new, 87 metre air traffic control tower;
- 60 aircraft stands.

British Airways is the only airline that will use the Terminal 5 facilities and its move to the new facility means that around 40 per cent of Heathrow's passengers will travel from the new terminal. This has presented BAA (British Airports Authority – the airport's owner) with an opportunity to undertake a major £6.2 billion redevelopment programme, including the construction of Heathrow East, a completely new facility that will replace the existing Terminals 1 and 2.

Weblink

Check out this website for more details of Terminal 5 at Heathrow.
www.baa.com

Activity 15.7

The government has announced plans to consult on building a third runway at Heathrow Airport. Carry out some research and write a 500-word newspaper article that outlines the case for and the case against this development. Explain how a third runway would affect and influence passenger transport within the UK.

This activity is designed to provide evidence for P2.

Factors

The following sections of this unit investigate a number if factors that affect passenger transport in the UK, including:

- Political;
- Legal;
- Environmental;
- Social;
- Economic.

Political factors

Political factors are those that are controlled or dictated by governments – at European, national, regional or local level.

At European level, the European Union (EU) passes laws and regulations (known as directives) that are directly concerned with, or have an impact on, passenger transport in the UK. These include regulations on, for example, the amount of time people are allowed to work (Working Time Directive), consumer protection for UK and overseas holidays (The Package Travel Directive), passenger vehicle speed limiters, vehicle pollution levels, drivers' hours and transport safety. There is currently a proposal for a new EU directive that would bring air travel into the EU Emissions Trading Scheme from 2011. Like the industrial companies that are already covered by the scheme, airlines will be able to sell surplus allowances if they reduce their emissions and will need to buy additional allowances if their emissions increase. The directive is a move towards encouraging the air transport industry to make a fair contribution to efforts to cut greenhouse gas emissions.

At national level, the UK government provides subsidies (payments) to some transport operators to allow them to offer services to the travelling public. This is particularly the case with trains and buses. Subsidies benefit local people and tourists alike, since without the subsidies, it would not be cost-effective for the transport companies to run the services. Subsidies are also offered by local councils and regional development agencies.

Governments also practise 'deregulation' in transport, which is when they move ownership of transport services from the public to the private sector. It is perhaps most associated with airlines, which historically have been state-owned. Through a process of 'privatisation', many UK airlines and other transport companies are now operated in the private sector, e.g. British Airways, Virgin Trains, etc. Deregulation is intended to increase competition between companies and ultimately produce better quality services and lower fares for passengers.

Deregulation of bus and coach travel, which took place in the USA in 1982 and in Britain under the Transport Act of 1985, has liberalised the market for travel and offered passengers a wide choice of operators. In the case of Europe, EU legislation allows a coach company from any member state of the EU to offer coach services in any other EU country.

FOCUS ON INDUSTRY

Stagecoach and deregulation

Stagecoach was one of the first companies to take advantage of transport deregulation in the UK in the 1980s and in the early years of the decade operated coach services in Scotland, as well as longer distance services to London. The Transport Act of 1985 deregulated bus services, which had previously been owned and operated by councils and local transport authorities. One of the early services launched by Stagecoach was Magicbus, which operated in Glasgow and offered cut-price fares to passengers. In the late 1980s, Stagecoach bought a number of former National Bus Company businesses, including Hampshire, Cumberland, United Counties, Ribble and Southdown. Stagecoach was one of the first major transport operators to expand overseas, buying the UTM bus company in Malawi.

Weblink
Check out this website for more details of the Stagecoach group of companies.
www.stagecoachgroup.com

Deregulation of the UK rail industry came with the privatisation of the railways under the Railways Act 1993. Following privatisation, the former British Rail was divided into two main elements, the first consisting of the national rail network (track, signalling, bridges, tunnels, stations and depots) with the second element being the train operating companies (TOCs) whose trains run on the network, e.g. Virgin Trains, GNER, South West Trains and First Great Western.

Legal factors

We discussed earlier in this unit that the European Union (EU) passes directives that affect passenger transport in a number of ways. These directives ultimately end up as laws and regulations in the EU member states, including the UK. One important area of law that affects passenger transport is the impact of the Disability Discrimination Act (DDA). Part 3 of the Act concerns public transport premises and public transport vehicles, other than aviation and shipping. The law states that public transport buildings, such as train stations, bus stations, airports and ferry ports, must be made accessible to disabled people. This also means that any services that are provided at these places must also be accessible to disabled people, for example travel information and booking facilities. The Act does not mean that

Assisted train travel (courtesy of ATOC)

all passenger transport vehicles such as trains, buses, coaches, aeroplanes, ferries and taxis must be accessible. There are separate regulations that set out how buses, coaches and trains need to be adapted, and the dates by which this needs to be done.

Weblink

Check out this website for more information on the impact of the DDA on passenger transport. www.dptac.gov.uk

Activity 15.8

Research two UK passenger transport companies and find out what services and facilities they offer passengers with disabilities and special needs.

This activity is designed to provide evidence for P2.

Environmental factors

The future of the environment is a major talking point today, not least the environmental impacts of passenger transport. Many scientists believe that the carbon emissions from cars and aircraft contribute towards global warming – the gradual rise in the earth's temperature. This, in turn, may lead to the melting of the polar ice caps and the gradual rise in sea levels, threatening low-lying coastal areas in particular. Developments in a variety of transport modes have given tourists the opportunity of travelling quickly to faraway places at a relatively low cost in comparative safety. New locations and destinations in the UK have been opened up for tourism, particularly since the introduction of the low-cost airlines and the growth in domestic air travel. Just as the travel and tourism industry must work towards greater sustainability, so too must the transport sector on which it relies so heavily. Transport operators are working hard to introduce cleaner types of travel, using more fuel-efficient vehicles that produce fewer harmful emissions.

FOCUS ON INDUSTRY

Bio-fuel used in aviation

The first commercial airline to be powered partly by bio-fuel flew from London's Heathrow Airport to Amsterdam in February 2008. A Virgin Atlantic Boeing 747 used fuel derived from a mixture of Brazilian babassu nuts and coconuts to complete the journey. The plane had one of its four engines connected to an independent bio-fuel tank that it said could provide 20 per cent of the engines' power. Earlier in the same month Airbus tested another alternative aviation fuel, a synthetic mix of gas-to-liquid. Sir Richard Branson, Chairman of Virgin, said that the flight was an important step for the airline industry and would enable companies that were serious about reducing their carbon emissions to go on developing the fuels of the future.

Weblink

Check out this website for more information on Virgin Atlantic. www.virgin-atlantic.com

Social factors

The development of the UK passenger transport system over the last 150 years has created a variety of social benefits for people travelling on holidays, short breaks and day visits, including:

● Increased mobility – people now have greater freedom to explore town and country areas on public transport and in their private cars. Figures from the Department for Transport indicate that nearly 30 per cent of the UK population do not own or have access to a car, relying instead on public transport;

● Equality – falling real prices of travel and cars have opened up transport opportunities to people from all income levels, religious backgrounds and ethnic origins, whether living in urban or rural areas. People with mobility problems have benefited from the greater freedom offered by the private car and improving facilities on public transport services;

- Enhanced holiday/leisure experience – developments in transport have played a crucial role in the development of a travel and tourism industry that is responsive to customer needs, provides a wide range of products and services to destinations throughout the world, and enhances people's quality of life.

The growth in the number of people using the various methods of transport has brought a sharper focus on passenger issues. Consumers in all sectors feel more empowered in expecting high levels of personal attention and customer service, and more confident in making complaints. Transport operators need to respond to this wider trend and with more elderly and mobility-impaired people travelling, the transport industry will need to continue to increase standards of passenger care. Training plays a vital role in helping staff to offer excellent standards of customer service to passengers.

Economic factors

At the time of writing, the world price of oil has broken through the $100 a barrel mark for the first time ever. This has pushed up the price of fuel for UK car owners to record levels, making many people think twice about using their car for a day trip, short break or longer holiday. Transport and travel companies are feeling the squeeze as well. Some airlines and tour operators are passing on the extra fuel costs to customers, through surcharges and supplements.

Economic issues to do with investment and jobs have always been at the forefront of transport developments. Entrepreneurs such as Thomas Cook, Samuel Cunard, Harold Bamberg of Eagle Airways, Freddie Laker of Skytrain (the first transatlantic, low-cost airline) and Richard Branson of Virgin, have invested heavily in transport services that have been used by millions of tourists. Transport is the lifeblood of the travel and tourism industry, helping to create thousands of service jobs in the UK and in tourist destinations across the globe. Transport has allowed destinations to develop their travel and tourism potential to the full, stimulating investment in airports, hotels, tourist attractions, travel agencies, tour operators, restaurants, night clubs, etc. In the UK, transport, like tourism, is an important part of economic development, particularly in regions of the country that have suffered from the decline of traditional industries such as mining, ship building and textiles.

Activity 15.9

With reference to one recent development and one factor, explain how the UK passenger transport sector responds to each.

This activity is designed to provide evidence for M1.

SECTION 3 | # Understand the relationships between UK passenger transport networks and the travel and tourism industry

From the construction of the first road networks in Roman times, the introduction of the railways in the mid-19th century, the growth of private motoring throughout the 20th century to the development of jet aircraft from the 1950s onwards, the growth of the travel and tourism industry has been closely linked to developments in transport networks. The provision of safe, reliable, comfortable, fast, convenient and

Year	Car (%)	Train (%)	Coach/bus (%)	Sea/air (%)
1951	28	48	28	-
1961	49	28	23	-
1971	63	10	17	-
1981	72	12	12	-
1991	78	6	12	-
1998	71	7	14	-
2004	71	13	6	-
2006	79	8	7	3

Source: Adapted from VisitBriatin data

Figure 15.2 – Modes of transport used for holiday travel in the UK 1951-2006

The popularity of different modes of transport changes over time, in response to new developments in technology, government priorities and customer demand. Figure 15.2 gives an indication of how the demand for different types of transport for tourism has changed since 1951 in the UK. It shows that holiday trips by car have increased dramatically from 28 per cent in 1951 to 79 per cent in 2006. Both rail and coach/bus tourist trips have decreased over the same time period, although rail travel has begun to show an upturn in popularity in recent years.

accessible modes of transport, plus an adequate transport infrastructure, is a vital prerequisite for successful tourism development in the UK.

The term 'passenger transport networks' refers to the fact that transport services do not operate in

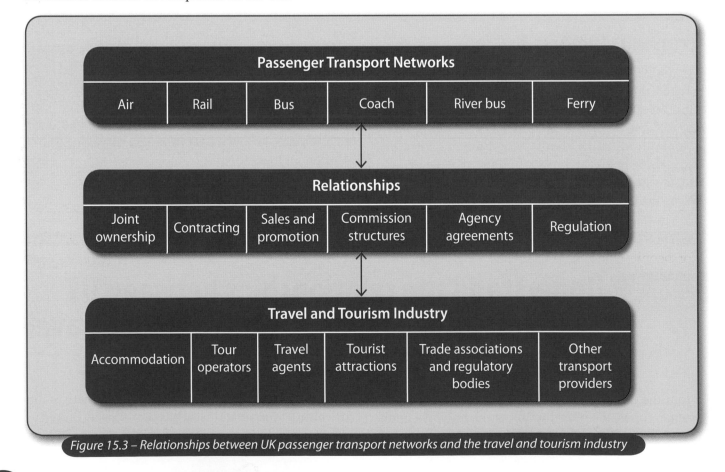

Figure 15.3 – Relationships between UK passenger transport networks and the travel and tourism industry

isolation from each other, but form part of larger transport systems. These can be made up of the same type of transport, for example the UK rail network, or comprise a combination of different transport types, e.g. the network of passenger transport services available at an airport – taxis, rail, coach, air, etc.

Figure 15.3 shows the relationships between UK passenger transport networks and the travel and tourism industry, indicating the different modes of transport and the various components of the travel and tourism industry.

UK passenger transport networks

We discussed at the beginning of this unit that the UK has a variety of air, rail, coach and water-based transport services, each with its own network structure. The UK government is committed to an integrated transport industry that offers a full range of reliable and efficient choices for people when making their travel decisions. In its Future of Transport White Paper published in 2004, the government agreed to the following objectives:

1. The road network – providing a more reliable and free-flowing service for both personal travel and freight, with people being able to make informed choices about how and when they travel;
2. The rail network – providing a fast, reliable and efficient service, particularly for inter-urban

Figure 15.4 – UK's principal motorways

journeys and commuting into large urban areas;
3. Making walking and cycling real alternatives for local trips;
4. Providing improved international and domestic links at ports and airports.

Figure 15.4 gives an overview of the UK motorway network, while Figure 15.5 shows our principal airports and ports.

Figure 15.5 – The UK's principal airports and ports

Relationships

There are many business relationships between UK passenger networks and the various components of the UK travel and tourism industry, as the following examples demonstrate:

- Joint ownership – e.g. a coach operator owning its own hotels;

- Contracting – e.g. a tour operator entering into a contract with a rail company to offer short breaks in major UK cities;

- Sales and promotion – e.g. a rail operator running a joint advertising campaign with a tourist attraction;

- Commission structures – e.g. a ferry company agreeing what level of commission it will pay to travel agencies for tickets sold;

- Agency agreements – a travel agent entering into an agreement with a coach company to sell coach holidays;

- Regulation – the Civil Aviation Authority (CAA) inspecting the safety standards at an airline.

Activity 15.10

Using your own examples, explain the relationships between UK passenger transport networks and the UK travel and tourism industry. Recommend and justify realistic measures to enhance relationships between passenger transport and the UK travel and tourism industry. Evaluate the extent to which passenger transport in the UK supports the economic growth of tourism, making reference to specific examples.

This activity is designed to provide evidence for P3, M2 and D1.

The travel and tourism industry

Figure 15.3 on page 160 shows the various components of the UK travel and tourism industry – accommodation, tour operators, travel agents, tourist attractions, trade associations, regulatory bodies and transport providers. Each of these parts of the industry interacts with transport networks in the ways described above. A component of travel and tourism may well have multiple relationships with transport providers. A tour operator, for example, may:

- Have agency agreements with travel agents;
- Be regulated by the terms of the Package Travel Regulations and other legislation;
- Agree commission structures with coach companies;
- Run sales and promotional campaigns with rail operators;
- Enter into contracts with ferry companies;
- Jointly own a car hire firm.

Ferry services are sold through travel agencies (courtesy of Brittany Ferries)

SECTION 4 ▸ # Understand how passenger transport provision affects the popularity and appeal of a specific UK tourist destination

The range of transport services available to and within a destination, as well as their cost, frequency and the levels of service offered, can have an important influence on its popularity with visitors. Resorts in remote areas, that have poor road and rail access, will struggle to attract the levels of tourist trade necessary to develop a full range of tourist facilities and amenities. On the other hand, a destination such as Liverpool, with frequent rail, air, ferry and road passenger transport services to and from the city, is in a good position to attract visitors from the UK and overseas.

Passenger transport provision

We have seen already in this unit that the UK has a wide variety of transport services available to reach tourist destinations and travel around once there. These rail, road, air and sea services are provided mainly by private sector businesses, with support and help from public and not-for-profit organisations. Whatever service is used, and whether it is to reach a destination in the first place or travel around once there, all tourists look for passenger transport services that are frequent, convenient, fast, reliable, safe and offer good value for money for the services provided. Transport operators make their services available via a variety of distribution channels, including online booking on the internet, booking offices at stations and terminals, and via travel agents and other retailers. Companies tend to charge the highest prices when demand is at its greatest and offer reduced rates for off-peak travel.

UK tourist destinations

The UK has a very wide variety of tourist destinations that appeal to British people and overseas visitors, for example:

- Capital cities – i.e. London, Edinburgh, Belfast and Edinburgh;
- Coastal resorts – e.g. Brighton, Blackpool, Rhyl, Torquay, Cleethorpes;
- Purpose-built resorts – e.g. Butlin's, Center Parcs, Forestry Commission parks;
- Countryside areas – e.g. National Parks, Areas of Outstanding Natural Beauty, Heritage Coasts, forests, mountain areas, lakes and waterways;
- Historical/cultural destinations – e.g. Stratford-upon-Avon, Bath, Ironbridge, Stonehenge, York;
- Business travel destinations and conference venues – e.g. London, Manchester, Birmingham, Leeds, Cardiff, Edinburgh, Glasgow, Belfast.

It is possible for a travel and tourism destination to fall into more than one of these categories. Bournemouth, for example, is a typical English south coast seaside resort as well as being an important business tourism and conference destination.

Cardiff is a popular tourist destination with good transport links

Activity 15.11

Describe the different types of passenger transport provision in two of the following tourist destinations:

1. York;
2. Belfast;
3. Brighton;
4. Scarborough;
5. Bath.

With reference to one of your chosen destinations:

(a) Assess the effectiveness of passenger transport in the destination and the effect on its popularity and appeal to tourists;
(b) Evaluate the contribution of passenger transport provision to the destination's popularity and appeal, making recommendations for improvements.

This activity is designed to provide evidence for P4, M3 and D2.

Popularity and appeal of destinations

A destination's popularity and appeal depends on a wide range of factors, some within its control and some not. These include:

- Natural attractions – places such as the Lake District and Snowdonia have wide appeal to visiting tourists;

- Built attractions – heritage and more modern attractions, such as theme parks and amusements, can increase a destination's appeal;

- Media attention – destinations that feature in TV programmes, magazines and newspapers, become more appealing as places to visit, e.g. the area of Yorkshire featured in the TV series Last of the Summer Wine;

- Location and accessibility – proximity to large centres of population increases the popularity of tourist resorts;

- Transport provision – destinations that are well-served by reliable and frequent passenger transport services are more likely to attract visitors.

Activity 15.12

With reference to named examples, explain how passenger transport provision can influence the popularity and appeal of UK tourist destinations.

This activity is designed to provide evidence for P5.

Case Study

Blackpool

Introduction

Blackpool is the UK's best-known seaside resort and home to the UK's most popular tourist attraction – Blackpool Pleasure Beach, with 5.5 million visitors in 2007. The resort itself welcomes around 10 million visitors every year to its two beaches and wide variety of tourist attractions and events, which include Blackpool Tower, Sandcastle Waterpark, Blackpool Zoo and the Sea Life Centre. The resort is also famous for its illuminations, designed to attract visitors outside of the peak holiday period. Blackpool is also a popular business tourism destination, hosting conferences, business meetings and exhibitions. The resort boasts a wide variety of entertainment venues for visitors, including the Opera House, Pavilion Theatre, Horseshoe Bar, Grand Theatre and Tower Circus. There are more than 30 nightclubs, plus numerous pubs, cafés and restaurants, plus a 10-screen Odeon cinema. Blackpool has a pedestrianised town centre shopping area with high-street chains and specialist shops. The resort has a wide range of sports facilities, including 3 18-hole golf courses, 2 golf driving ranges, outdoor bowling, ten-pin bowling, a sports centre and more than 50 tennis courts.

Types of visitors

The 10 million tourists who visit Blackpool every year are primarily attracted to the resort because of its reputation for fun, excitement and entertainment. Most visitors come to Blackpool on 1-3 night short breaks, day trips or to visit friends and relatives (VFR). The resort attracts visitors across a wide age range – from young people on hen and stag nights to families and older people drawn by Blackpool's appeal as an entertainment centre. Coach parties and other groups make use of Blackpool's bigger hotels, such as

Liberty's on the Square, the Savoy Hotel and the Park House Hotel. The resort also has a buoyant business tourism market, catering for exhibitions, conferences, sales conventions and business meetings.

Rail travel

Blackpool is connected to all parts of Britain via the rail network. Intercity trains to Preston link with a local shuttle service to the resort. There are approximately 10-12 trains per day from London (via Preston) to Blackpool, with a journey time in the region of 4 hours and 30 minutes. There are currently 35 services per day from Manchester, including Manchester Airport, to Blackpool, with a journey time of 1 hour and 15 minutes. The local shuttle service linking the resort to Preston runs every 30 minutes and is a half-hour journey.

Blackpool railway station (courtesy of ATOC)

Road travel

Blackpool is one of the few UK resorts that has a motorway direct to the town – the M55. This gives car drivers and coach passengers easy access to the resort. The M55 connects to the M6 and, from there, to all areas of the UK. National Express services operate to and from Blackpool throughout the year, linking the resort to the 1500 UK destinations currently offered by the coach operator.

Air travel

Blackpool Airport is situated 2.5 miles from the town centre and has a new terminal building capable of handling 350,000 passengers per year. Currently, scheduled services include flights from Aberdeen, Southampton, Dublin, Gerona, the Isle of Man, Malaga, Murcia, Alicante, Palma and Belfast. Airlines that offer services include Ryanair, Jet2 and Manx2. Nearby airports that offer a wider range of services include Manchester (58 miles), with direct train connections to Blackpool, and Liverpool (62 miles), linked to the resort via the M6 and M55 motorways.

Ferries

Blackpool is within reach of a number of ferry ports with crossings from Ireland, the Isle of Man and the Netherlands, for example:

- From Larne in Northern Ireland – Fleetwood (7 miles) and Cairnryan (211 miles);
- From Dublin in the Republic of Ireland – Liverpool (57 miles) and Holyhead (155 miles);
- From Douglas on the Isle of Man – Liverpool (57 miles) and Heysham (43 miles);
- From Belfast in Northern Ireland – Stranraer (333 miles);
- From Dun Laoghaire in the Republic of Ireland – Holyhead (155 miles);
- From the Hook of Holland in the Netherlands – Harwich (294 miles).

Case Study Questions and Activities

1. After carrying out some further research, describe five types of passenger transport provision in Blackpool.
2. Explain how passenger transport provision can influence the popularity and appeal of UK tourist destinations like Blackpool.
3. Assess the effectiveness of passenger transport in Blackpool and the effect on its popularity and appeal to tourists.
4. Evaluate the contribution of passenger transport provision to the popularity and appeal of Blackpool, making recommendations for improvements.

This case study is designed to provide evidence for P4, P5, M3 and D2.

Weblink

Check out this website to help answer the questions in this case study and for more information on Blackpool as a tourist destination.

www.visitblackpool.com

Activity 15.13

Using the case study of Blackpool as a guide, research and compile your own case study of another popular seaside resort in the UK. In your case study you should:

(a) Describe five types of passenger transport provision in the destination;

(b) Assess the effectiveness of passenger transport in the destination and the effect of its popularity and appeal to tourists;

(c) Evaluate the contribution of passenger transport provision to the destination's popularity and appeal, making recommendations for improvements.

This activity is designed to provide evidence for P4, M3 and D2.

Unit summary

This unit has examined the UK passenger transport sector and its links with travel and tourism. This has involved exploring the various types of passenger transport provision in the UK and the features of transport, such as cost, levels of service and accessibility. You have also investigated developments and factors that affect passenger transport, such as high-speed rail developments and subsidies. The unit has also explored the relationships between passenger transport and the travel and tourism industry, including joint ownership, contracting and agency agreements. Finally, you have examined how passenger transport provision affects the popularity and appeal of tourist destinations. Throughout the unit you have been shown many industry examples, while the case studies of the Stagecoach Group plc and Blackpool highlight key issues in passenger transport.

If you have worked methodically, by the end of this unit you should:

- Know about passenger transport operations within the UK;
- Understand the developments and factors affecting and influencing passenger transport in the UK;
- Understand the relationships between UK passenger transport networks and the travel and tourism industry;
- Understand how passenger transport provision affects the popularity and appeal of a specific UK tourist destination.

You are now in a position to complete the assignment for the unit, under the direction of your tutor. Before you tackle the assignment you may like to have a go at the following questions to help build your knowledge of passenger transport issues.

Test your knowledge

1. How has the development of the private car influenced travel for UK holidays and day visits?
2. Name three airlines that offer domestic air travel in the UK.
3. Explain the relationship between transport networks and the UK travel and tourism industry.
4. Name three organisations that have responsibility for the regulation of transport in the UK.
5. Why do you think that rail travel for tourist trips is growing in popularity?
6. What is a train operating company (TOC) and which TOCs operate in your local area?
7. Explain the role of Network Rail in the UK rail industry.
8. What factors are contributing to the rapid growth in air travel in the UK?
9. Why is there increased demand for regional airports in the UK.
10. List five features that passengers consider when deciding which type of passenger transport to choose.
11. How can the passenger transport sector reduce carbon emissions?
12. Explain how new technology affects the passenger transport sector.
13. What are the implications for transport operators of the increased measures needed to ensure health, safety and security in transport?
14. Give three examples of relationships between transport providers and components of the travel and tourism industry in the UK.
15. What effect is the high price of oil having on passenger transport operations?

Answers to these questions can be found on the Book 2 Tutor's CD-ROM that accompanies this book (ISBN 9780955019050). Full details can be found at www.tandtpublishing.co.uk

Passenger Transport Issues for the Travel and Tourism Industry

Introduction

This assignment is made up of a number of tasks which, when successfully completed, are designed to give you sufficient evidence to meet the Pass (P), Merit (M) and Distinction (D) grading criteria for the unit. If you have carried out the activities and read the case studies throughout this unit, you will already have done a lot of work towards completing the tasks for this assignment.

Scenario

You have been lucky in finding a summer placement job working for one of the top travel trade newspapers in the country. You will be reporting to Brenda Brook, the newspaper's transport correspondent. Brenda is working on a feature on passenger transport for the next edition of the newspaper.

The feature is divided into four main areas:

1. Passenger transport operations within the UK;
2. Developments and factors affecting and influencing passenger transport in the UK;
3. The relationships between UK passenger transport networks and the travel and tourism industry;
4. How passenger transport provision affects the popularity and appeal of a specific UK tourist destination.

Brenda wants you to carry out some research for the feature and present the information to her as a series of Word documents that she can edit and incorporate into the feature, plus a case study. She has asked you to complete the following four tasks.

TASK 1

Your first document is a report in which you must:

Describe passenger transport operations within the UK. This must cover passenger transport provision, features of the various types of transport, who operates them and how they are regulated.

This task is designed to provide evidence for P1.

TASK 2

The document for this task must:

(a) **Describe** three significant developments and three factors affecting and influencing passenger transport within the UK.

This task is designed to provide evidence for P2.

To be considered for a Merit grade for this task, your document must also:

(b) **Explain** how the UK passenger transport sector responds to developments and factors.

This task is designed to produce evidence for M1.

TASK 3

The document for this task must:

(a) **Explain** the relationships between UK passenger transport networks and the travel and tourism industry.

This task is designed to provide evidence for P3.

To be considered for a Merit grade for this task, your document must also:

(b) **Recommend** and **justify** realistic measures to enhance relationships between passenger transport and the UK travel and tourism industry.

This task is designed to produce evidence for M2.

To be considered for a Distinction grade for this task, your document must also:

(c) **Evaluate** the extent to which passenger transport in the UK supports the economic growth of tourism, making reference to specific examples.

This task is designed to produce evidence for D1.

TASK 4

Your final task should be presented as a written case study in which you must:

(a) As an introduction to the case study, **explain** how passenger transport provision can influence the popularity and appeal of tourist destinations generally;

(b) **Describe** five types of passenger transport provision in a specific UK tourist destination.

This task is designed to provide evidence for P5 and P4 respectively.

To be considered for a Merit grade for this task, your case study must also:

(c) **Assess** the effectiveness of passenger transport in your chosen tourist destination and the effect on its popularity and appeal to tourists.

This task is designed to produce evidence for M3.

To be considered for a Distinction grade for this task, your case study must also:

(d) **Evaluate** the contribution of passenger transport provision to the popularity and appeal of your chosen tourist destination, making recommendations for improvements.

This task is designed to produce evidence for D2.

UNIT 18

The Appeal and Importance of UK Visitor Attractions

INTRODUCTION TO THE UNIT

Visitor attractions play a vital role in the travel and tourism industry, offering excitement, fun, education and activities for all types of people from the UK and overseas. It is often an attraction that tempts people to visit a tourist destination in the first place. Attractions can be purpose-built, such as a theme park or family entertainment complex, or naturally-occurring, for example National Parks, forests and lakes. Together, they offer a wealth of unique experiences for domestic and overseas visitors to Britain.

In this unit you will learn about different types of visitor attractions, and the products and services they offer. You will discover how attractions use different kinds of interpretation techniques to inform, educate and entertain visitors, including displays, leaflets and costumed guides. You will also investigate the appeal of attractions to different types of visitors and the key features that affect their decision to visit, such as location, opening times, transport links and admission charges. Finally, the unit explores the importance of visitor attractions to the popularity and appeal of UK tourist destinations. Supervised visits to local and national attractions, and talks by people working in the attractions sector, will help you to understand how attractions operate, plus the techniques they use to attract and retain visitors.

WHAT YOU WILL STUDY

When you have completed this unit you should:

1. **Know the products and services provided by different types of visitor attraction;**
2. **Know the range and purpose of techniques used for visitor interpretation;**
3. **Understand the appeal of visitor attractions to different types of visitor;**
4. **Understand the importance of visitor attractions to the popularity and appeal of UK tourist destinations.**

You will be guided through the main topics in this unit with the help of the latest developments, statistics, industry examples and case studies. You should also check out the weblinks throughout the unit for extra information on particular organisations or topic areas and use the activities throughout the unit to help you learn more.

ASSESSMENT FOR THIS UNIT

This unit is internally assessed, meaning that you will be given an assignment (or series of assignments) to complete by your tutor(s) to show that you have fully understood the content of the unit. A grading scale of pass, merit or distinction is used when staff mark your assignment(s), with higher grades awarded to students who show greater depth in analysis, evaluation and justification in their assignments. An assignment for this unit, which covers all the grading criteria, can be found on page 204. Don't forget to visit www.tandtONLine.co.uk for all the latest industry news, developments, statistics and hot links to websites in this unit to help you with your assignments.

Icebreaker

This unit investigates the appeal and importance of UK visitor attractions – from theme parks and National Parks to cathedrals and museums. Working by yourself, or in small groups under the direction of your tutor, see how you get on with the following tasks to help you make a start on this unit:

- Have a go at coming up with your own definition of a 'visitor attraction';
- Name six built attractions found in the UK;
- Thinking about an attraction close to where you live, make notes on who owns the facility, its purpose and the types of visitors it attracts;
- Working in a small group, discuss what you think is meant by 'interpretation' and its link with visitor attractions ;
- Think of three points that would be important to you when deciding whether or not to visit an attraction;
- Name six natural attractions found in the UK;
- Working in a small group, discuss the importance of visitor attractions to the UK tourist industry.

When you've finished, show your answers to your tutor and compare your answers with what other students in your class have written.

SECTION 1

Know the products and services provided by different types of visitor attraction

There are an estimated 6,400 visitor attractions in the UK, including popular attractions such as Alton Towers, the London Eye, Edinburgh Castle and the Eden Project in Cornwall. It is important to remember that many tourist attractions throughout Britain are not multi-million pound businesses, but smaller enterprises such as museums, craft galleries, shops, leisure facilities and farm attractions that are crucial to the economic prosperity of many parts of the country. Together, they form the 'critical mass' of attractions in an area that encourage tourists to explore and perhaps stay overnight, thereby adding more value to the local economy. The former English Tourist Board's definition of a 'visitor attraction' shows that such places should be promoted to local people as well as to tourists:

'a permanently established excursion destination, a primary purpose of which is to allow public access for entertainment, interest or education, rather than being a primary retail outlet or a venue for sporting, theatrical, or film performances. It must be open to the public, without prior booking, for published periods each year, and should be capable of attracting day visitors or tourists, as well as local residents'.

Products and services

Managers of visitor attractions aim to maximise the revenue from their customers in order to make a profit and re-invest money into new facilities for visitors. They do this by offering a variety of primary, secondary and additional products and services.

The main facility, and principal reason for visiting the attraction, is known as the 'primary product'. If you visit a theme park, for example, the primary product is made up of the rides that provide excitement and fun. The primary product at a museum are the exhibits on display, while the prime reason for visiting a stately home is to see the architecture and furniture in the building, and learn about the way of life of the people who lived there in the past. The primary product of natural attractions is the beauty of the landscape that people have come to enjoy.

The primary product doesn't change a great deal over time, but attraction operators have to regularly update their 'product' in order to give people a reason to visit again. If a theme park, for example, did not introduce new rides and facilities on a regular basis, it would soon lose its customers and become unprofitable. Attractions often stage events that appeal to different types of visitors as a way of revitalising their primary product and generating extra income.

FOCUS ON INDUSTRY

Events at Chatsworth House

As well as welcoming visitors to the stately home and gardens, Chatsworth House in Derbyshire runs a series of special events that appeal to a wide variety of visitors, for example:

- Horse trials;
- An angling fair;
- A country fair;
- Concerts;
- Behind-the-scenes days;
- Farm shop events and demonstrations;
- Garden events;
- Sewing school courses;
- Vintage car rallies;
- Farmyard and woodland walks.

Offering such a wide variety of events helps to the keep the primary product refreshed and gives visitors who have been before a good reason for making a return visit.

Weblink

Check out this website for more information on events and facilities at Chatsworth House. www.chatsworth.org

Secondary and additional products and services are very important to visitor attractions, since they enhance the visitor experience and generate additional revenue. They include:

- Shops – selling gifts, souvenirs and products linked to the attraction, e.g. knitwear at a woollen mill and wine at a vineyard;
- Food and drink – for sale in restaurants, cafés, fast-food outlets, ice cream parlours, etc. The larger attractions feature well-known catering brands, such as McDonalds, Burger King and KFC;
- Children's play areas – often provided at no extra charge to provide somewhere for youngsters to let off steam and for parents to have a break;
- Picnic areas – places for individuals and groups to eat their own food. Picnic areas increase a person's 'dwell time' at an attraction, i.e. the total amount of time spent on site;
- Toilets – the availability and cleanliness of toilets is very important to visitors. Poor facilities create a bad impression with visitors and affect the number of repeat visits;
- Parking – visitors may have to pay to park their cars or this facility may be provided for free. Depending on the size of the attraction, there may be transport from the car parks to the main entrance, e.g. by land train, monorail or coaches.
- Services for visitors with special needs – providing accessible attractions is now a legal requirement under the Disability Discrimination Act and makes good business sense as well;
- Corporate hospitality and room hire – hosting business functions, meetings, conferences and even weddings is an excellent way for attractions to increase their income, particularly out of season when visitor numbers may be low;
- Photography – another income-earning activity,

especially in theme parks, where visitors are given the chance to buy a photo of themselves while on a ride;

- Education services – school, college and university groups make up a sizeable proportion of the visitors to many attractions, so providing facilities such as a classroom, guided walks, illustrated talks and fact sheets adds to the visitors' experience, as well as making good business sense.

Visitors usually have to pay an extra charge for most ancillary products and services, thereby generating extra revenue for the attraction. This 'secondary spend' as it is sometimes known, can be very profitable for the attraction – profit margins on, for example, selling gifts, food and drink, can be far higher than margins on entrance fees to the attraction.

FOCUS ON INDUSTRY

At-Bristol's corporate events

At-Bristol is a 'hands-on' science and discovery attraction located in the regenerated harbour area of Bristol. The attraction offers a wide variety of corporate events, including:

- Banquets and receptions;
- Conferences, meetings and presentations;
- Product launches, trade fairs, location shoots and concerts;
- Incentive outings, team-building activities and debate forums;
- Wedding receptions, family functions, wedding and naming ceremonies.

At-Bristol also has access to public areas surrounding the attraction that can be used for corporate events. Millennium Square can seat up to 4,500 people or accommodate 7,500 standing, while the smaller Anchor Square is designed to seat 1,000 people or accommodate 2,000 standing. Both squares are used for large events such as open-air concerts and exhibitions of public art.

Weblink

Check out this website for more information on At-Bristol and its corporate events.
www.at-bristol.org.uk/corporate

Activity 18.1

Choose three visitor attractions spread across the country and find out what facilities and services they offer for corporate events. Make a fact sheet on each of the attractions giving full details of the corporate facilities on offer.

This activity is designed to provide evidence for P1.

Types of visitor attractions

Tourist attractions can be either built or natural. Built attractions include facilities that have been developed specifically for tourism and leisure, e.g. theme parks, and buildings that were designed for another purpose, but which have since become popular with visitors, such as castles, cathedrals and other historic buildings. The British countryside, and in particular its 'protected' areas such as National Parks, Areas of Outstanding Natural Beauty and Heritage Coasts, is a major attraction for millions of people every year. The opening up of the countryside under the recent 'right to roam' legislation is likely to encourage more people to visit the countryside and its natural attractions.

Built attractions

There are many different types of built attractions found throughout Britain, for example:

- Historic monuments and properties;
- Theme parks;
- Heritage attractions;
- Gardens, wildlife and environmental attractions;
- Entertainment facilities;
- Sports centres;
- Cultural attractions.

Historic monuments and properties

Britain is renowned for its wide range of historic monuments and properties, which have great appeal to British people and overseas visitors. The majority of historic monuments are in public ownership, with many London properties under the management of Historic Royal Palaces, an independent charity that looks after the Tower of London, Hampton Court Palace, the Banqueting House, Kensington Palace and Kew Palace. Many castles and stately homes in England and Wales are cared for by the National Trust, CADW Welsh Historic Monuments and English Heritage, which manage sites and provide facilities for visitors. Some historic properties are in private ownership, including Chatsworth House and Blenheim Palace. The following are some of the UK's most popular historic monuments and properties:

- Tower of London;
- Edinburgh Castle;
- Windsor Castle;
- Roman Baths at Bath;
- Stonehenge, Wiltshire;
- Chatsworth House, Derbyshire;
- Tatton Park, Cheshire;
- Blenheim Palace, Oxfordshire.

Churches, cathedrals, ancient monuments and sites are also important attractions for visitors, for example St Paul's Cathedral in London, Glastonbury Tor in Somerset and the sites of past battles.

Edinburgh Castle is a popular historic monument

Theme parks

A theme park is a visitor attraction offering permanent rides and entertainment in a themed setting or range of settings, providing something for the whole family. Most theme parks charge one price for unlimited access to all rides and attractions in a fun environment. Theme parks have been a success story in the UK since the first was opened at Thorpe Park in Surrey in 1979. Based on a concept that was first developed in the USA, theme parks offer visitors a wide range of permanent rides and entertainments in a themed setting or range of settings, with a single entry charge giving access to all facilities. Most large UK theme parks have experienced growth in their attendances since the late 1980s, through constant updating of their facilities and visitor services. There is evidence, however, that the theme park market is becoming saturated in some parts of Britain, leading to price discounting by parks and the introduction of other incentives to maintain their market shares.

Although each UK theme park has its own particular attractions, there are certain common characteristics that theme parks exhibit, for example:

- Parks offer a mix of facilities and activities, e.g. 'white knuckle' rides, live entertainment, animals, gardens, events, children's play areas, education centres, corporate hospitality, retail and catering;

- Most parks operate on a seasonal basis between Easter and the end of October;

- Most visitors are family groups from the C1/C2 social classes;

- Group bookings account for between 10-25 per cent of all visitors;

- Typically, parking for 3,000-4,000 cars is provided;

- Site areas range from as little as 12 acres to 800 acres plus, with 130-140 acres being a typical size;

- Parks are generally close to the motorway network, ensuring very large two-hour catchment populations (up to 15 million);

- Length of stay on site averages between 6 and 7 hours, presenting park operators with ample opportunities for generating secondary spend, e.g. at catering and retail outlets.

In addition to Blackpool Pleasure Beach, the UK's most popular attraction, other popular UK theme parks include:

- Alton Towers, Staffordshire;
- Thorpe Park, Surrey;
- Chessington World of Adventures, Surrey;
- Oakwood Leisure Park, Pembrokeshire,
- Pleasureland Theme Park, Southport;
- Pleasure Beach, Great Yarmouth;
- Drayton Manor, Staffordshire;
- Legoland Windsor.

Fun at Legoland Windsor

Heritage attractions

Britain has a rich and varied heritage that appeals to many visitors from home and abroad. Right across the country there are large and small attractions that celebrate past events, industrial processes, traditions and landscapes, for example:

- Ironbridge Gorge Museum in Shropshire;
- Jorvik Viking Centre in York;
- Welsh Slate Museum in Llanberis, north Wales;
- Beamish Open Air Museum in County Durham;
- Quarry Bank Mill in Cheshire;
- National Maritime Museum at Greenwich, London;
- Lulworth Cove Heritage Centre, Dorset;
- New Lanark World Heritage Village, Scotland;
- Giant's Causeway Visitor Centre, Northern Ireland;
- Big Pit National Coal Museum (see case study on page 177).

Jorvik Viking Centre in York

Heritage attractions tend to focus on a particular theme or activity and use a variety of interpretation techniques to tell a story or explain a process (you will learn more about interpretation later in this unit). English Heritage is the publicly-funded agency that that advises the government on all matters concerning heritage and the historic environment. It also manages, and makes available to the public, more than 400 historic sites in England, including Barnard Castle, Stonehenge and Dover Castle. CADW does a similar job in Wales.

Some of Britain's finest heritage attractions have been awarded UNESCO World Heritage Site status in recognition of their unique contribution to the world's natural and built heritage. The UK currently has 27 World Heritage Sites, which include Ironbridge Gorge, the Tower of London, the Royal Botanic Gardens at Kew and Hadrian's Wall.

Ironbridge is a World Heritage Site

Case Study

Big Pit National Coal Museum

Introduction

Big Pit National Coal Museum, based around a real coal mine in the South Wales valleys, is one of the UK's leading industrial heritage museums. It is located close to the town of Blaenavon, which was awarded World Heritage Site status in 2000. Big Pit welcomes incoming tourists from all over the world and domestic visitors from across the UK.

Development of the attraction

The museum was established in 1983 after closure of the working mine in 1980. However, until 2001, lack of funding meant that many of the buildings on the surface were left untouched and out of bounds to the public. A period of closure followed, during which a £7 million redevelopment was carried out, and the museum was fully re-opened in February 2004. Since 2001, Big Pit has been part of the National Museums and Galleries of Wales (NMGW) group. It benefits, like all NMGW sites, from free access for visitors funded by the Welsh Assembly Government. Big Pit has welcomed nearly 2.4 million visitors in its 22-year history and the introduction of free entry to the museum has boosted visitor numbers considerably in recent years. In 2004, the museum had a record 141,000 visitors, made up of individuals, parties and education groups. In 2005, Big Pit won the prestigious £100,000 Gulbenkian Prize for Museum of the Year. The total number of visitors to Big Pit between April 2007 and February 2008 was 142,142.

Facilities for visitors

The highlight of a visit to Big Pit is the hour-long underground tour which is led by ex-miners. Visitors descend 300 feet in the original pit cage and are guided along underground roadways, through air doors and past engine houses, all built by generations of miners. On the surface, there are colliery buildings of all types open to visitors, including the winding engine-house, blacksmiths' workshops and the original pithead baths. The baths were the first to be installed at the site and date back to 1939. They currently house Big Pit's main exhibition space where the history of the coal mines of South Wales is explored and the stories of the communities that grew up around them are told, from the earliest days to the miners' strikes and pit closures of the 1980s. Big Pit also has multimedia displays of modern mining. Although the museum is on the side of a steep hill, much of it is accessible to those with mobility problems and visually/hearing-impaired visitors are catered for. A maximum of four wheelchair users are allowed underground at any one time for safety reasons and the site welcomes assistance dogs, although they cannot be taken on the underground tour. The museum has two catering outlets and a gift shop. There are toilets on all three levels of the site and baby changing facilities are available on two levels.

Educational visits

Big Pit hosts educational visits from primary school children to university groups. It offers a resource room for teachers, group leaders, students and other specialists who wish to carry out research work at the museum. The room contains reference books, maps, original documents and has internet access. The museum's Education Officer handles all education enquiries and provides teaching resources for schools.

Case Study Questions

1. Describe the products and services provided for visitors to Big Pit.
2. What different types of 'interpretation' does Big Pit offer to its visitors?
3. Why is it important for heritage attractions like Big Pit to offer facilities for education visits?
4. In what ways has Big Pit benefited from being a member of the National Museums and Galleries of Wales (NMGW) group?
5. Which other attractions are part of the NMGW group?

This case study is designed to provide evidence for P1 and P2.

Weblink

Check out this website to help answer the questions and for more information on Big Pit Mining Museum.
www.museumwales.ac.uk/en/bigpit

Gardens, wildlife and environmental attractions

Gardens, wildlife and environmental attractions are growing in popularity as people become more interested in the world around them and the impact that modern life has on the planet. Gardens range from the large-scale attractions such as Kew Gardens and the National Trust's Stourhead Garden in Wiltshire to the many small gardens open to the public as part of the National Gardens Scheme. Zoos have long been popular with visitors, but have changed their emphasis over the years to reflect the public's desire to see animals in a more natural setting. The following are some of Britain's most popular gardens, wildlife and environmental attractions:

- Eden Project in Cornwall;
- Chester Zoo;
- Kew Gardens in Surrey;
- London Zoo;
- The Deep in Hull;
- The Royal Horticultural Society (RHS) gardens at Wisley in Surrey;
- Royal Botanic Gardens in Edinburgh;
- The Botanic Gardens in Belfast;
- Stourhead Garden in Wiltshire;
- Glasgow Botanic Gardens.

Environmental attractions combine a fun day out with the chance to learn about issues such as conservation, energy use and sustainability. Examples of these types of attractions include the Centre for Alternative Technology (CAT) in Machynlleth, west Wales and the Eden Project in Cornwall (see case study on page 198).

Entertainment facilities

Entertainment facilities such as nightclubs, casinos, discos, theatres, concert halls, arenas and opera houses, all provide entertainment opportunities for visitors to an area and local residents. Indoor arenas, such as the NIA in Birmingham, the ExCel Arena in London's Docklands and Sheffield Arena, are major venues for concerts, attracting people from a wide catchment area. Much of the appeal of UK tourist destinations is the wide range of entertainment facilities they offer visitors. Seaside resorts such as Scarborough, Blackpool and Brighton, for example, attract tourists with a variety of live shows, concert events and 'night life' opportunities. Smaller towns and cities also attract day visitors from their immediate area to enjoy the entertainment at nearby cinemas, theatres, night clubs and arts centres.

Sports centres

As well as being popular with local residents, sports centres also add to the appeal of towns and cities in the UK, helping to attract overnight and day visitors. Swimming baths and leisure centres offer visitors indoor facilities when the weather outside is poor. There has been considerable investment in sport and leisure facilities in the UK in recent years, with the introduction of wave machines, jacuzzis, health suites, flumes and saunas into centres run by public and private sector operators. On a national scale, sport and recreation facilities are being used to help change the image of certain parts of Britain and attract further inward investment, for example both the Don Valley Stadium in Sheffield and the National Cycling Centre in Manchester are part of major urban regeneration projects. Many areas of east London are undergoing major regeneration as part of the developments for the 2012 London Olympic Games.

Cultural attractions

Some parts of Britain have a variety of cultural attractions that appeal to both UK and international visitors. Links with famous people, cultural diversity, associations with the arts and music, are all used to build an image of a destination and attract tourists. Shakespeare's birthplace in Stratford-upon-Avon, for example, is a magnet for UK and overseas visitors alike, while historic Bath, the Cardiff Singer of the World Competition and the Edinburgh Festival attract tourists from all over the world. Many tourists visit the haunts of Dylan Thomas in Wales and Thomas Hardy in Dorset. The cultural diversity in cities such as Leeds, Manchester, Cardiff, London and Bradford is used as a springboard for themed events and short breaks, e.g. curry weekends in Bradford and visits to the Chinatown areas of London and Manchester.

Museums and art galleries are amongst the most popular cultural attractions with visitors. They display ancient and modern artefacts in a variety of settings, using a range of techniques to inform, educate and entertain visitors. The following are amongst Britain's most popular cultural attractions:

- Tate Modern;
- British Museum;
- Science Museum;
- National Gallery;
- Tate Gallery at St Ives in Cornwall;

The Science Museum in London (courtesy of SSPL/Science Museum)

- The Burrell Collection in Glasgow;
- Natural History Museum;
- The Lowry, Salford Quays, Manchester;
- Museum of Welsh Life at St Fagan's, Cardiff;
- Ulster Folk and Transport Museum, Northern Ireland.

Activity 18.3

Carry out some research into three cultural attractions in the UK. For each attraction, produce an illustrated fact sheet that describes (1) the primary, secondary and additional products on offer to visitors; (2) corporate hospitality facilities; (3) services and facilities for visitors with special needs.

This activity is designed to provide evidence for P1.

Natural attractions

Britain has an abundance of natural attractions, from Land's End to John O' Groats. Domestic and overseas visitors are attracted to the beautiful coastline, the rugged mountains, peaceful lakes and the picturesque valleys. Many of these areas have been given special status to protect their environment and provide facilities for their enjoyment by the public, e.g. National Parks, Areas of Outstanding Natural beauty and Heritage Coasts. The job of overseeing these 'protected' areas in England lies with Natural England, while the Countryside Council for Wales (CCW) does a similar job in the Principality. In Scotland, Scottish Natural Heritage (SNH) is responsible for National Parks and other protected areas, and the Environment and Heritage Service (EHS) takes the lead on protected area matters in Northern Ireland.

Weblink
Check out these websites for more information on the work of these four agencies in landscape protection, tourism and recreation.
www.naturalengland.org.uk; www.ccw.gov.uk;
www.snh.org.uk; www.ehsni.gov.uk

National Parks

The term 'National Park' is used to describe different types of protected areas throughout the world, from vast areas of uninhabited wilderness in the USA to smaller, lightly-populated areas in the UK. The main concept of all National Parks is one of combining conservation of the landscape with access for recreation and enjoyment – a combination that is sometimes difficult to achieve!

To date, twelve National Parks have been designated in England and Wales since the 1949 National Parks and Access to the Countryside Act. This includes the Broads, which was set up under a special Act of Parliament in 1988, and the New Forest, designated a National Park in March 2005. The government is currently consulting on establishing a new South

Dartmoor National Park

from visitors and their vehicles. The Peak District National Park is a good case in point being located between the large conurbations of Sheffield and Manchester.

Activity 18.4

On a blank map of the UK, mark and name the National Parks in England, Wales and Scotland, plus the proposed Mourne National Park in Northern Ireland. Registered tandtONLine users can download a blank UK map from www.tandtonline.co.uk

This activity is designed to provide evidence for P1.

Downs National Park. The word 'national' does not mean that the Parks are owned by the government – most of the land within National Park boundaries is privately owned and often under severe pressure

Case Study

Brecon Beacons National Park

Introduction

The Brecon Beacons National Park (BBNP) is one of three National Parks in Wales. It covers an area of 1,347 square kilometres and includes the towns of Brecon, Crickhowell and Hay-on-Wye. There are approximately 32,000 people living within the Park. Its landscape is dramatic and varied, with gentle upland slopes, steep escarpments (the highest point is Pen-y-Fan at 886 metres), glaciated valleys, peat bogs and heather moorland. Water features widely in the landscape, with many rivers, lakes, waterfalls and reservoirs. The River Usk flows through the Park and the sources of the rivers Tawe, Nedd and Taff are found within its boundaries.

The man-made attractions of the area include remains from many different periods of history. These range from prehistoric cairns and hill forts to castles and churches. Remnants of more recent industrial times also survive, including quarries, tram roads and ironworks.

Importance of tourism in the BBNP

The Brecon Beacons National Park Authority (BBNPA) recognises that tourism is an essential industry in the area. It generates an annual income of £66 million and there are some 1,900 jobs in the National Park that are associated with tourism. The Authority therefore considers that the successful integration of tourism and the management of its impacts are critical to the economic and social future of the area. Developing tourism in a sustainable manner is seen as crucial to the Park's future.

A significant number of businesses in the Park rely directly on tourism. For example, there are over 100 outdoor pursuits centres/operators. Pubs, caravan park operators, attraction managers and event organisers all receive a proportion of their income from tourists. Shops and other retail outlets in the Park also rely on the trade they receive from visitors. Such businesses provide vital services to the communities within the National Park. Some 6.5 per cent of the people employed in the National Park area work in hotels and catering.

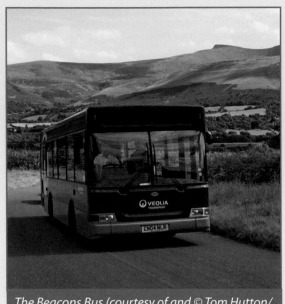

The Beacons Bus (courtesy of and © Tom Hutton/ BBNPA)

Attractions of the Park

The Park has a wide range of both natural and built attractions. Its main natural attractions are the mountains, moorland, waterfalls, rivers and caves. Visitors are attracted by the wide variety of wildlife in the National Park. Birds such as the red kite, peregrine falcons and buzzards can be found amongst the crags. Otters, salmon and kingfishers can be spotted along streams and rivers. Ring ouzels and purple saxifrage are found at Craig Cerrig Gleisiad National Nature Reserve. Large numbers of birds, including tufted ducks, wigeon and pochard, gather at Llangors Lake.

Built attractions include the castles, hill forts, historic houses and towns, plus the Monmouthshire and Brecon Canal. The canal has been restored between Pontypool and Brecon and narrow boats can be hired, or day trips taken, from a number of locations along its length. Purpose-built attractions include the National Park Visitor Centre at Libanus and Craig-y-nos Country Park, both managed by the BBNP. The Park has a number of popular market towns that appeal to visitors, including Brecon, Hay-on-Wye, Crickhowell and Llangors.

Visitors to the BBNP

The BBNP attracts visitors from a wide catchment area. Within just one hour's drive of the Brecon Beacons are the 2 million people who live in South Wales and the population of Bristol. The large urban conurbations of the West Midlands, including Birmingham, are within a 2-hour drive. The BBNP is the closest mountainous area to London and millions of people live within easy travelling distance of the Park. Visitors to the area include:

- Day trippers;
- People on holiday and staying within the Park boundaries;
- People on holiday, staying outside of the Park and making a day visit.

According to the findings of a survey conducted in 1994, the estimated number of visitor days to the BBNP is 3.6 million. It is impossible to calculate exactly how many visitors the Park receives because there are so many roads leading into the Park and no gated entry points. Visitor surveys are carried out to gather information on the types of tourists that visit the National Park and to obtain details of their stay.

Most of the day visitors to the Park visit more than once and some visit on a regular basis. The majority of visitors are in family or other small groups.

Interpretation in the Park

The BBNP's interpretation work is centred on the following facilities:

- The National Park Visitor Centre, Libanus – this Centre receives around 168,000 visitors per year. It is situated in the heart of the National Park and has superb views of the central Beacons (including Pen y fan). Visitors can learn about the National Park, find information about walks, activities and places to visit in the area, go for a walk on the common, visit the sensory Millennium Garden, enjoy a meal in the tea rooms or buy maps, local books and souvenirs in the shop. A range of festivals and events are organised at the Centre throughout the year. The Centre is a focal point for many of the tourists and day-trippers who visit the National Park. Other education and business groups visiting the site make use of its 60-seat lecture and conference room.

- Craig-y-nos Country Park – lies at the top of the Swansea Valley and provides services for a range of visitors. It is open every day of the year except Christmas Day and offers a variety of walks, guided and self-led. Environmental activities are provided for school groups. The Country Park's visitor centre contains an interactive exhibition area, a shop, classroom and activity areas. A number of public events are also held at the Country Park.

- YHA Danywenallt National Park Study Centre – located near Talybont-on-Usk, staff at this facility run residential education programmes for a wide range of education groups throughout the year. The centre is also used to host Interpretative Walking Courses, training courses and wildlife events.

- Information Centres – BBNP's three centres are located at Abergavenny, Brecon and Llandovery. Information staff advise visitors on the local countryside and heritage, and opportunities for recreation. They operate under the same roof as Tourist Information Centres (TICs) that are concerned mainly with providing advice on accommodation, attractions and touring.

Case Study Questions

1. What different types of 'interpretation' does the BBNP offer to visitors?
2. What types of visitors does the Park attract and why do they find it appealing?
3. What are the Park's main attractions and how important are they to the Park's popularity and appeal?
4. Analyse how effectively the products, services and interpretation techniques found in the Park are used to meet the needs of three different types of visitors.
5. Make realistic and justified recommendations for improvements to the products, services and interpretation techniques found in the Park to meet the needs of different types of visitors.

This case study is designed to provide evidence for P1, P2, M1 and D1.

Weblink

Check out this website to help answer the questions and for more information on the Brecon Beacons National Park.

www.breconbeacons.org

Material in this case study is adapted from the BBNP's Education Service publications.

Areas of Outstanding Natural Beauty (AONBs)

There are currently 41 AONBs in England and Wales. They range from the wild open moorlands of the North Pennines to the green belt countryside of the Surrey Hills and the intimate valley of the Wye, which straddles the border with Wales. There are nine AONBs in Northern Ireland, including Strangford Lough and the Lagan Valley. AONBs can be popular destinations for travel and tourism, although, unlike National Parks, they are not designated for their recreational value. In total, AONBs in England cover around 15 per cent of the landscape.

Weblink
Check out this website for more information on Areas of Outstanding Natural Beauty.
www.aonb.org.uk

Heritage Coasts

There are 46 Heritage Coasts in England and Wales. They are among the most precious assets for wildlife and landscape, as well as for tourism. Concern over the harmful impact of increasing numbers of visitors led to their designation and a plan of action which includes creating and repairing footpaths, cleaning up bathing water and removing litter. Currently, 32 per cent of England's scenic coastline is conserved as Heritage Coast.

SECTION 2 · Know the range and purpose of techniques used for visitor interpretation

The Association for Heritage Interpretation (AHI) defines interpretation as 'the art of helping people explore and appreciate our world'. Interpretation is all about giving visitors to all types of attractions not just an enjoyable experience, but one that will help them understand better the place they are visiting – some people say that it's all about 'telling a story' at a visitor attraction.

Purpose of interpretation

Interpretation is used in visitor attractions for a variety of reasons, such as:

1. Education and entertainment;
2. Entertainment;
3. Conservation;
4. Security;
5. To meet outreach activities.

Education and entertainment

First and foremost, interpretation in attractions sets out to educate visitors. This could be education in the formal sense, for example a party of school children being taken on a day visit to Longleat, or a less formal type of learning, such as a guided walk from a National Park visitor centre to explore the landscape and industrial heritage of the area. Interpretation can also entertain visitors – a well-trained and enthusiastic tour guide at a heritage attraction can add greatly to the visitors' experience by passing on information about the attraction in a stimulating and entertaining manner. This ability of interpretation to combine education and entertainment is sometimes referred to as 'edutainment' by people working in the attractions sector of travel and tourism.

Interpretation at the Jorvik Viking Centre in York

Conservation

Interpretation goes hand-in-hand with conservation of, for example, an area of a National Park, a particular wildlife habitat, a museum exhibit, historic building, etc. Interpretive techniques such as audio-visual displays, visitor centres, guided tours and leaflets, can be used to explain conservation issues to visitors and 'educate' them into what they can do to help matters, e.g. avoiding 'sensitive' wildlife areas, not touching museum exhibits, donating to conservation societies, etc.

Security

Visitor attraction operators are legally responsible for providing a safe and secure environment for their staff and visitors, plus any other people who visit the site. Security is a particular issue in relation to the following:

- Visitors and their possessions;
- Money taken for admission and in retail/food outlets;
- Artefacts and equipment in the attraction;
- Information relating to the business and its customers;
- Staff and their possessions.

Interpretative techniques can play a part in the security of a visitor attraction by, for example, using signage and training staff to guide visitors away from prohibited areas of the facility.

Outreach activities

Interpretation is sometimes used by attractions to encourage certain sections of a community who do not visit in large numbers to come to the attraction and learn more. Outreach activities – when staff go out into communities to spread their message – are an important part of this process. Sections of the community who may be under-represented at an attraction could include ethnic minorities, young people, school children or visitors with special needs. As an example, the Corinium Museum in Cirencester, Gloucestershire employs an Outreach Officer whose job is to take the services offered at the museum to communities and individuals outside of the confines of the museum itself, through activities, talks and other events. The aims are to make facilities, skills, artefacts, information and lifelong learning opportunities available to the Cotswolds community as a whole and to raise awareness of the museum and its facilities.

Interpretation techniques

Visitor attractions as diverse as farms, ancient monuments, gardens, museums, wildlife reserves, stately homes, National Parks, forest areas and theme parks, all offer interpretation facilities for visitors using a variety of techniques, including:

- Displays;
- Actors and curators;
- Interactive technology;
- Guides and tours;
- Leaflets, maps and signage;
- Activities and events.

There are many factors that need to be taken into consideration when choosing which interpretive techniques to use in an attraction, for example:

1. Location – facilities inside an attraction may not work in an outside setting;
2. Cost – the budget that the attraction has to work within;
3. Target audience – design, content and language will differ from one type of visitor to another;
4. Longevity – deciding how long the interpretation will be in place;
5. Reliability and maintenance – making sure that breakdowns are kept to a minimum;

5. Degree of interaction required – whether active of passive interpretation is needed;
6. Security – issues such as theft of equipment and vandalism.

Displays

Displays at attractions provide visitors with information in text, pictures, model and graphic form. They are a good way of conveying detailed information about an attraction or its exhibits and are often found in museums and art gallerie

Displays in the 'Making the modern world' gallery at the Science Museum (courtesy of SSPL/Science Museum)

Actors and curators

Using people in attractions gives visitors an immediate and informative experience. Actors and costumed guides, sometimes referred to as animateurs, are often found in heritage attractions, such as Beamish Open Air Museum, Blist's Hill Museum in Ironbridge and Wigan Pier, where they mingle with visitors and help to create an atmosphere of what life was really like in days gone by. Curators pass on their specialist knowledge of a museum or similar attraction, thereby enhancing the visitor experience.

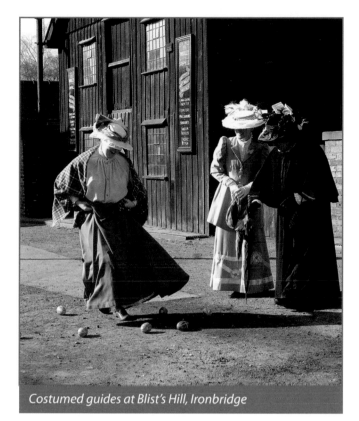

Costumed guides at Blist's Hill, Ironbridge

Interactive technology

Technology encourages visitors to interact with exhibits or artefacts to learn more about them. This is particularly appealing to children and young people who often have very enquiring minds! Technology is used in a number of ways in attractions, for example:

- Interactive displays – 'hands on' facilities that allow visitors to touch and interact with exhibits;

- Virtual displays – using 3-D computer technology to simulate an event or setting, for example a virtual tour of a house or castle ruins showing how it would have looked in the past;

- Auditory – defined points at which to listen to information or sound guides (sometimes in different languages) that can be carried by the visitor while they are at the attraction;

- Electronic – using computer-generated images, audio-visual displays or animatronics, i.e. moving models of past and present animals, for example dinosaurs.

An interactive display at the Wales Millennium Centre, Cardiff

Guides and tours

Guides and tours are types of interpretation that give visitors the chance to delve more deeply into an attraction and its facilities. Guides can take a number of forms, including:

- Guided tours – group activities where a guide leads visitors on a tour of an attraction. These person-to-person tours are one of the best ways of interpreting an attraction, but guides need to be well-trained;

- Self-guided tours – when visitors use a leaflet or series of signposts to take themselves on a tour of an attraction. Self-guided tours are particularly popular at countryside attractions and give people the chance to walk at their own pace.

As well as adding to the visitor experience, tours can also be used to manage visitors at an attraction. For example, guides can control where, when and for how long visitors dwell at a site. This is particularly important in the case of small attractions with limited space for large numbers of visitors. Visitors to Anne Hathaway's cottage in Stratford-upon-Avon are escorted around the property by fully-trained guides to enhance their experience and to control visitor numbers and throughput. Self-guided trails can be planned so as to divert visitors away from environmentally sensitive areas of an attraction.

Tour guides can interpret an area to visitors

FOCUS ON INDUSTRY

Interpretation at English Heritage

English Heritage is a public body, funded by the Department for Culture, Media and Sport (DCMS), and is responsible for over 400 historic properties in England (CADW: Welsh Historic Monuments does a similar job in Wales). English Heritage has developed a wide range of visitor services, including site interpretation and publications, in order to enhance visitor satisfaction and increase the likelihood of repeat visits. There are:

- Defined minimum standards of presentation for all properties;

- Explanatory graphic displays, audio tours, audio-visual presentations and exhibitions;
- Colour guidebooks and souvenir guides, many of which have been revised to be more attractive and readable;
- Children's activity sheets at some sites;
- Guided walks at many sites;
- Brief, plastic-covered guides are provided at some sites where entry is free, designed to be used on site and left for the next visitor.

English Heritage is the largest developer and user of audio tours for interpretation of historic properties, with more than 50 sites now offering this service. At Battle Abbey, Stonehenge, Framlingham Castle, Down House and Eltham Palace, there are interactive audio tours using the hand-held 'wand' system, which gives visitors the flexibility to choose which information they want to listen to, accessed by a numbered keypad. In addition, English Heritage is working to provide audio tours created specially for visitors with visual impairments, thereby increasing access to its sites.

Weblink

 Check out this website for more information on interpretation at English Heritage.
www.english-heritage.org.uk

Activity 18.5

Log on to the English Heritage website (www.english-heritage.org.uk) and choose six properties/sites for some further research. Make a chart showing the different interpretation facilities that each property/site offers.

This activity is designed to provide evidence for P2.

Leaflets, maps and signage

Printed leaflets and maps are a relatively cheap type of interpretation to produce, but may not have the visual impact of other interpretive techniques, e.g.

audio-visual displays or guided tours. Visitors on self-guided tours and trails are often provided with a printed leaflet at the start of their journey.

Good signposting not only helps visitors to find their way around an attraction, but can also form part of the interpretation at the facility. The materials used for the signs may reflect those found in the local area, for example slate signs in a mining museum, wood in a forest environment, iron in an industrial heritage attraction, etc. Signs can be expensive to produce, but are an important part of any visitor attraction.

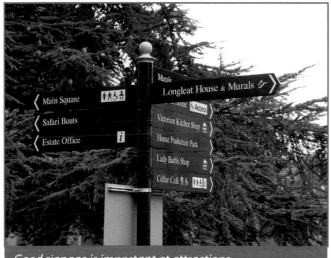
Good signage is important at attractions

Activities and events

As well as providing another source of income for attractions, activities and special events can play an important role in interpretation. All types of attractions, from castles to countryside visitor centres, organise events that add to the visitors' experience and understanding of the area. Recent events at Beamish Open Air Museum in County Durham included a traction engine rally, May Day celebrations, a quilting exhibition, an archaeology weekend and a ploughing match.

Weblink
Check out this website for more information on events at Beamish.
www.beamish.org.uk

Jousting at Warwick Castle

Special needs

Visitors with special needs may need particular interpretation facilities if they are to get the most out of their visit to an attraction. Depending on the nature of their special needs, these facilities could include:

- Large print information leaflets and displays;
- Braille information and magnifiers;
- Tactile maps and exhibits;
- Audio guides and hearing loop systems;
- Sensory exhibits;
- A MiniCom telephone number for bookings.

Under the terms of the Disability Discrimination Act, attractions must make their facilities accessible to all visitors, regardless of their circumstances. Providing specialist interpretation facilities for these customers, although not a legal requirement for attraction operators, is seen as an important part of their work to encourage all sections of the community to visit.

Understand the appeal of visitor attractions to different types of visitor

It is clear that not all visitor attractions will appeal to every type of person in the UK or tourist from overseas. Some people will look for thrills, fun and excitement by visiting theme parks and entertainment venues, while others will prefer the peace and quiet of trips to the countryside, stately homes and gardens. To be successful, any attraction must be clear precisely which type or types of visitors it is targeting and provide the right facilities and amenities to meet their target markets' needs. Market research is used to gather information on existing and potential visitors to attractions, and is an essential first step in identifying customers' needs.

Having established its target market(s), a visitor attraction must develop a 'product' that its customers will appreciate and enjoy. It will need to give attention to a number of considerations, including:

- The main products and services offered by the attraction;

- Extra features aimed at particular types of visitors, e.g. coach parties, school visits, visitors from abroad, conferences and corporate hospitality;

- Special events and activities, e.g. historic car rallies, balloon festivals, music concerts, etc;

- Catering facilities, e.g. restaurants, pizza parlours, ice cream outlets, cafés, etc;

- Other facilities, e.g. baby changing, wheelchairs, buggies, car parking, transport links, facilities for visitors with special needs, etc.

Appeal

It is the features of a visitor attraction that make it appeal (or not) to visitors. An attraction that has few features and whose operators have not invested in new facilities and services will struggle to survive. Key features that influence the appeal of an attraction are shown in Figure 18.1 and discussed in the following sections of this unit.

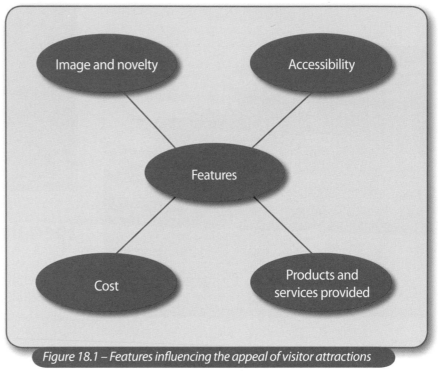

Figure 18.1 – Features influencing the appeal of visitor attractions

Accessibility

In the case of visitor attractions, 'accessibility' is an all-embracing term covering:

- Geographical access – location, transport routes and parking;

- Physical access to the attraction – opening seasons and times, plus access for people with mobility problems and other special needs;

- Access for all sectors of the community – regardless of, for example, their age, gender, race or income level. This is often reflected in the attraction's pricing policy, e.g. reduced prices for certain categories of visitors.

The location of natural attractions and many cultural sites is predetermined, but developers can choose where to build new visitor attractions, subject to planning regulations. An attraction that is located close to a busy urban area will have a large population on which to draw, but may also be in competition with many other attractions. Visitors look for attractions that are conveniently located and have good car and public transport access. Good signposting to and within the attraction is also important.

Visitors look for speedy access arrangements when visiting an attraction so as not to waste time. Any 'shuttle' transport that is provided must run at frequent intervals and facilities for buying entrance tickets must be well staffed in order to keep queuing time to a minimum. Larger attractions give visitors the chance to pre-book by telephone or on the internet so as to save time queuing when they arrive. Access to attractions is an important issue for visitors with special needs – many attractions now offer comprehensive services for these visitors to comply with the Disability Discrimination Act.

Most visits to attractions in the UK are made using a car or coach. Car drivers look for plenty of space for parking and easy access to and from the site. This is particularly true for visitors with special needs, who require parking facilities close to the attraction entrance. Coach companies that transport schools and other groups to attractions expect good access and parking facilities as well, plus some facilities for their drivers to take a break in comfort.

Not all visitor attractions are open all year round. Their operators consider that it is not economic to open for the small numbers of visitors who may visit in the winter. The types of visitors who come to attractions vary according to the time of year. Families come at weekends and during school holidays, whereas school and college groups visit during term time. Retired people have more flexibility in when they can visit and often take advantage of off-peak discounts to make their trip during quiet mid-week periods. Events for corporate guests take place throughout the time an attraction is open to the public.

Range of products and services

Different customers make use of the different products and services on offer at attractions. Families, for example, tend to make use of a wide range of facilities, such as baby changing, toilets, places to eat and lost children points. Visitors from overseas may need to use an attraction's interpretation facilities if they are provided in their own language, e.g. an audio tour. Enthusiasts of one kind or another make a beeline for the main facility at attractions, e.g. 'white knuckle' rides, traction engines at a steam rally or the paintings at an art gallery.

We saw earlier in this unit that there are many types of interpretation available at visitor attractions. Individuals and groups who really want to get an educational experience out of their visit to an attraction will look for comprehensive guide books, guided tours and static displays. Children are drawn to 'hands on' exhibits and artefacts that they can touch. Overseas visitors may need interpretative materials to be available in different languages.

Staging events is an excellent way of attracting visitors to an area and gaining significant revenue from entrance fees and secondary spending opportunities, such as car parking fees and the sale of food, drink and a variety of merchandise. Events are particularly useful for destinations that don't have extensive built and natural attractions to tempt visitors or are located in remote areas away from major centres of population. Events cater for an extremely wide variety of visitor interests – everything from sport, music and food to history, gardens and books. Britain has music events that appeal to all tastes, from the Cardiff Singer of the World Competition to the Glastonbury and V music festivals. Sporting events such as the British Grand Prix at Silverstone, football and rugby matches at the Millennium Stadium in Cardiff and the tennis championships at Wimbledon, attract thousands of visitors from the UK and overseas. Major cultural events such as the Edinburgh Festivals and Notting Hill Carnival have international reputations.

Events are popular at attractions (courtesy of English Heritage)

Cost of visiting

The cost of visiting an attraction is an important consideration that will affect its appeal to visitors. Most attractions operate a variable pricing policy, offering different entry prices depending on when a person is visiting, e.g. peak season and off season rates, discounts for early evening and mid-week visits, etc. Attractions also charge different prices according to the type of visitor, as the following example from the Eden Project illustrates (2008 prices):

	Individuals	Groups (10+)
Adults	£15.00	£11.00
Children under 5 years	free	free
Children 5 – 18 years	£ 5.00	£ 4.00
Full-time students	£ 7.00	£ 6.00
Seniors (60 + years)	£ 10.0	£ 8.00
Family	£36.00	-

Attractions in the public sector, such as leisure centres and museums, sometimes offer concessionary rates for local people, including lone parents and unemployed people.

Image and novelty

An attraction's image will often encourage people to visit. The image of an attraction is generated from a variety of sources, such as its leaflets and website, press articles, TV and radio advertising, mail shots and links with personalities. Attractions that feature in movies often reap the rewards with increased visitor numbers, e.g. parts of the James Bond film Die Another Day were filmed at the Eden Project in Cornwall. Liverpool's attractions, including the Tate Liverpool, The Beatles Story and Merseyside Maritime Museum, are currently benefiting from the city's designation as the European Capital of Culture 2008.

New attractions have a certain novelty value with visitors, but the secret is maintaining visitor numbers over the long term. UK attractions that have caught people's imagination in recent years as being excellent examples of their type include the London Eye, Eden Project, The Deep in Hull, the National Waterfront Museum in Swansea, the BALTIC Centre for Contemporary Art in Gateshead, the Spinnaker Tower in Portsmouth, to name but a few.

High quality information, both before they visit and while on-site, helps visitors to plan their visit to an attraction and make informed decisions about what to do while they are there. Visitors need certain basic information – opening times, prices, location, refreshment facilities – as well as more specific information on what the attraction has to offer visitors. Much of this information is made available on attractions' websites and in printed leaflets and guides. Websites have the advantage of publishing changes to basic information at short notice and can be used as a publicity tool to encourage people to visit an attraction. As well as providing information to the general public, attractions may have to supply other travel trade companies, including coach companies and tour operators, with details to incorporate into their own tour programmes. Members of the press will also request information from time to time.

Chessington World of Adventures

Introduction

Chessington World of Adventures is part of the Merlin Entertainments Group of visitor attractions. The attraction started life as Chessington Zoo, which was opened in July 1931 as a private venture by Reginald Goddard who invited the public to view his private animal collection. After the Second World War, Chessington soon became known for the different types of entertainment it could offer, including a circus, a funfair and a miniature railway, as well as the zoo. Despite these developments, the attendance figures of over 800,000 began to decline in the early 1970s and the Zoo was in need of further investment.

In 1978 the Pearson Group bought Chessington and when they later bought Madame Tussauds, they put all their leisure interests together to form the Tussauds Group. Planning for the redevelopment of Chessington began in 1981 and six years later the £12 million upgrade was completed and officially opened by HRH Prince Edward. The opening coincided with the opening of the M25 motorway, which gives easy access to the attraction from various parts of the country. Approximately 18 million people live within a 2-hour drive of the site. Every year the attraction welcomes more than 1 million visitors and employs at least 1,000 members of staff.

Location and access

Chessington is located 12 miles from London, two miles from the A3 and M25 motorway. The attraction offers free parking for visitors. The park is accessible by public transport – regular South West Trains services run from Waterloo, Clapham Junction and Wimbledon to Chessington South Station, a 10-minute walk from the attraction. Chessington is served by regular bus services from nearby Kingston and Epsom. The attraction welcomes disabled guests and provides a range of services to make their time at Chessington as enjoyable as possible. Full details are given in the attraction's detailed guide for disabled visitors.

Products and services at Chessington

The primary product at Chessington consists of the various rides, events and entertainments aimed at the family market; these include Dragon's Fury, Dragon Falls, Vampire, Bubbleworks, Rameses Revenge and Tomb Blaster. The park has categorised its rides and attractions according to an 'adventure rating'. The four levels of adventure are:

1. Mini adventurer (for tiny tots);
2. Junior adventurer (for younger adventurers);
3. Family adventurers (for all the family – height and size restrictions may apply);
4. Experienced adventurers (for the older adventurer).

The managers of the attraction aim to launch a new attraction every year in order to refresh the product and give people a reason for making a return visit. Once the type of ride has been agreed, it can take as long as three years for the project to be completed, so careful long-term planning is crucial. Ancillary products and services at Chessington include places to eat, games, photography, corporate hospitality and services for visitors with special needs. The attraction offers the opportunity for students studying travel and tourism, business or animal husbandry to visit the site and take advantage of an educational talk as part of their trip.

Facilities for corporate events

Chessington offers tailor-made packages for corporate visitors, including team building/activity days, day delegate packages and fun days. Groups of all sizes can be catered for, including major events involving up to 10,000 visitors.

Case Study Questions and Activities

1. Describe the target markets that Chessington World of Adventures is aiming to attract and explain how the facilities are geared to meet the needs of each target market.
2. List the specific facilities and services the attraction offers visitors with special needs.
3. Explain the appeal of Chessington World of Adventures to three different types of visitors.
4. Explain how Chessington could adapt to appeal to a wider range of visitor types.
5. Carry out some further research on Chessington's facilities for corporate customers and prepare detailed lists of what is available.

This case study is designed to provide evidence for P1, P3 and M2.

Weblink

Check out this website to help answer the questions in this case study and for more information on Chessington World of Adventures. www.chessington.co.uk

Different types of visitors

Visitor attractions appeal to different people for different reasons; one family may enjoy a day out at London Zoo, for example, while another might prefer a trip to the nearby Natural History Museum; yet another family may choose somewhere else entirely, perhaps a trip on the London Eye or a visit to the London Transport Museum. Whatever the reasons behind the choice of an attraction, all sites have a wide range of types of visitors, each with different characteristics. For a typical visitor attraction, these could be:

- Incoming tourists to the UK – overseas visitors tend to be attracted by Britain's natural and built heritage and often use London as a convenient starting point for their holiday;

- Educational parties – are important sources of revenue for attractions, particularly outside the peak season. Many attractions offer an education service to school and college groups, which includes fact sheets on the attraction, illustrated talks by members of staff and reduced price entry;

- Groups with special interests – these may be on an organised event or travelling independently. Examples include members of gardening clubs visiting stately homes and car enthusiasts going to a vintage car rally at an attraction;

- Families – are a key market for many attractions, particularly theme parks and other entertainment venues. Attractions must offer a range of facilities to appeal to all members of the party;

- Different age groups – from the youngest baby to senior citizens, visitor attractions must cater for a wide age range in their visitors;

- Visitors with special needs – must be provided with a range of facilities to make their visit as enjoyable as possible;

- Corporate customers – are a very good source of revenue for many attractions, which provide facilities for training days, exhibitions, product launches, team-building events and staff incentives.

This list gives an indication of the difficult task of satisfying the needs of each of these different types of visitor, often referred to as 'markets', and stresses the importance of precise market research to identify exactly who visits an attraction and whether they are happy with the 'product'.

Children getting involved at an English Heritage attraction

FOCUS ON INDUSTRY

Types of visitors to Alton Towers

Alton Towers in Staffordshire is one of the UK's most popular paying attractions. The types of visitors to the attraction can be broken down as follows:

- Individuals;
- Coach groups;
- Companies for corporate events;
- School parties;
- Group organisers.

The age profile of visitors to Alton Towers is as follows:

Age (yrs)	Percentage
Under 7	4.8
8-12	4.0
13-17	19.2
18-24	28.9
25-34	21.1
35-44	14.3
45-54	5.9
Over 55	1.9

Alton Towers attracts people from all over the UK and has extensive facilities and services for visitors with special needs.

Weblink

Check out this website for more information on Alton Towers.
www.altontowers.com

Activity 18.6

Choose one of the UK National Parks and write a short report that explains its appeal to three different types of visitors. Explain in your report how the National Park could adapt to appeal to a wider range of visitor types.

This activity is designed to provide evidence for P3 and M2.

Understand the importance of visitor attractions to the popularity and appeal of UK tourist destinations

Visitor attractions play a crucial role in the popularity and appeal of UK tourist destinations, whether these are towns and cities, such as Shrewsbury and Bath, countryside areas, for example the Lake District National Park and Dartmoor, or whole regions, such as the south west of England or north Wales. Attractions – natural and built – are often what tempts people to visit an area in the first place.

Visitor attractions are important to UK tourism for a number of reasons, including:

1. Attracting visitors from overseas;
2. Stimulating domestic tourism;
3. Supporting the regeneration of areas;
4. Contributing to the local and national economy;
5. Promoting cultural exchange;
6. Conservation.

Attracting visitors from overseas

The number of overseas visitors to the UK increased from 30 million in 2005 to an all-time record of 32.7 million in 2006. Spending by overseas visitors was also at a record level of £16 billion in the same year. Overseas visitor numbers to Britain have been grown steadily for more than 20 years, from just 11.5 million in 1981 to today's record of 32.7 million. Britain's image to overseas visitors is very appealing – from the pageantry associated with our great capital cities to the quaint towns and villages throughout the UK, tourists from overseas continue to be attracted to this country.

Many overseas visitors put Britain's heritage attractions as the number one reason for visiting – famous buildings such as St Paul's Cathedral, the castles at Caernarvon and Windsor, the Elizabethan architecture in Shakespeare's birthplace of Stratford-upon-Avon, rural and industrial heritage are all focal points for overseas tourists. The Royal Family, with their palaces and ancestral homes, including Buckingham Palace and Hampton Court, are also an important attraction for tourists from abroad.

Museums, art galleries, the ballet, rock concerts and events such as the Proms and Cardiff Singer of the World, are all part of Britain's rich and varied culture and customs which attract the overseas visitor. Sporting events, including Wimbledon, international rugby and football matches, Henley Royal Regatta and the Open Golf Championship, are popular with overseas visitors. Many visitors are also attracted by Britain's excellent shopping facilities, not only in London's West End, but also in historic cities such as Chester, Cambridge, Oxford, Edinburgh, Bath and York.

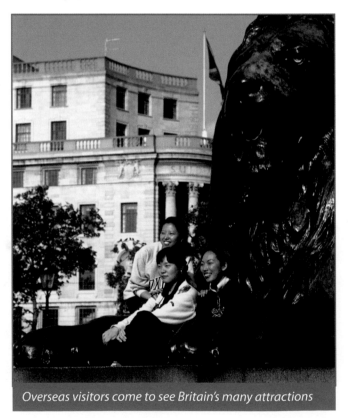

Overseas visitors come to see Britain's many attractions

Stimulating domestic tourism

Spending on domestic tourism – British people making trips within the UK – was worth £68 billion in 2005. In 2006, UK residents took:

- 53.3 million holidays of one night or more, spending £10.9 billion;
- 19.2 million overnight business trips, spending £4.6 billion;
- 49.6 million overnight trips to friends and relatives, spending £4.8 billion.

Attraction	2006
Blackpool Pleasure Beach	5,730,000
Tate Modern	4,915,376
British Museum	4,837,878
National Gallery	4,562,471
Natural History Museum	3,754,496
River Lee Country Park	3,500,000
Xscape Castleford	3,476,000
Science Museum	2,440,253
Victoria & Albert Museum	2,372,919
National Portrait Gallery	1,601,448

Figure 18.2 – Top 10 free admission attractions

Attraction	2006
Tower of London	2,084,468
St Paul's Cathedral	1,626,034
Pleasure Beach Great Yarmouth	1,400,000
Flamingo Land Theme Park & Zoo	1,302,195
New MetroLand	1,288,980
Windermere Lake Cruises	1,267,066
Kew Gardens	1,215,206
Chester Zoo	1,161,922
Eden Project	1,152,332
Canterbury Cathedral	1,047,380

Figure 18.3 – Top 10 paid admission attractions

Total spending on day trips, many of which were to natural and built visitor attractions in the UK, amounted to £44.3 billion. Figures 18.2 and 18.3 show the number of visitors to the top free admission and paying attractions in the UK for 2006.

The south west of England is Britain's most popular tourist region in terms of number of visits and spending by tourists – in 2006 there were 20.3 million trips to the region and tourism spending was nearly £3.7 billion. The most popular paid visitor attractions in 2006 were as follows:

1. Eden Project   1,152,332
2. Studland Beach   1,000,000
3. Stonehenge   879,393
4. Longleat   779,488
5. Roman Baths at Bath   843,693

Activity 18.7

With reference to your own tourist board region, make a illustrated presentation that explains the impact that visitor attractions have had on the popularity and appeal of the area. Also in the report, evaluate the success of visitor attractions to the popularity and appeal of your region, making recommendations for improvement.

This activity is designed to provide evidence for M3 and D2.

Supporting regeneration

Visitor attractions often feature in multi-use regeneration projects, particularly in urban areas of the country. They are built alongside new entertainment venues, eating places, shopping outlets and sports facilities as part of urban regeneration projects, e.g. at Cardiff Bay, Bristol Harbourside, the Don Valley in Sheffield and Albert Dock in Liverpool. Rural areas also benefit from attractions, as the following case study on the Eden Project demonstrates.

Cardiff Bay attractions are part of the area's regeneration

Case Study

The Eden Project

Introduction

The Eden Project is one of the UK's most popular tourist attractions, welcoming more than 5 million visitors since it opened in March 2001. Built on the site of a former China clay works near St Austell in Cornwall, Eden was part-funded by a grant of £43 million of National Lottery money from the Millennium Commission. The attraction's centrepieces are the largest two conservatories in the world, known as 'biomes', that recreate different climates from around the world and house a variety of exotic plant species. Visitors can wander around the site or join one of the guided tours. As well as being a visitor attraction, Eden is also an educational resource in the widest sense of the word and a living exhibition of sustainable development.

Eden's organisation and mission

Eden promotes itself as 'a global garden for the 21st century, a gateway to a sustainable future and a dramatic setting in which to tell the fascinating story of mankind's dependence on plants'. Its primary message is:

'Eden explores the human dependence on plants, and in doing so reveals our global interdependence. This in turn leads us to interpret economic, social and environmental impacts on a wider stage, not only out of curiosity and a shared humanity, but also because these factors affect us all'.

The Eden Project is the home of the Eden Trust, a UK-registered charitable trust – the Trustees are ultimately responsible for Eden's actions and its sustainable future. The project was the brainchild of Tim Smit, now Eden's Chief Executive, who had previously put his energies into developing the Lost Gardens of Heligan, also located in Cornwall, into a leading garden attraction. The Eden Trust has recently established the Eden Foundation, which will be the focus for all future activities at the attraction, working with a range of partner organisations to explore new approaches to sustainable living.

Products and services at Eden

The biomes are undoubtedly the most recognisable feature of the Eden Project and the primary product that attracts visitors. At 50 metres high, the hot tropics biome houses plants from South America, West Africa, Malaysia and the Tropical Islands, including bananas, coffee, balsa, mahogany, orchids, spices and tropical ferns. The smaller, warm temperate biome showcases the cradle of civilisation around the Mediterranean, with citrus, olives, herbs and vines, a rich variety of plants from the South African regions, drifts of colourful Californian annual plants and also banks of fruits, vegetables, pulses and grains. Each plant has its own story and the attraction uses a wide variety of interpretation techniques to inform visitors to the full.

Visitors approach the attraction via the visitor centre, which includes the Eden Shop – already one of the site's most successful and highly-regarded ventures. The shop offers a combination of environmentally-

The biomes at the Eden Project

friendly products from around the world, local produce and Eden-branded merchandise. Also within the visitor centre is the ticketing hall, plant areas, a coffee shop and the Gallery Restaurant offering panoramic views of the biomes below. Further refreshment facilities are located in the building that links the two biomes, including Morocco Red – a restaurant serving tastes from around the world, but using local produce – and a café Zzub Zzub, offering a range of light meals and snacks. Other catering points can be found outdoors, with the emphasis on quality, 'Cornishness', freshness and value for money. Extensive toilet and baby changing facilities are available in the visitor centre and elsewhere in the attraction. More than half of the attraction's staff are first aid trained and there are also fully-qualified paramedics on site at all times.

Eden's education programme

Approximately 250 schoolchildren visit the Eden Project every day, from Cornwall, across the UK and even from overseas. The aims of the attraction's formal education programme are to:

1. Link the National Curriculum with the real world, real issues and current stories;
2. Run enrichment programmes for teachers;
3. Explore the ways people learn and develop effective learning and communication;
4. Motivate and engage people of all ages, abilities, ethnicity and background.

In addition to science education programmes, Eden covers a number of other areas of the curriculum, including art, history, numeracy, literacy, design and technology.

Case Study Questions and Activities

1. What facilities and services does Eden offer visitors with special needs?
2. What interpretation techniques does Eden offer its visitors to make their visit as enjoyable and instructive as possible?
3. What activities does Eden carry out to minimise its impact on the local environment and community?
4. Describe the different categories of visitors that you think are likely to be attracted to the Eden Project, explaining precisely what appeals to each category.

This case study is designed to provide evidence for P1, P2 and P3.

Weblink
Check out this website to help answer the questions in this case study and for more information on the Eden Project.
www.edenproject.com

Contributing to the local and national economy

As well as providing excitement, fun and education for millions of domestic and overseas tourists every year, the 6,500 visitor attractions found in the UK generate significant economic benefits for the local and national economy, including employment, generating revenue, investment and regeneration.

Providing jobs is one of the key positive impacts of the UK attractions sector. Precise figures on the numbers employed in visitor attractions are very difficult to gauge, since there is no category for jobs in attractions in government figures. However, 2003 data indicates that there were 86,700 people employed in libraries, museums and other cultural facilities. Most of these jobs are full-time, but many attractions, including theme parks and water parks, employ mostly seasonal workers. This often leads to a high turnover of staff and sometimes makes it difficult for attraction operators to persuade their employees to commit to training courses on a regular basis.

Economic impact of the Eden Project

Research results released in 2004 show that the Eden Project (see case study on page 198) has injected nearly half a billion pounds worth of business back into the economy of Cornwall and the south west region of England. Eden has received £55.4 million of funding from the National Lottery via the Millennium Commission since it was built in 2001, but is estimated to have generated more than £460 million in economic impact on the local economy. Eden's operators estimate that, if visitors numbers remain as they have been since opening, the attraction's first 10 years of full operation should generate over £2 billion in economic output.

Eden has contributed to the economy in many ways. The attraction pays out £8 million in wages to local people every year, employing 600 temporary staff in the peak season and 380 people full-time all year round. Eden also uses local suppliers wherever possible, with knock-on effects to other businesses. The project has been responsible for attracting thousands of visitors to Cornwall. In 2006 there were 1.15 million visitors to the attraction, 90 per cent of whom had travelled into the county and more than half of the 90 per cent said that Eden had influenced their choice of holiday.

Weblink
Check out this website for more information on the economic impact of the Eden Project .
www.edenproject.com

There is a trend in UK tourism towards all-year-round tourism, particularly associated with the growth in short breaks and additional holidays. It is not uncommon now for British people to take a holiday abroad plus two, three or even four short breaks in the UK every year, either to the countryside or in cities (or a mixture of the two). This helps create more permanent employment in visitor attractions, since the operators can be sure of revenue outside the traditional peak season. This is particularly true for attractions that include activities that are not weather-dependent, e.g. mountain biking, canoeing, white-water rafting and orienteering. The same applies to attractions that cater for the schools market – schoolchildren visit during term time when visitor numbers tend to be lower, thereby helping to spread revenue and jobs throughout the year.

As well as providing jobs, another important positive economic impact of visitor attractions is the revenue generated from visitors and investors. The money spent by visitors at an attraction and in the surrounding area is re-circulated in the local economy via the 'multiplier effect', for example when people employed in attractions spend their wages in local shops and on local services.

Visitor attractions have benefited enormously from the National Lottery. To date, some £20 billion has been awarded to 'good causes', which has included investment in many visitor attraction projects in sport, the arts, heritage and the environment.

Weblink
Check out this website for more information on the National Lottery and the 'good causes' it supports.
www.national-lottery.co.uk

FOCUS ON INDUSTRY

Economic and social impact of cathedrals in England

Research published in Heritage Counts examined the economic and social value to local communities of the 42 Anglican cathedrals in England. There were 8.8 million visits to these cathedrals in 2003, although separate research by the Church of England, which included Westminster Abbey, indicated that the number of visits was as high as 12.5 million. Spending by visitors attracted to the local area by the presence of a cathedral was estimated at £91 million per year to the local economy, while the total economic impact was estimated to be £150 million, supporting some 5,500 jobs.

Weblink
Check out this website to find out more about Heritage Counts.
www.heritagecounts.org.uk

Promoting cultural exchange

Attractions give visitors the chance to experience past and present-day cultures, through viewing artefacts and objects, taking part in activities and using 'hands on', interactive exhibits. Cultural attractions, such as museums and art galleries, have a twin role of conserving items of value and making them available to the general public. The government encourages visits to attractions by 'sponsoring' some of the UK's most popular cultural attractions, i.e. the Department for Culture, Media and Sport (DCMS) provides funding to the attraction so that it can offer everybody free access. Since it was introduced in 2001, this free admission policy has been a great success – visits to museums have increased by 75 per cent nationally. In 2004, there were 34 million visits to all the museums and galleries sponsored by the DCMS and in the same year nearly 6 million more visits were made to England's formerly charging museums and galleries than in the year before the charges were dropped. Visits to museums that have always been free, such as the National Gallery, the Tate and the British Museum, rose by 9 per cent over the same period.

The British Museum in London (courtesy and © British Museum)

For many tourists, learning about an area's culture by visiting its attractions is an essential feature of their holiday experience. Incoming tourists to the UK are particularly keen to explore our heritage and culture, learning about our language and traditions. As people become better educated and more discerning, the travel and tourism industry must respond by offering both domestic and incoming tourists products that meet their needs for a more culturally-enriching experience at attractions.

Conservation

As well as conserving historic buildings, museum exhibits and wildlife habitats, visitor attractions can help conserve traditional activities in local communities, for example arts, crafts and customs. In the Peak District of Derbyshire, the ancient custom of 'well dressing' dates back hundreds of years and is a major attraction for visitors and local people. Wells are decorated with flower petals, berries, moss, cones and seeds, which are pressed into clay held in a wooden framework. Well dressing is celebrated in more than 60 towns and villages throughout Derbyshire, including Hope, Eyam and Tideswell. Many attractions that celebrate our industrial heritage, for example Ironbridge Gorge, sell traditional items that are made locally, thereby continuing past skills and practices.

Activity 18.8

Write a short report with the title 'The importance of visitor attractions to UK tourism'. You should comment generally on why attractions are important to tourism and use examples to illustrate your points.

This activity is designed to provide evidence for P4.

Unit summary

This unit has explored the visitor attractions sector and recognised the important role that attractions play in the economic and cultural life of the country. You have examined the products and services offered by attractions, and investigated different types of UK attractions. You have learned about the purpose of interpretation and have examined the various interpretation techniques that can be used in natural and built attractions to enhance visitors' understanding and enjoyment. You have considered the appeal of attractions to different types of visitors, including incoming tourists, educational groups and visitors with special needs. Finally, the unit has explored the importance of visitor attractions to the popularity and appeal of UK tourist attractions. Throughout the unit you have been shown many industry examples, while the case studies on the Big Pit National Coal Museum, the Brecon Beacons National Park, Chessington World of Adventures and the Eden Project, highlight key issues in the operation of visitor attractions.

If you have worked methodically, by the end of this unit you should:

- Know the products and services provided by different types of visitor attraction;
- Know the range and purpose of techniques used for visitor interpretation;
- Understand the appeal of visitor attractions to different types of visitor;
- Understand the importance of visitor attractions to the popularity and appeal of UK tourist destinations.

You are now in a position to complete the assignment for the unit, under the direction of your tutor. Before you tackle the assignment you may like to have a go at the following questions to help build your knowledge of UK visitor attractions.

Test your knowledge

1. List the five most popular charging attractions in the UK in 2006.
2. What is the difference between 'primary', 'secondary' and 'additional' products and services at a visitor attraction?
3. What type of corporate hospitality events are staged at visitor attractions?
4. List five popular UK heritage attractions.
5. What is a World Heritage Site?
6. Name five popular UK cultural attractions.
7. Why do you think the Eden Project has been so successful since it opened in 2001?
8. List the five most popular free attractions in the UK in 2006?
9. How do tourist attractions help the regeneration of urban and rural areas?
10. List three ways in which visitor attractions contribute to the local and national economy.
11. Name five popular sporting attractions and events in the UK.
12. What are the key points to bear in mind when deciding which interpretation techniques to select for a visitor attraction?
13. What interpretation techniques are particularly suitable for visitors with special needs?
14. What are the key features of an attraction that make it appealing to visitors?
15. How does seasonality affect the type of visitors to an attraction?

Answers to these questions can be found on the Book 2 Tutor's CD-ROM that accompanies this book (ISBN 9780955019050). Full details can be found at www.tandtpublishing.co.uk

The Appeal and Importance of UK Visitor Attractions

Introduction

This assignment is made up of a number of tasks which, when successfully completed, are designed to give you sufficient evidence to meet the Pass (P), Merit (M) and Distinction (D) grading criteria for the unit. If you have carried out the activities and read the case studies throughout this unit, you will already have done a lot of work towards completing the tasks for this assignment.

Scenario

Your uncle Jim works for a consultancy firm that specialises in advising governments in the new European Union (EU) member states on tourism projects. Three of the Baltic countries that have recently joined the EU – Latvia, Lithuania and Estonia – are planning to join forces to develop and promote new tourist attractions in their countries. Your uncle is heading the project to advise the countries and has invited you to help him over the summer.

The project focuses on four main areas:

1. The products and services provided by visitor attractions;
2. The range and purpose of techniques used for visitor interpretation;
3. The appeal of visitor attractions to different types of visitors;
4. The importance of visitor attractions to the popularity and appeal of UK tourist destinations.

He wants you to complete the following four tasks.

TASK 1

(a) Produce two case studies that **describe** the products and services provided by one built and one natural visitor attraction;

This task is designed to produce evidence for P1.

(b) In your case studies, **describe** the techniques used for visitor interpretation at the built and natural visitor attractions you chose for Task 1 (a).

This task is designed to provide evidence for P2.

To be considered for a Merit grade for this task, you must also:

(c) In your case studies, **analyse** how effectively the products, services and interpretation techniques of your chosen built and natural attractions are used to meet the needs of three different types of visitors.

This task is designed to provide evidence for M1.

To be considered for a Distinction grade for this task, you must also:

(c) In your case studies, make realistic and justified recommendations for improvements to the products, services and interpretation techniques used by your chosen built and natural attractions to meet the needs of different types of visitors.

This task is designed to provide evidence for D1.

TASK 2

Prepare and deliver an illustrated presentation in which you must:

(a) **Explain** the appeal of one selected natural and one built visitor attraction to three different types of visitors. You may use the same attractions that you chose in Task 1 to complete this task.

This task is designed to provide evidence for P3.

To be considered for a Merit grade for this task, your presentation must also:

(b) **Explain** how one built or natural attraction could adapt to appeal to a wider range of visitor types. You may use one of the attractions that you chose for Task 2 (a) to complete this task.

This task is designed to produce evidence for M2.

TASK 3

Produce a written report in which you must:

(a) **Explain** why visitor attractions are important to UK tourism.

This task is designed to produce evidence for P4.

To be considered for a Merit grade for this task, your report must also:

(b) **Explain** the impact visitor attractions have had on the popularity and appeal of a UK destination or area.

This task is designed to provide evidence for M3.

To be considered for a Distinction grade for this task, your report must also:

(c) **Evaluate** the success of visitor attractions to the popularity and appeal of the destination or area you chose for Task 3 (b), making recommendations for improvements.

This task is designed to provide evidence for D2.

UNIT 24

Handling Air Passengers

INTRODUCTION TO THE UNIT

Air travel is one of the fastest-growing sectors of the travel and tourism industry. The number of passengers travelling by air is growing steadily, encouraged by lower prices, higher quality services and expanded route networks. To cope with growing passenger numbers, airports and their associated facilities are being developed in the UK and across the world. Regional airports in particular are experiencing rapid development, driven by the growth of low-cost airlines. Providing air passengers with an efficient and stress-free experience when flying is seen as a major priority by airlines and airports.

This unit helps you to understand the process that passengers go through when travelling by air. You will investigate the options available to customers when travelling to and from airports, including transport networks and inter-terminal transport. You will also examine the embarkation process and the roles of airport and airline staff in helping passengers, for example with luggage procedures and ensuring health, safety and security. Facilities and services available to passengers during their flight vary between airlines and this unit gives you the opportunity to examine these in greater detail. Finally, the unit will help you understand airport and airline services and facilities during the passengers' disembarkation process.

WHAT YOU WILL STUDY

When you have completed this unit you should:

1. **Know the options available to customers when travelling to and from airports;**
2. **Understand the process of embarkation and the roles of airport and airline staff;**
3. **Know the facilities and services available to passengers during the flight;**
4. **Know the airport and airline services and facilities during the disembarkation process.**

You will be guided through the main topics in this unit with the help of the latest developments, statistics, industry examples and case studies. You should also check out the weblinks throughout the unit for extra information on particular organisations or topic areas and use the activities throughout the unit to help you learn more.

ASSESSMENT FOR THIS UNIT

This unit is internally assessed, meaning that you will be given an assignment (or series of assignments) to complete by your tutor(s) to show that you have fully understood the content of the unit. A grading scale of pass, merit or distinction is used when staff mark your assignment(s), with higher grades awarded to students who show greater depth in analysis, evaluation and justification in their assignments. An assignment for this unit, which covers all the grading criteria, can be found on page 236. Don't forget to visit www.tandtONLine.co.uk for all the latest industry news, developments, statistics and hot links to websites in this unit to help you with your assignments.

Icebreaker

This unit investigates passenger processes when travelling by air – a sometimes stressful experience, but well worth it when you reach your final destination! Working by yourself, or in small groups under the direction of your tutor, see how you get on with the following tasks to help you make a start on this unit:

- Write a short paragraph that explains the sort of work that a member of airport staff working at check-in would do in a typical day;
- Name three types of public transport that airline passengers could take to get to or from an airport;
- Make a list of the members of airport/airline staff that a passenger would come into contact with when taking a flight from London to Aberdeen;
- What are 'embarkation' and 'disembarkation'?
- Think about the particular airport and airline facilities and services that are needed by passengers with special needs;
- Name two types of inter-terminal transport found at airports;
- Name three roles and responsibilities of airline cabin crew.

When you've finished, show your answers to your tutor and compare your answers with what other students in your class have written.

SECTION 1

Know the options available to customers when travelling to and from airports

Air passengers look for convenience when choosing their departure airport, often preferring a local airport that is closer to home over one that may have more facilities, but involves a longer journey to reach. Bigger airports are able to offer a wider range of facilities and services, such as facilities for business travellers, private lounges, covered walkways and on-airport accommodation. In the first section of this unit we investigate the many options that are available to customers when travelling to and from airports, covering facilities such as transport, car rental and accommodation.

Transport to and from airports

An airport must be as accessible as possible for its customers, whether they are arriving by public transport or private vehicle. Arriving by public transport, for example by coach or train, is considered

Birmingham Airport's monorail link between the train station and terminals

a more environmentally-friendly option, but airports must offer a full range of transport facilities for their customers, including:

- Frequent rail services;
- Good access roads and car parking for private vehicles;
- Bus and coach services;
- Taxis and other private hire vehicles.

The Gatwick Express

FOCUS ON INDUSTRY

The Gatwick Express

Since 1984, passengers using London's Gatwick Airport have been able to use the Gatwick Express rail service – a non-stop rail link between London's Victoria Station and Gatwick Airport. Used by 5 million people every year, the journey takes 30 minutes and trains run every 15 minutes in both directions between 0500 hrs and 0035 hrs. The service is owned and operated by National Express, best known for its inter-city coach services. Gatwick Express employs 300 members of staff to operate the 160 services it runs per day on the 27-mile stretch of track.

Weblink

Check out this website for more information on the Gatwick Express train service.
www.gatwickexpress.com

The following case study on Manchester Airport gives details of the many transport options available to people departing from and returning to this busy airport.

Case Study

Transport Options at Manchester Airport

Introduction

Manchester Airport is part of the Manchester Airports Group (MAG), the country's largest UK-owned airport operator. The Group's four airports – Manchester, East Midlands, Bournemouth and Humberside – currently serve a total of more than 28 million passengers every year. Manchester Airport alone handles some 22 million travellers annually. There are currently 100 airlines offering direct flights to 225 destinations worldwide from Manchester Airport – more destinations than any other UK airport.

With around 19,000 people employed directly on site, the airport is a major contributor to the regional economy of the north-west of England and beyond.

The airport contributes £3.2 billion to the UK economy and supports over 130,000 jobs. According to independent analysis, MAG could grow further to generate £6.3 billion in economic value and support 260,000 jobs by 2015. MAG supports the UK government's commitment to the principles of sustainable development in the aviation industry, striking a balance between economic, social and environmental considerations. The Group is publicly-owned by the ten local authorities of Greater Manchester and is privately managed on their behalf. The biggest shareholder is the Council of the City of Manchester, with a 55 per cent stake in the business. MAG also runs businesses in property development and management, baggage handling, car parking, airport security, fire fighting, engineering, advertising and motor transport.

Travelling to and from Manchester Airport

Departing and returning air passengers can reach and leave Manchester Airport using a variety of transport services, including travel by train, car, taxi, bus and coach.

Train travel

'The Station' is Manchester Airport's integrated transport hub, with frequent train services linking the airport with over 100 destinations across the north of England and beyond. Frequent, direct rail services to the airport run to and from Sheffield, York, Newcastle, Leeds, Huddersfield, Bolton, Preston, Blackpool and the Lake District. These services are operated by TransPennine Express and Northern Rail, running 24 hours a day and 7 days per week. Up to six trains an hour link the airport to Manchester Piccadilly station in the city centre and from there to the national rail network. The airport has 'skylink' moving walkways that link The Station to the terminal buildings. Passengers flying from Manchester Airport can book their onward rail rickets online and collect them from self-service ticket machines in the baggage reclaim halls. Alternatively, train tickets can be bought from the booking office in The Station.

Cars and taxis

Manchester is one of the UK's most accessible airports, located at the heart of the motorway network (see Figure 24.1). Example motorway distances in miles between the airport and main city centres include:

- London – 185
- Birmingham – 80
- Cardiff – 172
- Sheffield – 38
- Leeds – 40
- Newcastle – 185

The airport has a spur road that connects it to the M56 motorway and from there to the M6 and M60.

The airport has taxi ranks outside all three terminals, allowing passengers easy access to their check-in desk to start their journey or a speedy departure when returning to the airport. Fares for journeys within the Manchester Licensed Area are shown on the meter inside the taxi. For journeys outside Manchester, there is a published tariff of maximum fares that is displayed at all taxi ranks. Passengers may use any taxi service of their choice for departure or arrival, but this must be booked in advance. The airport advises customers to meet their taxi driver inside the arrivals hall as waiting restrictions apply on all roads close to the terminal buildings. A private company, Airportcarz, offers a taxibus service that operates at all three of Manchester's terminals. Journeys with Airportcarz must be pre-booked at the company's desk inside the arrivals hall of any of the terminals. Bookings for this service can also be made online.

Figure 24.1 – Manchester Airport's position in the UK motorway network

Bus and coach services

Manchester Airport is well served by a network of local and regional buses running every day from early morning until late at night, including weekends and bank holidays. The services are provided by Skyline and Arriva, which now offers a 24-hour bus service operating between Altrincham and the airport. A map of the local and regional bus services at Manchester Airport is available at www.manchesterairport.co.uk/manweb.nsf/All+Content/BusNetworkMaps

A large number of coach services operate daily from The Station, Manchester Airport's integrated transport hub, linking the airport with destinations within the north-west region and major UK cities further afield via the National Express network. Coach travel is a cost-effective way of getting to and from the airport, and most coaches are equipped with reclining seats, air-conditioning and onboard toilets and washroom facilities. There is a National Express ticket desk located in The Station, open from 0700 hrs to 2200 hrs every day. However, to guarantee a seat, the company advises booking in advance online or via an agent.

Case Study Questions and Activities

1. Describe the transport options available to customers when travelling to and from Manchester Airport.
2. What transport facilities does the airport offer for customers with special needs who need to travel to and from the airport?
3. What are options available to passengers travelling between terminals at Manchester Airport?
4. What is a typical journey time on the train from Manchester Airport to London, Birmingham and Leeds?
5. What is a typical journey time by National Express coach from Manchester Airport to Edinburgh, Nottingham and Lancaster?

This case study is designed to provide evidence for P1.

Weblink

Check out this website to help answer the questions and for more information on travelling to and from Manchester Airport.
www.manchesterairport.co.uk

Activity 24.1

Using the case study of Manchester Airport as a guide, carry out some research into another major international airport in the UK and compile a fact sheet on the transport options available to passengers departing from, and returning to, the airport.

This activity is designed to provide evidence for P1.

Car parking

Airport car parking facilities are normally divided into short-stay and long-stay. Short-stay parking bays are located closest to the airport terminals and are the most expensive. Long-stay car parks are often located some distance from the main terminals and

passengers are transferred to the airport by shuttle buses that run at frequent intervals and are designed to accept passengers and their luggage in relative comfort. VIP (very important person) parking facilities are available at most airports for dignitaries and celebrities, located closest of all to the main terminal buildings and perhaps even having their own entrance/exit.

The growth in demand for airport parking has led to an increase in the use of off-airport parking, usually provided by private operators. This is when a passenger leaves their car (and its keys) with a member of car parking staff at a convenient point in the airport. The car is then driven to a nearby parking compound that is away from airport property and has 24-hour security surveillance. The car is brought from the compound and returned to the customer at the end of his or her trip. Off-airport parking is usually the cheapest type of airport parking and is preferred by people travelling on a budget. Most airports have an area for 'setting down' departing passengers, but these now tend to be located away from the entrance to terminals for security reasons.

The growth in the use of the internet has encouraged more people to pre-book their airport parking online, thereby receiving a discount on the normal tariffs. Travellers simply use the credit card they used for their online booking to enter and leave the car park. Customers who have not pre-booked can pay for their parking at pay stations located in car parks and terminal buildings.

Activity 24.2

Carry out some research on an airport that is close to your home area and produce a fact sheet that describes the car parking facilities on offer to customers, giving sample prices.

This activity is designed to provide evidence for P1.

Inter-terminal transport

Larger airports that have more than one terminal have to provide transport for passengers who need to travel between terminals. This could be by bus, minibus or moving walkway. There is usually no

Inter-terminal transport at Heathrow

charge for this inter-terminal service, the cost being absorbed by the airport operator.

Car rental at airports

Car rental is an important service that airports must offer passengers. As with on-airport and off-airport parking discussed earlier in this unit, the cheapest car rental deals are usually found away from the main airport terminals – where the multinational car hire firms are found, e.g. Hertz, Avis and Europcar. Passengers pay higher rental rates for the convenience of a terminal pick-up and drop-down, plus the greater confidence associated with dealing with a well-known car rental brand.

A car rental desk at Stansted

Many airlines and airports offer a limousine service for VIP customers who are prepared to pay for the privilege. Virgin Atlantic Airways offers its first class passengers a range of free transport options to reach their airport.

FOCUS ON INDUSTRY

Complimentary ground transfers with Virgin Atlantic

Passengers who are flying first class with Virgin Atlantic Airways – their 'Upper Class' service – can pre-book a range of complimentary transport options for either end of their journey.

Chauffeur-driven car transfers are available to/from the following airports: Heathrow, Gatwick, JFK, Newark, Boston, Washington DC, Miami, Orlando, San Francisco, Los Angeles, Las Vegas, Bridgetown, Antigua, Tobago, Grenada, St Lucia, Hong Kong, Johannesburg, Cape Town, Dubai, Shanghai, Tokyo, Delhi, Mumbai, Sydney, Jamaica, Mauritius, Havana and Dubai.

In addition the following high speed transfer options are available:

Flights to/from Heathrow

"Limobike" motorcycles; Heathrow Express train from London Paddington.

Flights to/from Gatwick

"Limobike" motorcycles; Gatwick Express train from London Victoria.

Flights to/from Narita

Limousine bus services; Keisei liner train from Tokyo Ueno or Nippori stations; Narita Express trains to/from Tokyo, Shinagawa, Shinjuku, Yokohama, or Ofuna stations; Baggage delivery service (One item of luggage per person can be delivered to a choice of specified locations nationwide).

UK-based passengers arriving at destinations in the USA

Free car hire (2 days free per single flight).

Flights to/from South Africa

Free car hire (2 days free per single flight).

Weblink
Check out this website for more information on travelling with Virgin Atlantic Airways. www.virgin-atlantic.com

Accommodation at airports

Having accommodation close by is an important facility that airports need to offer travellers, whether they are on business or leisure trips. People travelling a long distance to an airport, or who have to catch an early flight, appreciate the chance to rest before their journey. Many hotels and motels located close to airports offer accommodation packages that include car parking for the duration of the passengers' trip. This can often work out cheaper than using the airport's normal car parking facilities. It is common for airport hotels to run shuttle buses between their premises and the airport terminals at regular intervals.

FOCUS ON INDUSTRY

Accommodation at Manchester Airport

Hotels with an airport shuttle service near Manchester Airport include:

- Crowne Plaza Manchester Airport (1.2 km);
- Holiday Inn Manchester Airport (1.2 km);
- Bewleys Hotel (1.3 km);
- Hilton Manchester Airport Hotel (1.5 km);
- Etrop Grange Hotel (1.9 km);
- Stanneylands Hotel (3.4 km);
- Britannia Airport Hotel Manchester (6.5 km);
- Best Western Cresta Court Hotel Manchester (6.5 km);
- The Britannia Country House Hotel (7.2 km);
- Stay Inn Manchester (14.9 km);
- Village Hotel & Leisure Club Hyde (17.4 km).

Weblink

Check out this website for more information on accommodation close to Manchester Airport. www.manchesterairport.co.uk

SECTION 2 | Understand the process of embarkation and the roles of airport and airline staff

Embarkation is the process that air passengers go through when boarding an aircraft. The process starts when they arrive at their departure airport and finishes when they take their seat on the aircraft, as shown in Figure 24.2. As you can see from the chart, some parts of the embarkation process are 'landside' and some 'airside'. Landside refers to areas of an airport that are accessible to the general public, whereas airside areas are only open to passengers with valid boarding cards (or equivalent) and airline/airport staff with the necessary identification (ID) documents.

Disembarkation is the reversal of the embarkation process and begins when passengers land at their destination and leave their plane (see page 232 for more information on disembarkation and the stages involved). The embarkation process involves a number of stages and airport facilities, and is the responsibility of a variety of airline and airport staff, as we discover in the following sections of this unit.

Departure airport facilities

Once passengers have arrived at their departure

Figure 24.2 – The embarkation process

terminal with any luggage that they may be carrying, their next step is to check in for their flight at the appropriate check-in desk. Screens in the departure hall indicate which check-in desks are handling which flights. Each flight will have a final time for passengers to check in, after which access to the flight is withdrawn – this could be up to 2 hours in the case of long-haul flights to as little as 30 minutes for some low-cost airlines. Airlines are very strict about final check-in times and it is the responsibility of passengers to allow sufficient time for their journey to the airport, allowing for traffic jams and congestion when necessary. If passengers arrive after the final check-in time for their flight, they will be prevented from flying on that service and may be offered a later flight.

The staff at the check-in desks may be employed directly by the airline or may be working for a ground handling company that provides services to the airlines and/or the airport. One of the biggest ground handling companies is Servisair, which provides support at more than 140 airports around the world, including Manchester, Birmingham, Newcastle and many other UK airports.

FOCUS ON INDUSTRY

Servisair

Servisair offers a range of ground handling services to airports and the aviation industry generally, handling more than 100 million air passengers per year across the world. The company's passenger services include checking in, ticketing, boarding, lost and found, security screening, hotel accommodation, meal vouchers and requests from customers with special needs. Its technical services include baggage handling, repositioning aircraft, flight operations, aircraft cleaning and staff supervision.

Check-in desks at Heathrow

Weblink

Check out this website for more information on Servisair.

www.servisair.com

Once passengers have checked themselves in, plus any luggage they may be carrying, they proceed through security to the departures area or lounge. The point at which they go through security is the point at which they move from landside to airside. Most departure areas in airports are arranged as a main public lounge with facilities such as toilets, eating places, currency exchange facilities and shops. There are also screens with information on departing aircraft, showing the time of departure, whether on-time or delayed and the number of the gate from which it will be leaving. There may also be facilities for children in the departure area, such as play areas, video screens and games machines. Chapels of many religious denominations are also found in larger international airports. Many airports have private lounges set aside for business travellers, first class passengers and VIPs, equipped with dining areas, business facilities and internet access. Some of these are available to economy class passengers on payment of a supplement.

Airports have a variety of retail outlets – the bigger the airport, the more shops on offer. Retail outlets provide a useful service to passengers and are also an important way for the airport to gain extra revenue. Landside shops that are available to the general public are not allowed to sell tax-free goods – these are only available to passengers who have passed through security control and have reached the airside departure lounge area.

Airport tax-free shopping

Stansted Airport

As well as shops, airports offer their customers a variety of places to eat and drink, usually run by concessionaires, i.e. private businesses that enter into a contract with the airport to provide the facility and agree to pay a proportion of profits back to the airport. Many well-known retail brands are found in UK airports, including W H Smith, Dixons, Starbucks, Accessorize and Pret A Manger.

Activity 24.4

Carry out some research into the shops and eating places found in the new Terminal 5 at London's Heathrow Airport, presenting your findings as a passenger fact sheet.

This activity is designed to provide evidence for P2.

Facilities for travellers with specific needs

There are certain categories of air travellers who have specific needs, such as infants, unaccompanied children, pregnant women and those with impaired mobility or in need of communication assistance. 'Unaccompanied minors' is the term used for children who are travelling on a flight without a parent, guardian or adult friend/relation. Their wellbeing during the flight is entrusted to a member of cabin crew. Traditionally, unaccompanied minors have been welcomed on flights – perhaps children travelling to visit a relative abroad or returning to the UK from a school overseas. Full-service airlines, such as British Airways and bmi, tend to have the most comprehensive services for unaccompanied minors, whereas most of the low-cost airlines do not allow unaccompanied minors on flights at all.

Activity 24.5

Visit the British Airways website www.ba.com and make notes on the current policy and charges for its unaccompanied minors' service – now called Skyflyer Solo.

This activity is designed to provide evidence for P2.

Children and infants may need special facilities during the embarkation process, such as priority boarding, buggy hire, baby-changing facilities and bottle warming. These services vary between airlines and airports, and passengers travelling with young children are advised to seek assistance and information prior to their flight.

Weblink

Check out this website for information on Virgin Atlantic's facilities for child passengers. www.virgin-atlantic.com/en/gb/passengerinformation/travellingwithchildren/index.jsp

Many airlines have special rules for pregnant travellers. For example, the low-cost airline flybe states that no action is required on the part of pregnant women below 27 weeks of pregnacy, but that a doctor's note certifying fitness for travel is needed from week 28 up to and including week 33. This must be presented at check-in. The airline does not carry passengers once the pregnancy has reached or exceeded week 34.

At the time of writing, airlines are not fully covered by the legislation contained in the Disability Discrimination Act, although the Act does state that public transport buildings, including airports, must be made accessible to disabled people. It makes good business sense to provide facilities and services for passengers with special needs – some of the low-cost airlines have been slow to respond and have received bad publicity on this issue.

Help points and telephones are provided in some airports for people who need assistance to check in for their flight, perhaps because of mobility problems or communication difficulties. Once checked in, the responsibility for assistance passes to the airline. Policies on providing assistance to passengers with special needs varies greatly between airlines, but they all make the point that passengers should inform the airline at the earliest possible opportunity in order to receive the best possible attention.

FOCUS ON INDUSTRY

Assistance for passengers with special needs at Stansted Airport

Facilities for the hard of hearing

Induction loops are fitted in many areas of the terminal and satellites and are identified by the sympathetic ear sign. All telephones throughout the airport are fitted with induction couplers. Public text phones are situated in the international arrivals area and in the satellite two departure lounge. A number of airport staff are proficient in BSL stage one and the majority have been trained in deaf awareness. Many of the staff are able to finger spell.

Facilities for the blind and partially-sighted

Guide and hearing dogs are the only dogs allowed in the terminal buildings. The airport directional signs are black on yellow providing optimum contrast to assist all users. Reserved seating areas aim to provide low-level flight information screens, but if you have difficulty seeing the monitors, please advise your airline at check-in.

Getting to your gate

There is a transit train system which connects passengers from the departure lounge to the satellites where the boarding gates are located. The same service operates for returning passengers:

- All trains are fully wheelchair-accessible;
- Each train has two help points situated at either end of the car;

- Normal train service is every three minutes and is free;
- If your aircraft is not linked to a satellite, your airline or their handling agent will arrange your transfer. Please advise them of your requirements at the time of check-in and ask if there is a charge for this service.

Reserved seating areas

Reserved seating areas, clearly identified by the use of special needs pictograms, are available for special needs passengers and are located throughout the airport in the general seating areas. These areas aim to provide the following:

- An induction loop;
- Arms on both sides of seats;
- Space for wheelchair users;
- Low-level flight information monitors.

Security checks

The safety and security of our passengers is our number one priority. All passengers must pass through security control before they enter the departure lounge. Wheelchair users will inevitably activate the archway metal detector, and security personnel are obliged to hand search passengers who activate the alarms: therefore chair and passenger will be searched. You can ask to be searched in private, away from the main security control area if you prefer.

Toilet facilities

Unisex accessible toilets are provided on the main concourse and within the departures lounge. Parents travelling with children are welcome to use the unisex accessible toilets.

Weblink

Check out this website for more information on facilities for passengers with special needs at Stansted Airport.
www.stanstedairport.com

Routine processing functions

There are a number of routine functions that airport, airline and other staff have to complete during the embarkation process, including:

- Check-in;
- Security;
- Boarding;
- Information provision;
- Itinerary changes.

Earlier we discussed the traditional check-in process at the airport, when passengers present their documents and any luggage to a member of staff at a check-in desk, usually after having queued for some time. In the last few years there have been major changes to check-in procedures, with airlines now encouraging passengers to check-in online and even print their boarding card before they leave home. Some low-cost airlines make a charge for manual check-in to encourage passengers to use online check-

Automated check-in at Heathrow

in. Automated, self-service check-in machines are also replacing check-in staff at airports. Automating the check-in process saves the airlines money and gives the passenger a better experience. In the new Terminal 5 at Heathrow, British Airways is expecting that 80 per cent of passengers will opt for self-service check-in. As such, the terminal is equipped with 96 self-service kiosks and 54 standard check-in desks.

Security

Having checked-in and received (or printed their own) boarding cards, passengers go though passport control and on to security screening. Carry-on luggage and items such as mobile phones, laptops and coats, are passed through x-ray scanners by security personnel to detect any illegal items. Passengers themselves pass through a screening process and if any metal items are detected, an alarm sounds. All passengers are also liable to random searches, which could involve removing their shoes. Luggage that is taken into the hold of the aircraft is also subjected to security screening.

Luggage procedures at airports

Handling luggage at airports is a time-consuming and at times frustrating operation, as anybody who has lost their baggage will tell you! The general move towards online and self-service check-in means that baggage 'drop desks' are replacing the traditional check-in desks at airports. Making sure that a passenger's luggage arrives in good condition and at the correct location is the responsibility of the airline or its ground handling agent, for example Aviance, Servisair and Swissport.

Dangerous and restricted goods

The rules on what can be taken on to an aircraft are covered by international agreements and in the UK it is the job of the CAA (Civil Aviation Authority) to make sure that these are followed. CAA inspectors have the power to seize packages if they have reason to be suspicious. Most incidents are a result of ignorance of the rules, but there are occasions when passengers deliberately try to bring items on board knowing the risks involved.

For safety reasons, there are a number of items that are completely prohibited from being taken on to an aircraft. These include:

- Compressed gases, including camping gas cylinders, butane, liquid nitrogen, propane gas and gas lighters;
- Corrosives such as acids, alkalis, mercury and wet-cell batteries;
- Explosives, munitions, flares, fireworks;
- Flammable liquids and solids, such as flammable aerosols, lighting or heating fuels, matches, paint thinners, fire lighters;
- Oxidising materials such as bleaching powder and peroxides;
- Poisons and infectious substances, such as arsenic, cyanide, insecticides, weed killer and live virus materials;
- Radioactive materials;
- Gas-powered devices (other than hair curlers) such as culinary blow torches or soldering irons;
- Other restricted articles such as magnetic material, offensive or pornographic materials.

The regulations governing dangerous and restricted goods are constantly reviewed and are liable to change. Passengers are advised to contact their airline to find out the up-to-date situation before they begin their journey.

Certain items are not allowed on to the aircraft as hand baggage, but can be taken on as hold luggage. These include bottles of contact lens solution, hairsprays, certain food items, some drinks and sharp items such as scissors, knives and tweezers.

Luggage allowances

Luggage or baggage allowances are determined by the airlines and depend on a number of factors, such as the class of travel, aircraft type, route, government regulations and the airline's own health and safety regulations. In general, airlines set a free baggage allowance, expressed either by weight, number of pieces of luggage or a combination of the two. Passengers are normally allowed to take one piece of hand luggage with them onboard the aircraft, which must be within certain dimensions and/or weight.

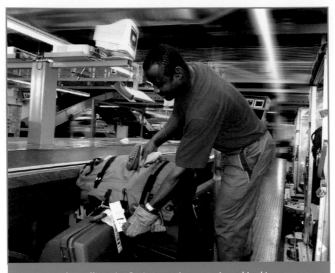
Luggage handling (© Swissport International Ltd.)

The whole area of luggage allowances has become much more complicated in the UK in recent years – the low-cost airlines in particular have seen this as an area where they could make extra revenue and have reduced allowances, in the hope of making money on excess baggage charges, i.e. the fees paid by passengers when they exceed their luggage allowance. Airlines also charge for larger items of luggage, known as outsize baggage, which can include bicycles and ski equipment.

Airline and airport personnel and staff roles

Airports are very busy places employing hundreds and sometimes thousands of people – Heathrow alone currently employs more than 70,000 staff. Figure 24.3 lists some of the main types of staff found at airports and their respective roles. All play a vital part in helping passengers through the embarkation and disembarkation processes as efficiently as possible.

Customer service agents

Customer service agents, also known as passenger service agents or passenger handling agents, are responsible for checking in airline passengers and their luggage. At the check-in desk, agents:

- Greet passengers;
- Deal with passenger enquiries, such as queries on departure times and changes to flights;
- Check passengers' tickets and passports;
- Allocate seats to passengers (where appropriate);
- Weigh passengers' luggage, check it in and make any excess charges if necessary;
- Print out luggage labels and attach them to the luggage;
- Issue boarding cards;

Personnel	Roles
Airline staff	Providing information, selling tickets, boarding passengers, dealing with queries, flight operations, despatching flights
Ground handlers	Dealing with passenger queries, checking in, issuing tickets, hotel accommodation sales
Customer service agents	Checking in passengers, processing documentation and luggage
Baggage handling agents	Ensuring luggage is despatched effectively and efficiently
Security staff	Screening passengers and luggage, looking for suspicious passengers
Immigration officers	Checking the status of passengers entering the country
HM Revenue & Customs officers	Responsible for duties on goods brought into the country
Retail staff	Selling goods and services in airport shops

Figure 24.3 – Airport personnel and their roles

- Ask a set of questions about security, such as 'did you pack this luggage yourself?', 'could anybody have interfered with your luggage at any time?'; 'are you carrying any of the following prohibited items in your luggage?', etc;
- Prepare any necessary customs paperwork;
- Point out which gate the plane will be departing from and at what time;
- Direct passengers to passport control and security;
- Deal with late passengers.

Customer service agents may also work at the boarding gate, announcing when a plane is ready to board and checking passengers' boarding cards. They may also escort passengers to their waiting plane and could have extra responsibilities for passengers with special needs, such as those in wheelchairs. They may also be asked to supervise children who are travelling unaccompanied by an adult. Customer service agents are responsible to a supervisor and work closely with other check-in staff, flight dispatchers, ground escorts, security staff and airline operations personnel.

A customer service agent (© Swissport International Ltd.)

Air Handling plc

Job description

Title of post:	Security Officer
Post no:	SO/09/09
Location:	Various
Responsible to:	Security Manager

Job summary

- Play your part in the security of the airport so that customers, staff and vehicles can use the facilities safely;
- Screen all people, vehicles and items that enter restricted areas using x-ray machines, other screening technology and hand searches;
- Check ID and/or travel documents for all passengers and staff entering the restricted areas;
- Understand passengers' needs – especially those with small children – and keep queuing times to a minimum;
- Patrol the terminal and surrounding areas to ensure buildings are secure and potential risks are identified;
- Assist in emergency situations such as evacuating the terminals;
- Help people with questions about directions and airport facilities;
- Demonstrate a flexible and helpful attitude, assisting in the smooth running of the airport;
- Maintain high professional standards at all times, including personal appearance;
- Record any incidents in a clear and concise manner.

Requirements

1. Full-colour vision;
2. Good observation and object recognition;
3. The ability to stand for long periods of time, reach up and bend down during body searches and lift hand luggage;
4. Pass our security background checks in line with Department for Transport (DfT) regulations;
5. Ability to read, understand, write and speak fluent English;
6. Experience of working in a customer service role is desirable;
7. Are you the kind of person who can:

    - Make suggestions that will help others improve?
    - Use your ingenuity to improve the area you work in?
    - Understand how to meet and exceed the expectations of passengers?
    - Challenge yourself to produce excellent results?
    - Take account of your colleagues' priorities when doing your job?

Salary and benefits

- Competitive salary and benefits package is offered;
- Full training will be given in line with DfT guidelines;
- Shift-work to cover 24-hour operation.

Dated: 1st September 2008

Figure 24.4 – Job description for an airport security officer

Airport security staff

Security staff play an important role in making sure that the passenger embarkation process is as safe and secure as possible. Security procedures at airports have become much stricter since the events of September 11th 2001 in the USA and passengers must act appropriately while security screening takes place. In addition to screening passengers and their luggage on their way to the departure lounge, security staff are responsible for vehicles, retail premises and all airport buildings and equipment. They work in partnership with the police, national security services, immigration officers and HM Revenue & Customs staff in the course of their work.

The job description in Figure 24.4 gives an overview of the roles and responsibilities of an airport security officer.

Activity 24.6

Choose two of the categories of staff from Figure 24.3 and compile two fact sheets that describe the roles that the staff concerned play during the embarkation of customers. Include the type of detailed information shown in Figure 24.4.

This activity is designed to provide evidence for P2.

SECTION 3 Know the facilities and services available to passengers during the flight

Having arrived at the airport, checked in, passed through passport control, been screened at security and arrived at the aircraft via the boarding gate, passengers are now able to relax and enjoy their flight. The facilities on board the aircraft are designed to make the journey as comfortable and safe as possible.

Boarding

Closer to their time of departure, passengers move from the departure lounge to the gate allocated to their aircraft. There are few facilities at departure gates, simply rows of seats and a work station with a member of staff given the task of boarding passengers on to the aircraft. Boarding may be via an airbridge from the departure gate or across the tarmac and up steps to the aircraft. The advantage of using an airbridge is that passengers are not exposed to any inclement weather. Passengers may be transported from the

departure gate to their aircraft in an airport bus that is specially designed for the purpose.

Boarding the aircraft is the final stage of embarkation. Airline staff known as dispatchers are responsible for making sure that a flight departs on time and

At the boarding gate (© Swissport International Ltd.)

with the correct number of passengers on board. All passengers must show their boarding cards at this stage – without it, a passenger won't be allowed to board their aircraft.

Boarding procedures vary between airlines. Full-service airlines, such as Virgin Atlantic, British Airways and bmi, allocate specific seats to passengers at check-in, whereas the low-cost airlines, for example easyJet, Ryanair and bmibaby, do not allocate seats at all. For safety reasons, some seats on aircraft are not suitable for all passengers, such as older people, children or those with limited mobility, as the following section of the easyJet website explains:

'Because safety is our main priority at easyJet, there are some seats that are not suitable for all passengers. These are marked with grey headrests as opposed to orange ones and are located at the front row of the aircraft, on the wing exits and on the last row. These seats are only suitable for use by able-bodied adults as you may be required to assist the crew in the highly unlikely event of an emergency. Passengers may only sit in one of these restricted seats at the discretion of the cabin staff'.

Boarding passengers are usually divided into groups in order to make the process as efficient and fair as possible. More recently, some low-cost airlines have introduced a priority boarding service, aimed at people who are prepared to pay extra to be amongst the first to board the aircraft. easyJet, for example, operates a strict priority boarding system, with passengers being boarded in the following order:

- Group SB – passengers who have purchased Speedy Boarding (currently £4 per passenger per flight) or Speedy Boarding Plus (annual subscription);
- Group SA – passengers travelling with babies;
- Group A – reserved for passengers who have checked in online, and the first 30 people who check in at the airport;
- Group B – all other passengers.

Airlines can provide assistance to passengers who have special needs, but advise passengers to inform them at the earliest opportunity in order to receive the care and attention they need. Every airline has very detailed rules governing people with special needs, who may include:

- Passengers with wheelchairs;
- Travellers with limbs in plaster;
- Special needs passengers travelling with carers;
- Those with a visual or hearing impairment;
- Passengers with asthma;
- Diabetics;
- Passengers with a specific food allergy.

Activity 24.7

Carry out some research on two airlines (one low-cost and one full-service) and compare the facilities and services each offers for passengers with special needs.

This activity is designed to provide evidence for P2.

Staff who work at the boarding gate are trained to look out for any passengers who may be acting suspiciously or who appear to be under the influence of alcohol. Drunken passengers, or those who are considered to be a risk to other passengers, will not be allowed to board the aircraft. Boarding gate staff may also need to give more attention than usual to first-time and nervous flyers. Announcements may have to be made to inform late passengers that their flight is about to depart. If there are still passengers missing when the gate closes, their luggage is taken off the aircraft and they miss their flight. Once on the aircraft, passengers may use overhead lockers and the space underneath their seats to stow their cabin baggage. Cabin crew staff will make sure that all the aisles on the aircraft are kept clear in case of emergencies.

Activity 24.8

Write a short report that describes the boarding process on a low-cost airline and a full-service airline.

This activity is designed to provide evidence for P3.

On-board facilities

Facilities on board an aircraft will vary greatly according to a number of factors, such as:

- The airline;
- Class of travel;
- Route travelled;
- Type of aircraft;
- The length of the flight.

To illustrate this point, one passenger may be pampered with luxury food, fine wines and a bed in first class when flying between Singapore and London on board the new Airbus A380 with Singapore Airlines, while another passenger may be travelling on a short flight with Ryanair from Newquay in Cornwall to London Stansted with limited on-board facilities provided – but for a much lower price!

Class of travel has the biggest influence on the facilities that passengers can enjoy during their flight. In general, the higher the class of travel (and cost of the ticket) the better the facilities and services on offer – so, first class, premium economy and business class travellers have access to more facilities of a higher standard than passengers who are travelling economy class. The actual facilities and services provided vary between airlines and this is an area where they hope to gain an advantage over their competitors by, for example, having extra seat room, offering free food and drinks, and providing state-of-the-art entertainment technology. Figure

Class	Facilities and services
Upper Class	<ul><li>Complimentary ground transfer</li><li>Drive-through check-in</li><li>Access to airport *Clubhouse* lounge</li><li>Fully-flat bed</li><li>Leather seat with increased width of 22"</li><li>Laptop power access and large table to work</li><li>Multi-directional 10.4"TV screen</li><li>Unlimited access to dinner and drinks menu</li><li>Beauty therapy treatments</li><li>Upper Class *Snooze Pack*</li></ul>
Premium Economy	<ul><li>Dedicated check-in, priority boarding, disembarking and baggage reclaim</li><li>Leather seat with increased width of 21"</li><li>Dedicated cabin crew</li><li>Personal seat-back TV</li><li>Laptop power</li><li>Pre-flight drinks, liqueurs and fresh fruit</li><li>Choice of meals served on china dinnerware with stainless steel cutlery</li></ul>
Economy	<ul><li>Individual seat-back TV</li><li>Free meal and drinks (special diets catered for)</li><li>Free amenity kit (eyeshades, socks, toothbrush, toothpaste)</li><li>*Seatback* magazine, goodie bag for kids, newspaper</li><li>In-flight shopping</li></ul>

Figure 24.5 – Virgin Atlantic's on-board facilities and services

24.5 compares the facilities available to passengers travelling in different classes.

In general, low-cost airlines only offer one class of travel. These 'no frills' operators have reduced the number of free facilities on board their services in recent years, charging passengers instead for items such as drinks, food and pre-allocated seats. Charter airlines, running flights in conjunction with package tours, still tend to offer a free meal, but are beginning to charge for pre-allocated seating and 'premium' services, e.g. newspapers, seats with more leg room, etc.

On-board entertainment

Activity 24.9

Carry out some research into the services and facilities offered for passengers travelling in different classes on a full-service airline of your choice. Use the information you gather to compile a fact sheet giving details of what's on offer.

This activity is designed to provide evidence for P2.

Facilities for passengers with special needs

For safety reasons, airlines are only allowed to carry a certain number of passengers who have restricted mobility on each flight. This varies according to the size of the aircraft and the policy of the airline. In general, low-cost airlines offer only limited facilities and services for passengers with special needs, whereas full-service airlines have more comprehensive services. British Airways, for example, offers the following assistance to travellers with special needs:

- Passengers travelling with their own wheelchair – provided space is available, BA will store collapsible wheelchairs and mobility aids in the aircraft cabin. If no space is available, they are carried in the hold. Up to two mobility aids, e.g. wheelchair, can be carried free of charge in addition to the normal luggage allowance.

- Facilities on board aircraft – safety regulations stipulate that passengers with additional needs should not be seated at emergency exits or in cross aisles that form part of emergency routes. On-board facilities include wheelchairs on all long-haul, twin-aisled flights, adapted toilets on Boeing 747 aircraft and a number of seats with lifting armrests for ease of access. There are no adapted toilets on short-haul or domestic flights.

- Hearing-impaired passengers – BA can provide separate briefings about safety procedures, subtitles on the English version of the in-flight safety video, induction loop facilities and headphones that are compatible with standard hearing aids switched to the 'T' position.

- Visually-impaired passengers – BA can provide an escort to and from the aircraft, individual safety briefings and assistance during the flight. In addition, Braille cards are available on some flights and assistance is given to visually-impaired and blind passengers.

- Travelling with guide/assistance dogs – Certified Assistance Dogs for blind, deaf or disabled passengers travel free of charge in the aircraft cabin on all British Airways services within the UK. In addition, Assistance Dogs that are compliant with the Pet Travel Scheme may be carried in the cabin of the aircraft on certain international routes.

All passengers are advised to consider their health during a flight, especially those on long-haul trips. DVT (deep vein thrombosis) has become a particular concern in recent years. It is potentially life-threatening and is thought to be caused by staying in the same position for a long time. All airlines offer guidance on how to reduce the risk of DVT on a flight, by carrying out exercises at regular intervals to keep limbs active. easyJet provides the following general advice for air travellers:

- Wear loose and comfortable clothing;
- Drink plenty of water – moderate your intake of tea, coffee, cola drinks and alcoholic beverages, as caffeine and alcohol can lead to dehydration;
- Stretch your arms and legs regularly;
- If you wear contact lenses, you may find it more comfortable to remove them before the flight as the air in the cabin can be drying.

Facilities for children

Safety is an important consideration for children travelling in aircraft. Cabin crew issue infant seat belts, cots and child seats as appropriate, and offer individual assistance to parents before take-off and during the flight. They can also provide a bottle warming service and point out the location of baby-changing facilities.

Keeping children entertained on flights can be a difficult task, so any on-board facilities that will keep them amused are welcomed by their parents, particularly when travelling on long-haul flights. Virgin Atlantic provides every child with an activity pack to keep them amused, while the seat-back TVs have dedicated channels for children of all ages, including computer games. Children's meals are also available, but need to be pre-booked.

Family entertainment on a Virgin flight (Courtesy of Virgin Atlantic Airways/Travmedia)

Activity 24.10

Explain the importance of providing facilities to meet specific passenger needs both on board and during the boarding process.

This activity is designed to provide evidence for M2.

Roles and responsibilities of personnel in flight

The members of staff that look after passengers during their flight are known as air cabin crew – the pilots are the flight crew. A senior member of cabin crew will lead his or her staff team in delivering a service to all passengers that includes:

Cabin crew on an XL Airways flight

- Ensuring health and safety – making announcements, checking equipment, etc;
- Giving information – for onward travel, immigration procedures, transit passengers, etc;
- Safeguarding the welfare of passengers – helping nervous passengers, providing assistance for passengers with special needs, etc;
- Providing medical assistance – from minor scratches to major incidents;
- Managing passenger behaviour – ensuring that unruly passengers are dealt with in an appropriate manner;
- Selling goods – items such as perfumes, gifts and souvenirs on a commission basis;
- Providing a food and beverage service – this will vary depending on the length of flight and class of travel.

Cabin crew are the main point of contact for air passengers and their primary role is to ensure the safety of their customers. Air cabin crew carry out a variety of duties that include:

- Overseeing the boarding of passengers on to the aircraft;
- Checking that the aircraft is clean and tidy, and stocked with food and drinks;
- Making sure that the cabin equipment and on-board medical stocks are in order;
- Supervising the boarding and disembarking of passengers;
- Making sure that passengers' hand luggage is securely stowed;
- Informing passengers of the aircraft safety procedures;
- Serving meals and drinks;
- Selling gifts and duty-free items during the flight.

Cabin crew work irregular hours, including nights, weekends and public holidays, and staff who work on long-haul flights may be away from home for long periods. The working environment is often quite demanding, with restricted space and a lot of time spent moving around the cabin attending to passengers.

bmi (part of the British Midland Airways Group) operates 1,700 flights per week and has a fleet of 41 aircraft. The company's air cabin crew are responsible for looking after passengers on aircraft and making sure that they have a safe and enjoyable flight. This involves checking cabin equipment, serving meals and drinks, looking after in-flight entertainment and making sure that passengers understand safety and emergency procedures.

When employing cabin crew, bmi stresses that they need to be flexible about working times as they are expected to work weekends, overnights and public holidays. bmi have the following requirements for anybody thinking of joining as cabin crew:

- Minimum age is 18 – there is no maximum age limit although the mandatory retirement age is 65 years of age;
- Between 5'2" and 6'2" in height with weight in proportion;
- Minimum qualifications are 4 GCSEs at grades A-C including English and maths (or equivalent);
- Applicants must hold a 10-year British or European passport before employment or have the indefinite right to live and work in the UK, as well as any relevant visas;
- A minimum of 12 months' experience in a customer-facing role;
- A high standard of physical fitness and a visual acuity of 6/9 in each eye, aided or unaided. Contact lenses are preferred, but glasses are acceptable;
- A good standard of fluency in the English language;
- Immaculate appearance.

Most cabin crew opportunities with bmi occur at their Heathrow base, but jobs at other airports are available from time to time. Currently, the airline has cabin crew staff based at the following airports: Heathrow, Manchester, Leeds-Bradford, Glasgow, Edinburgh, Teesside, Dublin and Belfast.

In recruiting cabin crew, bmi looks for people whose strengths and qualities match its own. Applicants must be approachable and have excellent personal skills, such as team-working ability, initiative and adaptability, plus high-level communication skills.

Cabin crew must be able to remain calm under pressure and deliver excellent customer service, while meeting the airline's values of speed with charm and style. Leadership skills are important for those seeking future promotion within the company.

The length of working days is very variable for cabin crew, depending on how many sectors they are rostered to complete (a sector is a one-way flight). Staff may have to start work as early as 5.00 am and may not finish until 11.30 pm. Charter flights may require reporting for duty/finishing at any time of the day or night. In addition, the working day may be affected by delays or changes to flights. With bmi, cabin crew are given a roster four to eight weeks in advance. Duty days will vary between early starts and late finishes, the number of sectors worked and may include standby duties at home or at the airport. The hours of work are governed by Civil Aviation Authority (CAA) regulations.

Activity 24.11

Research and compile a passenger information leaflet that describes the role of staff and the facilities available for customers during a flight with an airline of your choice.

This activity is designed to provide evidence for P4.

Activity 24.12

Compare the facilities available at London Heathrow and London Gatwick for passengers travelling to and from the airports, and during the embarkation process. With reference to either Heathrow or Gatwick, evaluate the effectiveness of processes for handling passengers during embarkation, making justified recommendations for improvement.

This activity is designed to provide evidence for M1 and D1.

Know the airport and airline services and facilities during the disembarkation process

When a flight arrives at its destination airport, passengers are allowed to disembark the aircraft when it has come to a complete stop and the seat belt warning signs have been switched off by a member of the cabin crew. Passengers may need assistance with a number of procedures concerned with disembarkation, including:

1. Passport and visa requirements;
2. Luggage reclaim;
3. Car hire, transport and other arrival facilities;
4. Passenger transfers.

Passport and visa requirements

Having left their aircraft, either by means of an airbridge or steps and perhaps an airport bus, passengers not making a connecting flight head for the immigration area of the arrivals hall. There are two separate queuing areas – one for European Union (EU) and British nationals, the second for all other destinations. Once at the immigration booth, an immigration officer checks passengers' passports and any visas and other supporting documentation relevant to their visit. Officers check that a visitor's passport will not expire during the person's visit to the UK. Any passenger who arrives in the UK with incorrect documents will be sent back to the country from which the flight originated and the airline may be fined for failing to follow procedures. Large queues can develop at busy times and airports ask passengers to be patient while these important checks are carried out to help ensure security for visitors and UK residents alike.

Immigration checks and procedures have become much more stringent in recent years as the threats from international terrorism and people trafficking have increased. Visitors to UK airports from countries outside the EU can expect much stricter checks than those returning from EU member states. The USA has introduced very strict regulations involving finger printing and passengers having their photographs taken. As a result, passing through US immigration can be a very lengthy process.

Luggage reclaim

Having passed safely through immigration, passengers with hold luggage make their way to the baggage reclaim area of the arrivals hall. In larger airports, there may be a series of carousels on which the luggage is delivered from the aircraft, with screens indicating which carousels to use for particular flights. Trolleys are available to help passengers transport their luggage from the arrivals hall. Outsized luggage will need to be picked up from a separate point in the luggage reclaim area.

Passengers pass through customs when they have picked up their luggage. As with immigration control, there are separate channels for passengers whose journey started in an EU country and those who are arriving from outside the EU. Passengers with goods to declare are asked to go through a separate (normally red) channel and speak to a customs officer. For passengers' safety and to ensure a quick journey though its airports, the British Airports Authority (BAA) – which runs 7 major UK airports including Heathrow, Gatwick and Stansted – advises returning passengers as follows:

- Never carry anything into the UK for somebody else;
- Never bring prohibited goods into the UK – if in doubt, ask at the customs enquiry point;
- If you are unsure about your duty/tax-free entitlement, go to the customs enquiry point;
- If you are connecting from one international flight to another international flight, you will not need to clear customs;
- If you are connecting from an international flight to a UK flight, you must clear customs and immigration.

Passengers whose luggage fails to arrive or has been damaged during the flight must contact a member of airline staff to resolve the matter. This involves filling in a Property Irregularity Report (PIR) form with full details. Most airlines send on delayed luggage at their expense to the passenger's home address and offer compensation for lost and damaged items. The amount of compensation is limited under the Montreal Convention and passengers may well find that their travel insurance offers better recompense.

Activity 24.13

Describe the procedures for lost and damaged luggage on one full-service and one low-cost airline of your choice.

This activity is designed to provide evidence for P5.

Arrival facilities

Passengers arriving at an airport may need access to a range of facilities and services, such as car hire, currency exchange, public transport, information and the location of car parks.

Currency exchange facilities at Stansted Airport

Most airports have official meeting points in each terminal to help returning passengers to find friends, relatives and business associates. These meeting points have screens displaying live flight information, the status of which could be:

- Expected – the flight hasn't landed yet;
- Landed – generally allow 30-40 minutes after landing for passengers to clear immigration control, baggage reclaim and customs;
- Baggage in hall – passengers should be in the arrivals areas shortly.

Activity 24.14

Research and compile information sheets that describe the disembarkation and transit processes at London's Heathrow and Gatwick Airports. Write a short report that analyses the effectiveness of the disembarkation processes at one of these two airports.

This activity is designed to provide evidence for P5 and D2.

Transit passengers

For some passengers arriving at an airport, it is not their final destination – these are transit passengers who remain within the confines of the airport to catch another flight, which could be domestic (within the UK) or international. Larger airports have transit areas for these passengers, with facilities such as toilets and washrooms, shops, catering outlets, internet access and information points. There are also screens with the latest information on flight departure times and boarding gates, plus airline ticket desks for passengers who need boarding cards or have any queries.

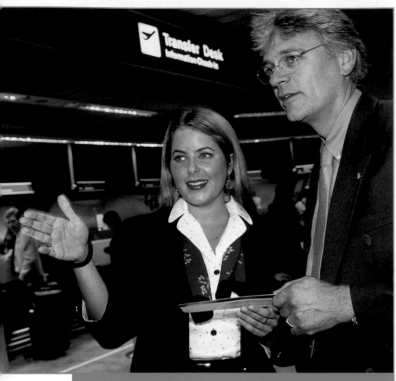

Assistance for a transit passenger (© Swissport International Ltd.)

Transit passengers who have checked their luggage in to their final destination at the start of their journey do not have to collect their luggage when transiting through an airport – it will be automatically routed to their connecting flight.

The procedure for connecting flights at UK airports depends on where a passenger is flying to and from:

- If the passenger arrived on a flight from within the UK they do not need to clear security control and can go directly to their departure terminal;

- If the passenger arrived on an international flight, they will need to go through a security check;
- If the onward flight is to another UK airport, passengers will also need to clear UK immigration.

Information for transit passengers at Heathrow

Activity 24.15

Write a short report to explain the importance of effective disembarkation processes at UK airports.

This activity is designed to provide evidence for M3.

Unit summary

In this unit you have examined the processes that passengers go through when travelling by air. You have considered the transport options available to passengers travelling to and from airports, such as rail networks, coach services, taxis and private hire services. The process of passenger embarkation has been covered in detail, from airport check-in to boarding the aircraft. You have investigated airport facilities and services for travellers with special needs, including mobility assistance and arrangements for unaccompanied minors. On-board passenger facilities offered by different airlines, for example entertainment, services for children and catering, have been compared. It is clear that class of travel is the single most important factor affecting passenger facilities, with first class and business travellers enjoying the widest range of services. The roles and responsibilities of staff, both at the airport and on the aircraft, have been examined in detail, including passenger service agents, cabin crew and security personnel. Finally, the unit looked at airline and airport services and facilities during the disembarkation process, such as luggage reclaim, immigration and customs. Throughout the unit you have been shown many industry examples, while the case study on Manchester Airport gives an overview of the various options available for travel to and from a busy international airport.

If you have worked methodically, by the end of this unit you should:

- Know the options available to customers when travelling to and from airports;
- Understand the process of embarkation and the roles of airport and airline staff;
- Know the facilities and services available to passengers during the flight;
- Know the airport and airline services and facilities during the disembarkation process.

You are now in a position to complete the assignment for the unit, under the direction of your tutor. Before you tackle the assignment you may like to have a go at the following questions to help build your knowledge of the handling air passengers.

Test your knowledge ?

1. What is 'embarkation'?
2. List six duties of cabin crew on an aircraft.
3. List the typical facilities and services provided in first class air travel.
4. Name three companies that provide ground handling services at UK airports.
5. What is the role of an aircraft dispatcher?
6. What are the three classes of travel offered by Virgin Atlantic Airways?
7. What is 'disembarkation'?
8. Name four airports that are operated by BAA (the British Airports Authority).
9. What are flybe's regulations concerning pregnant women flying?
10. What are 'unaccompanied minors'?
11. What are excess baggage charges?
12. What are the main duties of a passenger service agent at check-in?
13. What is the main role of HM Revenue & Customs officers at airports?
14. What is a Property Irregularity Report (PIR) form used for?
15. What is a transit passenger?

Answers to these questions can be found on the Book 2 Tutor's CD-ROM that accompanies this book (ISBN 9780955019050). Full details can be found at www.tandtpublishing.co.uk

Handling Air Passengers

Introduction

This assignment is made up of a number of tasks which, when successfully completed, are designed to give you sufficient evidence to meet the Pass (P), Merit (M) and Distinction (D) grading criteria for the unit. If you have carried out the activities and read the case studies throughout this unit, you will already have done a lot of work towards completing the tasks for this assignment.

Scenario

You have been lucky enough to find a summer placement job in the training department of a major international airport in the UK. The Training Manager, Jimmy O'Connor, is developing new training materials for airport staff and would like you to help him put together a set of electronic and written materials that could be used by new members of staff in induction training sessions. The materials will cover the following topic areas:

1. Transport options available when travelling to and from UK airports;
2. Passenger embarkation and the boarding process;
3. Facilities and services available to passengers on flights;
4. Disembarkation processes at UK airports.

TASK 1

For this task you are to prepare an illustrated presentation in which you must:

(a) **Describe** the options available to customers when travelling to and from airports and between airport terminals. You may focus on one specific airport or use examples from a range of airports. You must cover not only the different types of transport available, but also investigate car parking, car rental and airport accommodation;

This task is designed to provide evidence for P1.

(b) **Describe** the process of embarkation for all passengers and the role that airport and airline staff play during the embarkation of customers.

This task is designed to provide evidence for P2.

To be considered for a Merit grade for this task, your presentation must also:

(c) **Compare** the facilities available at two different airports for passengers travelling to and from the airports, and during the embarkation process.

This task is designed to provide evidence for M1.

To be considered for a Distinction grade for this task, your presentation must also:

(d) **Evaluate** the effectiveness of processes for handling passengers during embarkation at a specific airport, making justified recommendations for improvement.

This task is designed to provide evidence for D1.

TASK 2

For this task you are to research and compile two fact sheets. Your first fact sheet must:

(a) **Describe** the boarding process for air passengers. This can be in general terms or related to a specific airport;

This task is designed to provide evidence for P3.

In your second fact sheet you must:

(b) **Describe** the role of staff and the facilities available for customers during a flight. You should not focus on one particular airline for this task, but draw on examples from a variety of carriers.

This task is designed to provide evidence for P4.

To be considered for a Merit grade for this task, your fact sheets must also:

(c) **Explain** the importance of providing facilities to meet specific passenger needs both on board and during the boarding process. You should say why airlines provide these facilities, which should cover a range of reasons, such as health, safety and security, to comply with legislation and for commercial gain and competitive advantage.

This task is designed to provide evidence for M2.

TASK 3

Jimmy would like you to write a short report, in which you must:

(a) **Describe** the disembarkation and transit processes at UK airports. You may focus on one specific airport for this task or use examples from a variety of airports.

This task is designed to produce evidence for P5.

To be considered for a Merit grade for this task, your report must also:

(b) **Explain** the importance of effective disembarkation processes at UK airports. You should cover a range of reasons, such as security, passenger convenience and airport efficiency.

This task is designed to produce evidence for M3.

To be considered for a Distinction grade for this task, your report must also:

(c) **Analyse** the effectiveness of disembarkation processes at a particular UK airport.

This task is designed to provide evidence for D2.

UNIT 26
Current Issues in Travel and Tourism

INTRODUCTION TO THE UNIT

Travel and tourism is a dynamic industry that affects all our lives, whether we are on holiday, travelling for business or visiting friends and relatives. It is an industry that is made up of many different sectors – from accommodation and tour operations to attractions and transport. There are many issues that affect travel and tourism, some that have an impact on society and the environment, others that are specific to companies and organisations. People entering the industry at graduate level need to be able to understand the nature of the industry and the key issues that affect it.

This unit focuses on a range of current issues that affect travel and tourism, giving you the opportunity to study one issue in greater depth. You will develop skills that are appropriate to carrying out sustained and planned research, similar to those adopted in academic research. You will gain an understanding of the different approaches to research and the research tools that can be used to plan and carry out a travel and tourism research project. Your project will not only investigate an issue in depth, but also analyse the impacts of that issue on the travel and tourism industry, such as the development of new markets, loss of revenue and changing product ranges.

WHAT YOU WILL STUDY

When you have completed this unit you should:

1. **Understand methods that can be used to research a current issue affecting the travel and tourism industry;**
2. **Be able to conduct research into a current issue affecting the travel and tourism industry, using appropriate resources;**
3. **Be able to communicate findings on a travel and tourism issue using appropriate media and conventions;**
4. **Understand the impacts of a current issue on the travel and tourism industry.**

You will be guided through the main topics in this unit with the help of the latest developments, statistics and industry examples. You should also check out the weblinks throughout the unit for extra information on particular organisations or topic areas and use the activities throughout the unit to help you learn more.

ASSESSMENT FOR THIS UNIT

This unit is internally assessed, meaning that you will be given an assignment (or series of assignments) to complete by your tutor(s) to show that you have fully understood the content of the unit. A grading scale of pass, merit or distinction is used when staff mark your assignment(s), with higher grades awarded to students who show greater depth in analysis, evaluation and justification in their assignments. An assignment for this unit, which covers all the grading criteria, can be found on page 269. Don't forget to visit www.tandtONLine.co.uk for all the latest industry news, developments, statistics and hot links to websites in this unit to help you with your assignment for this unit.

Icebreaker

This unit explores current issues in travel and tourism – those that have arisen in the last five years and those that are likely to have an effect on the industry in the future. Working by yourself, or in small groups under the direction of your tutor, see how you get on with the following tasks to help you make a start on this unit:

- Make a list of six current issues that you think are important to the future development of the travel and tourism industry;
- Think about the different ways you could gather information from people about their travel habits;
- List the stages you would go through when asked to carry out some research into a current issue in travel and tourism;
- Name three sources of information that you could use when carrying out a travel and tourism research project;
- Make some notes on the role of the internet in travel and tourism research;
- What is the difference between primary and secondary research?
- Name three reliable sources of statistics on travel and tourism.

When you've finished, show your answers to your tutor and compare your answers with what other students in your class have written.

SECTION 1 — Understand methods that can be used to research a current issue affecting the travel and tourism industry

In this section we investigate the different methods that can be used to research a current issue affecting the travel and tourism industry, as well as highlighting a variety of current issues that could form the basis of a research study.

Research methods

Carrying out research is an important aspect of any subject area, and travel and tourism is no different. Research may be carried out for purely academic purposes, such as a researcher in a university investigating the impact of tourism on communities in a developing country, or can be directly related to the travel and tourism industry. Industry-related research could focus on exploring customers' changing demands for products, services

and destinations, or analysing the trend in sales of package versus independent holidays over a particular time period.

Research methods are the 'how' of the research process, i.e. stating how you are going to conduct your research in order to achieve your research objectives. Research can involve intervention, e.g. spending time with a tribe in Africa to appreciate the impacts that tourism is having on their culture, or non-intervention, for example carrying out an extensive review of the literature – books, journals, websites, etc. – on a particular travel and tourism topic. 'Action research', also known as participatory research, is considered to be 'learning by doing'. In other words, researchers identify a problem, do something to resolve it, see how successful their efforts were and, if not satisfied with the outcome, try again. What separates action research from mainstream research is its emphasis on scientific study, informed by research theories.

Research sources

There are many sources of information that can be used when carrying out research in travel and tourism, usually divided into primary and secondary sources. A research study may focus entirely on primary research sources, but, in reality, the majority of travel and tourism research consists of both primary and secondary research.

Primary sources

Primary sources refer to information that is collected for the first time, i.e. it is not already available from another source – this is secondary research.

Although there is an increasing amount of relevant and up-to-date secondary data available on tourism at international, national and local levels, it is likely that a researcher, at some stage in the research process, will need to collect information that is not already available in a published form. The collection and subsequent analysis of this information is known as primary research.

A researcher wanting to collect primary data has three main options available, namely:

1. Surveys;
2. Observation;
3. Focus groups.

Surveys

Conducting a survey is the most common method of collecting primary data when researching the travel and tourism industry. It involves the collection of data from a proportion of a total 'population', which researchers refer to as the sample. In this context, population means the total number of people who could be interviewed for a research project. For example, somebody researching visitors at a visitor attraction may decide to interview a 5 per cent sample

of all visitors to the attraction on a particular day during the season. If the total number of visitors is 10,000 (the population), 500 interviews (the sample) will need to be undertaken. Sampling is carried out because it is usually impractical to interview the whole population. It is a very precise statistical technique that we investigate further on page 245.

There are three main types of survey that can be used to collect primary data:

1. Face-to-face interview survey;
2. Self-completed questionnaire survey;
3. Telephone, e-mail and online surveys.

A face-to-face interview survey involves an interviewer asking questions of a member of the general public, known as the respondent, and recording his or her answers and comments on a questionnaire. This type of survey is very common in all sectors of the travel and tourism industry, from destination resorts to transport providers. Face-to-face interviews can be carried out in a number of different locations, for example in a tourist area, at a respondent's home or place of work, in the street or en route to a holiday area, perhaps at a frontier post or a toll booth. The face-to-face interview is a good way of obtaining both quantitative and qualitative data (see page 247).

Face-to-face interviews have a number of advantages when compared with other survey methods. One advantage is that the interviewer is able to answer any difficulties that the respondent may have with particular questions. The interviewer can also use prompts to encourage the respondent to elaborate on his or her answers, thereby gaining further valuable information. A further advantage is that visual aids, such as charts and photographs, can be used by the interviewer when asking questions. The main disadvantage of the face-to-face interview technique concerns cost. Recruiting and training interviewers can be expensive and the associated administrative load can be high. Face-to-face interviews are also more time-consuming than techniques such as telephone and online surveys. They are, nonetheless, used very widely by travel and tourism researchers as a means of providing valuable information that can be used for academic and industry purposes.

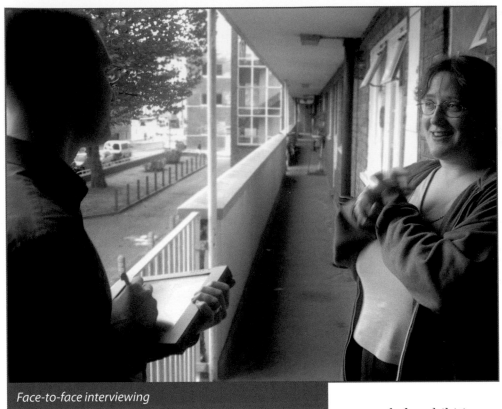
Face-to-face interviewing

Unlike face-to-face interviews, self-completed questionnaire surveys do not involve the use of interviewers, thereby making them a less expensive option for many travel and tourism researchers and businesses. They are also a more flexible technique, but they do have some disadvantages. Response rates are typically lower than for comparable face-to-face surveys – this can sometimes be improved by sending a reminder to the respondent. Also, if a respondent does not fully understand a question, there is no interviewer to ask for clarification. Self-completed questionnaire surveys are used extensively in travel and tourism, as a relatively low-cost method for obtaining both qualitative and quantitative data on customers and usage. Many visitor attractions use self-completed questionnaire surveys to gather feedback from their customers (see Figure 26.1).

The information contained in these questionnaires gives valuable feedback from clients and is often the starting point for changes to products or services. It is common to find self-completed questionnaires at attractions and in accommodation facilities, for customers to complete and either return by post, or

leave behind before they depart. Some travel and tourism organisations provide an incentive, such as a free gift or discounted travel, in order to increase the number of completed questionnaires.

Telephone surveys are gaining in popularity in the tourism industry, as a way of getting a fast response to an event, facility or service. They are used widely in the USA, but are largely restricted in the UK to trade activities, such as following up enquiries from buyers who have attended exhibitions, such as the World Travel Market in London or British Travel Trade Fair held every year in Birmingham. Companies specialising in selling timeshare also use telephone surveys to target likely customers. Conducting a survey by telephone can certainly give a speedy response and, if trained operators are used, many interviews are possible in a given time period. Disadvantages include the fact that it is not possible to use visual stimulus materials and the likelihood that people will feel that they have had their privacy invaded and will refuse to co-operate with the interviewer.

E-mail and online surveys are growing in popularity as the use of the internet develops. These types of surveys are a fast and relatively inexpensive way of gaining research data, but suffer from similar disadvantages to telephone interviewing, for example invasion of privacy. They do, however, offer researchers a simple method of collecting data from respondents spread right across the world. This is a particularly attractive benefit for travel and tourism researchers, since the scope and influence of the industry is truly global.

Your Visit

How satisfied were you with your visit overall?

- ☐ Very satisfied
- ☐ Dissatisfied
- ☐ Neither satisfied nor dissatisfied
- ☐ Satisfied
- ☐ Very dissatisfied

What was the highlight of your day?

....

What type of ticket(s) have you purchased today?

(N.B: Smaller attractions include Postman Pat® Village, Pets Corner, Longleat Railway, Motion Simulator, Butterfly Garden, Safari Boats, Adventure Castle & Blue Peter Maze, Longleat Hedge Maze, Old Joe's Mine).

- ☐ Longleat Passport
- ☐ Safari Park plus other smaller attractions
- ☐ Childrens attractions only
- ☐ Longleat House only
- ☐ Safari Park only
- ☐ Grounds and Gardens only
- ☐ Longleat House plus other smaller attractions

If you purchased the Passport Ticket, is this your?

- ☐ 1st visit ☐ 2nd visit ☐ 3rd visit ☐ 4th visit this season?

How much time did you spend at Longleat this visit?

- ☐ 1-2 hours ☐ 2-3 hours ☐ 3-4 hours ☐ 4-5 hours
- ☐ 5-6 hours ☐ 6-7 hours ☐ 7-8 hours
- ☐ More than one day, will come back for second visit

How did the following live up to your expectations?

	Excellent	Good	Fair	Poor	Very Poor	Not visited
Safari Park	☐	☐	☐	☐	☐	☐
Longleat House	☐	☐	☐	☐	☐	☐
Grounds and Gardens	☐	☐	☐	☐	☐	☐
Lord Bath's Murals	☐	☐	☐	☐	☐	☐
Safari Boats	☐	☐	☐	☐	☐	☐
Old Joe's Mine	☐	☐	☐	☐	☐	☐
Motion Simulator	☐	☐	☐	☐	☐	☐
Pets Corner	☐	☐	☐	☐	☐	☐
Longleat Railway	☐	☐	☐	☐	☐	☐
Butterfly Garden	☐	☐	☐	☐	☐	☐
Longleat Hedge Maze	☐	☐	☐	☐	☐	☐
Postman Pat® Village	☐	☐	☐	☐	☐	☐
Adventure Castle	☐	☐	☐	☐	☐	☐
Blue Peter Maze	☐	☐	☐	☐	☐	☐
Tea Cup Ride	☐	☐	☐	☐	☐	☐
Summer Show (21st July - 2nd Sept 2007)	☐	☐	☐	☐	☐	☐
Longleat House Scale Model	☐	☐	☐	☐	☐	☐
Family Bygones Exhibition	☐	☐	☐	☐	☐	☐
Life and Times of Henry, Lord Bath	☐	☐	☐	☐	☐	☐
King Arthur's Mirror Maze	☐	☐	☐	☐	☐	☐
Family State Chariot	☐	☐	☐	☐	☐	☐
Mystical Garden	☐	☐	☐	☐	☐	☐
Cellars Restaurant	☐	☐	☐	☐	☐	☐
Wessex Pavilion	☐	☐	☐	☐	☐	☐
Fast Food Units	☐	☐	☐	☐	☐	☐
Kiosks	☐	☐	☐	☐	☐	☐
Shops	☐	☐	☐	☐	☐	☐
Staff	☐	☐	☐	☐	☐	

Did you visit the Longleat catering outlets?

Wessex Pavilion	☐ Yes	☐ No
Cellars Restaurant	☐ Yes	☐ No
Fast Food Units	☐ Yes	☐ No

If not, please advise why? ....

How would you rate Longleat for Value for Money?

	Excellent	Good	Fair	Poor	Very Poor	Not visited
Overall Value for Money	☐	☐	☐	☐	☐	☐
Passport Ticket	☐	☐	☐	☐	☐	☐
Other Ticket Type	☐	☐	☐	☐	☐	☐
Catering	☐	☐	☐	☐	☐	☐
Shops	☐	☐	☐	☐	☐	☐

If anything about your visit failed to meet your expectations, please briefly tell us why.

....
....
....

Please use the space below if you have any comments or suggestions to improve the visit.

....
....

Other Information

How would you rate Longleat compared with other attractions?

- ☐ The best ☐ The same ☐ Worse ☐ Don't know

Have you ever visited Longleat before?

- ☐ YES ☐ NO

If YES, how long ago?

- ☐ 6 mths or less ☐ 7-12 mths ☐ 1-2 years
- ☐ 2-3 years ☐ 3-4 years ☐ 4-5 years
- ☐ 5-10 years ☐ Over 10 years

When will you next visit Longleat?

- ☐ This month ☐ Next month ☐ This year
- ☐ Next year ☐ Next 2 years ☐ 3 or more years
- ☐ Never ☐ Don't know

Were the brown tourist signs adequate for you to easily find your route to Longleat?

- ☐ Yes ☐ No ☐ If no, please advise why ....

Optional Information

(a) Updates by Email

If you would like to receive the latest news, events and special offers from Longleat throughout the season then please complete the section below so that your details can be added to our database

Name ....

Email Address ....

(please complete in capitals)

OR please visit the Family Fun Club section of the Longleat website (www.longleat.co.uk) and add your contact details yourself!

(b) Annual Updates by Post

If you would like to receive pre-season annual information on Longleat via post then please complete the section below so that your details can be added to our database

Name ....

Address ....

.... Postcode ....

Win Longleat Tickets 2008

If you would like to enter the monthly prize draw then please complete your details below

Name ....

Address ....

.... Postcode ....

If you DO NOT wish to receive further communications from Longleat then please tick this box ☐

Please place this Visitor Survey in any of the boxes throughout the Longleat Estate or post FREE to:
Longleat Marketing Department, FREEPOST (BS 8210) Warminster BA12 7ZZ

Please remember that if your responses are to count then we must receive completed questionnaires within 2 weeks of your visit.

Thank you.

Visitor Survey 2007

Estate Office, Longleat, Warminster, Wiltshire BA12 7NW
Tel: 01985 844400 www.longleat.co.uk

Figure 26.1 - An extract from a self-completed questionnaire

Questionnaires

Questionnaires are used in a variety of research projects, including online surveys, face-to-face interviews and self-completed surveys. Designing an effective questionnaire that will achieve its intended aim is a skilled operation. It can also be very time-consuming, checking to see that the questions are easy to understand and in an appropriate order. Specialists in the design of questionnaires recommend that researchers follow the sequence shown in Figure 26.2 to ensure an effective finished product.

As Figure 26.2 indicates, the questionnaire design sequence begins with listing the expected 'outcomes' of the survey, i.e. what it is hoped the survey will achieve. These are then used as the basis for the formulation of a set of questions, the answers to which will help achieve these outcomes. A draft questionnaire is produced next and used in a pilot survey – this is a 'dry run' of the main survey with a small number of respondents to check understanding and suitability of the questions. The draft questionnaire is then amended in the light of the pilot survey to produce a final version for use in the main research study.

The following is a list of guidelines that should be followed when designing questionnaires:

- Always put 'sensitive' questions, e.g. concerning age, occupation, marital status, etc., at the end of the questionnaire. Respondents will feel more comfortable about giving answers to such personal questions than if they appear at the beginning;
- Avoid ambiguous questions (questions with 'double meanings');
- Avoid using jargon;
- Make the questionnaire as short or as long as it needs to be; don't be tempted to include questions that, although interesting, will not help achieve the 'outcomes';
- Simple, objective, pre-coded (agree/neutral/disagree) questions will provide clearer answers than open-ended questions;
- Avoid 'leading questions', e.g. 'don't you agree that the hotel is comfortable?' is a question that invites a positive response;
- Do not include questions that are an impossible test of the respondent's memory, e.g. 'how much did you spend on drinks per day for the first week of your holiday?'
- Use language that is appropriate to the respondent.

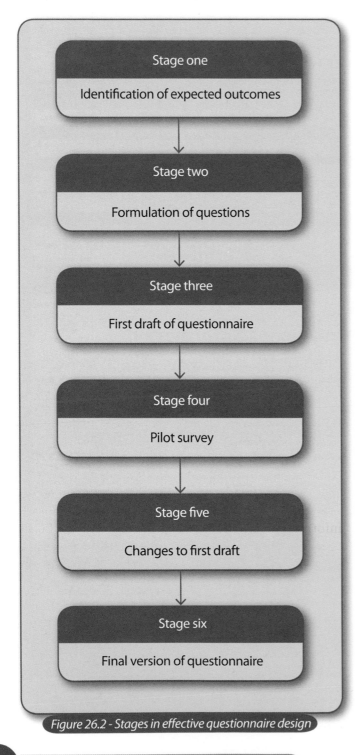

Stage one
Identification of expected outcomes

Stage two
Formulation of questions

Stage three
First draft of questionnaire

Stage four
Pilot survey

Stage five
Changes to first draft

Stage six
Final version of questionnaire

Figure 26.2 - Stages in effective questionnaire design

A questionnaire can have a combination of 'open' and 'closed' questions. Open questions invite the respondent to give any answer they choose, whereas closed questions ask the interviewee to choose from a range of answers, for example 'yes', 'no', 'don't know', etc.

Activity 26.1

Using the above guidelines, design a questionnaire to discover people's opinions of a current issue in travel and tourism, and conduct some pilot interviews to check that the questionnaire is suitable.

This activity is designed to provide evidence for P1.

Sampling

In the majority of travel and tourism research studies, it is not feasible to survey all the people who may, for example, use a tourist attraction or visit a particular destination. Instead, researchers must rely on the responses of a proportion of the total 'population', known as the sample. If the selection of the sampling unit (the target population to be surveyed), sample size (how many are to be interviewed) and sampling procedure (the method by which the respondents are selected) are based on proven statistical methods, the responses of the people interviewed should mirror those of the total population within known limits of accuracy. The sampling method chosen must reduce bias to a minimum. For example, if a researcher was asked to collect data on customer experiences for a hotel group with 325 establishments spread evenly across Europe, but carried out 80 per cent of the surveys in France, the results would clearly be biased and not representative of the group as a whole.

The sampling procedure may be either random or quota. For a random survey, individuals are pre-selected from a sampling frame, such as the electoral role or a company's database. The interviewer may be asked to carry out interviews at selected households chosen at random. Many UK government surveys are carried out in this way. When using the quota sampling method, the interviewer is given instructions as to the number of respondents he or she must interview in certain categories, for example defined by age, sex or social class.

The size of the sample will determine the level of accuracy of the data. Generally speaking, the larger the sample size the better, but the increase in accuracy becomes less significant as the sample size is increased. Provided that proven statistical methods have been used to select the sample, a survey consisting of approximately 2000 interviews will give an accurate reflection of the public's view of general matters to a 95 per cent confidence level (in other words, 19 out of 20 surveys will fall within a stated 'margin of error'). In reality, it would be rare for a researcher to carry out a survey with a sample size of less than 100, even if only broad impressions were needed.

Observation

Observation is a very useful, and often neglected, source of primary data in travel and tourism. In its simplest form, observation is a management practice that involves an organisation employing a person to study the behaviour of others as a way of improving its products and services. It is particularly suitable for visitor attractions such as theme parks, craft galleries and museums. It does not always involve people actually watching what others do and recording the details systematically. Nowadays, there are sophisticated techniques such as closed circuit television (CCTV) and time-lapse photography that can be used to produce valuable information on the flow of people and traffic at tourist facilities. Electronic tally counters are used in attractions, leisure centres and tourist information centres to monitor usage. On occasions, staff may be asked to 'mingle' with visitors or customers and to eavesdrop on their conversations without revealing their identity. People are often far more honest about their true feelings when talking in private, than they would be when asked questions as part of a visitor survey.

Observation can be used as an initial type of

exploratory research, perhaps visiting a Pacific island to view the impact of tourist boats on coral reefs or investigating the effects of tourism in a developing nation in Africa. This could lead to other types of quantitative research being planned, based on the findings of the original observations.

Observation has an important role to play in researching competitors' products. There are very few products, services and facilities in the travel and tourism industry that are truly unique, most having been based on an idea seen elsewhere. It is not uncommon for hoteliers, travel agents and airlines, for example, to use the facilities of competitors in order to pick up new tips and improve their own products. Tourism companies sometimes employ 'mystery shoppers' to anonymously visit competitor facilities (and sometimes even their own facilities!) to check on standards of service and the range of products on offer.

Focus groups

A focus group is a research technique used to collect in-depth information from a carefully-selected group of individuals. It is used to gain information on customers' purchasing habits, for example to explore the reasons why they choose one travel product or company in preference to another. This kind of in-depth information is not easy to obtain from questionnaire surveys or observation, but focus group sessions give respondents the time to reflect and consider in detail why they make the decisions they do. A focus group, or panel interview as it is sometimes called, usually consists of up to 10 individuals under the guidance of a trained interviewer, who will use a number of techniques to explore the innermost thoughts and values of the members of the group. The sessions are generally video-recorded for future analysis and will often cause companies to make changes to their product range or promotional activities. Neutral locations are chosen for the focus group sessions, thereby avoiding either positive or negative associations with a particular facility or site. Given the intensive nature of the focus group, it is an expensive method of gaining primary research data and tends, therefore,

to be used mainly by larger travel and tourism organisations, primarily in the private sector of the industry.

Secondary sources

Many travel and tourism research studies involve the collection of information from a mixture of primary and secondary sources. Secondary data is information that is already available, usually in written form, but increasingly now made available online and on CD-ROMs. Research that makes use of secondary data sources is sometimes referred to as 'desk research'. Sources include books, journals, the internet and newspapers. The main advantage offered by secondary research when compared with primary data collection methods is that it can save both time and money. There is a great deal of secondary research data available to researchers working in all sectors of the travel and tourism industry, some internal to organisations and some made available by a range of commercial and public sector sources.

Internal sources of secondary data

Some of the information that an organisation needs for research purposes may already be held within its various departments and management systems. An examination of existing files, databases and records should be a first priority before external research sources are consulted, in order to save time and money. The following internal information sources, held by any organisation that is operating professionally in the travel and tourism industry, may reveal useful data for research purposes:

- Sales receipts;
- Customer records;
- Mailing lists;
- Financial returns;
- Survey findings.

The advent of computerised management information systems (MIS) makes this kind of information so much more accessible and useful for research purposes.

External sources of secondary data

For travel and tourism researchers, secondary data from a variety of published sources is generally much easier to access than the internal company data described in the previous section of this unit. As the worldwide tourism industry continues to grow, there is an increasing amount of specific secondary research data on tourism generated to service this expansion, much of it now available on the internet. The World Tourism Organisation (WTO) and World Travel and Tourism Council (WTTC) supply statistical data on an international scale, while organisations such as the Organisation for Economic Co-operation and Development (OECD) and the Pacific Asia Travel Association (PATA) provide regional, international data. Statistics on tourism at a national level are made available by government departments or government-sponsored agencies. In the UK, researchers have access to a wide range of information on travel and tourism provided by government and commercial sources, including:

- Annual reports of the UK National Tourist Boards;
- Travel and tourism academic journals;
- Annual reports of the Regional Tourist Boards/ Regional Development Agencies (RDAs);
- The International Passenger Survey (IPS)
- The United Kingdom Tourism Survey (UKTS)
- Business Monitor MQ6 - Overseas Travel and Tourism published by HMSO;
- Annual reports of commercial travel and tourism organisations, for example British Airways, Thomas Cook, TUI UK and Merlin Entertainments Group;
- Reports from consultants such as Mintel and MORI;
- Travel and tourism textbooks;
- Trade and consumer newspapers;
- Trade associations including ABTA, AITO, and IATA
- The Statistical Office of the European Communities (EUROSTAT);
- Professional bodies such as the Tourism Society.

Sources of information in travel and tourism

Research data

The data collected as part of a research project can be either qualitative or quantitative. In reality, travel and tourism research projects often aim to collect data of both types.

Qualitative data

Qualitative data refers to a respondents' opinion of, or attitude towards, a particular facility, product, service or issue, rather than gathering numerical data (this is quantitative research). Focus groups and in-depth questionnaire surveys are excellent methods to use when collecting qualitative data for a research project.

Typical questions that would produce qualitative data are as follows:

1. How would you rate the standard of service you received at the holiday centre?

2. What are your feelings towards the further development of tourism in Antarctica?
3. How could the facility be improved for disabled people?
4. Which feature of the visitor attraction did you like the most?
5. What was your general impression of the resort complex?
6. What is your opinion of the food in the restaurant?

Qualitative research does not usually lead to clear and precise conclusions, and, as such, its results can be more difficult to analyse, when compared to quantitative research.

Quantitative data

Quantitative data refers to factual information gathered as part of a research project, such as the age of respondents, where they live, how far they have travelled to a destination, how much they have spent on holiday and the type of transport they have used. Research that involves gathering quantitative data provides more structured information than projects that collect qualitative information. Unlike qualitative research, which is concerned with gathering in-depth information from a relatively small number of respondents, researchers using quantitative methods often collect large amounts of data that is relatively easy to analyse with statistical software packages.

Types of current issues in travel and tourism

In this section we investigate a range of current and recent issues that affect the travel and tourism industry, with a view to you selecting one current, significant topic to use for the research project when completing the assignment in this unit. Remember that you can register at www.tandtonline.co.uk for free, regular travel and tourism industry updates to keep abreast of all the latest issues.

General issues

Travel and tourism is one of the world's biggest industries, made up of many different industry sectors – transport, attractions, travel agencies, tour operators, accommodation, etc. It impacts on everybody's lives, whether going on holiday, enjoying a day trip, travelling on business or visiting friends and relatives (VFR). Travel and tourism has influence at global, national, regional and local levels. Figures from the World Tourism Organisation (WTO) forecast a growth in tourism from 898 million international arrivals in 2007 to 1.6 billion in 2020.

The travel and tourism industry is affected by a wide variety of social, economic, political, environmental, cultural and technological issues, the most important of which are considered in the remainder of this section.

Changes in consumer demand

Better education, higher disposable incomes and greater access to new technology are changing the types of travel products being bought and the way in which they are purchased. Adventure travel is a major growth area of travel and tourism as people look for ever more adventurous and stimulating experiences in their leisure time. The term 'adventure

Canyoning is a popular type of adventure tourism

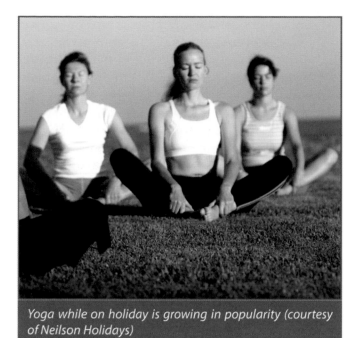

Yoga while on holiday is growing in popularity (courtesy of Neilson Holidays)

travel' can cover anything from a cruise along the Nile or a trek in the foothills of the Himalayas to scuba diving in Madagascar or bungee jumping in South Africa. New Zealand is a country that markets itself as an adventure tourism destination, offering a wide variety of activities such as canyoning, hot air ballooning, sea canoeing, paragliding and snowboarding.

Consumers are also looking beyond 'sun, sand and sea' holidays for new experiences as part of their travel plans. There is a growing trend in health and 'wellness' tourism – taking part in activities such as yoga is becoming popular while on holiday, as a way of escaping from the pressures of modern life. Tourists are also demanding higher standards when they travel, both in terms of the facilities they use and the customer service levels they experience.

Changes in consumer demand are also leading to a growth in independent travel, at the expense of package holidays. Increasing numbers of people now prefer to arrange their own holidays using guide books and the internet, rather than visiting a travel agent – this is known as 'dynamic packaging'. New destinations are also being discovered by people who are looking for a unique travel experience. The general growth in world travel over the last 50 years has introduced tourists to many new destinations at a growing pace. Long-haul travel is becoming commonplace as aircraft flight distances grow, tourists' appetites for new experiences increase and prices of air tickets fall.

Demographic trends

The ageing of the population in western, industrialised nations (the major tourism generating countries) is having an important effect on the demand for travel and tourism products and services. Changes in household composition, such as increased numbers of one-parent families and couples choosing not to have children or to delay having children until later in life, also influence tourism demand.

The ageing of the population is affecting demand for travel and tourism

Technological developments

Technology has had a major impact on the travel and tourism industry in recent years and will continue to do so in the future. The internet has revolutionised the way people research and book their holidays and other travel products. Continuing developments in transport will reduce travel times and make the remoter regions of the world more accessible to tourists. Sensitive planning will be needed to minimise the possible harmful effects on these destination areas.

Emerging economies

Emerging nations of the world, such as China and India, are set to become the economic power houses of the 21st century. Within a generation, China is forecast to overtake the USA as the world's biggest economy, and the World Bank predicts that as many as nine of the world's top fifteen economies will be from developing nations. Given that past patterns of international tourism growth have closely followed global economic prosperity, we are likely to see a very different pattern of demand for tourism at the international level in the future, with the emergence of a distinct east-west movement of tourists from the 'tiger economies' of the Far East. New European Union countries will also influence the demand for tourism as their economies grow and they invest in new tourism facilities.

Political stability

Governments around the world are becoming increasingly aware of the possibilities opened up by tourism for social and economic development, including job creation and foreign currency earnings. World regions that have a high proportion of countries with stable political regimes are likely to gain in terms of travel and tourism, at the expense of politically unstable nations, which will find it harder to attract tourists, who are becoming more conscious of safety and security issues when travelling.

Changing work patterns

Developments such as home working, the growth of short-term contracts and multi-tasking (one person carrying out a number of different job roles), are having significant effects on the nature of tourism demand, with a continuation of the trend away from long (4+ nights) holidays to short breaks. Many people are questioning their work-life balance and are using their leisure time in more creative ways.

Environmental issues

Issues concerning the environment are very topical at the moment and are high up the agenda of the travel and tourism industry. Governments and the public are concerned about issues such as global warming, the conservation of rain forests and the availability and costs of fossil fuels. Today's tourists are more aware of the impact they can have on destinations and are anxious to reduce their 'carbon footprint' as much as possible. 'Offsetting' is a way of transferring emissions by, for example, making a contribution to a development project in a third world country or a conservation charity.

Natural disasters, such as volcanic eruptions, floods and hurricanes, appear to be happening more frequently and can cause havoc to a country's travel and tourism industry. The Asian tsunami that affected Indian Ocean countries in late 2004 and Hurricane Katrina's devastation of New Orleans in 2005 are examples that are all too familiar. Although tourism can be badly affected very quickly when such disasters occur, the industry has proved itself to be very resilient in the face of adversity. Tourism in areas affected by natural disasters usually returns to its former state, on the back of investment in new hotels and other tourist facilities.

The growth in environmental awareness amongst tourists has led the industry to invest further in projects that promote 'sustainable tourism', such as eco-lodges that blend in with the environment, employ local people and use local produce whenever possible.

Airlines are working hard to reduce their carbon footprint

Tourism can help to alleviate poverty in developing countries

Tourism in developing nations

Developing countries, particularly in Africa, are enjoying an increasing share of the growth in world travel and tourism. The revenue from incoming tourists is helping to improve education, health and economic prosperity. Many developing nations see tourism as a way of helping to reduce poverty – this is known as 'pro-poor tourism'.

Weblink

Check out this website for more information on pro-poor tourism.
www.propoortourism.org.uk

Globalisation and integration of the industry

Moves by major players in the international tourism industry to increase their influence and domination of global markets can reduce consumer choice. On the other hand, greater deregulation of industry sectors, coupled with the emergence of a more discerning travelling public, is likely to result in greater choice for consumers.

Integration in the travel and tourism industry – vertical or horizontal – is becoming more common, as companies enter into mergers and takeovers to increase their market share and boost their profits. Recent examples have included the merger of Thomas Cook with MyTravel and the link-up between TUI/Thomson and First Choice. Integration can sometimes lead to reduced choice for consumers.

Health, safety and security

In the same way that natural disasters can adversely affect travel and tourism, so too can health scares. Britain's tourism industry was very badly affected in 2001 when the country experienced an outbreak of foot and mouth disease (FMD). Countryside areas were closed to the public and countless rural tourism businesses lost earnings of up to 90 per cent for the year. Further afield, in 2002 an outbreak of the disease SARS affected tourism in the Far East and had a knock-on effect on the countries to which people from this area visited, including the UK. Recent outbreaks of bird 'flu have caused similar problems in certain parts of eastern Europe.

The tragic events of September 11th 2001 in the USA have alerted the world to the threats from international terrorism. In 2002, Bali experienced a terrorist bombing that led to many deaths. Its tourism industry was devastated overnight and took many years to recover. Similar atrocities have occurred in Kenya and Madrid. The 7/7 2005 London bombings resulted in a 2 per cent fall in overseas visitor numbers for 2005, representing a loss to the UK economy of at least £300 million.

Domestic and incoming tourists tend to react differently to terrorist outbreaks. British people generally take a pragmatic approach to travel and tend not to cancel holiday bookings or change their plans to any great extent. Some overseas visitors, however, react quickly to security incidents and cancel bookings immediately.

The rise of the 'new tourist'?

In terms of the demand for travel and tourism, it is currently fashionable to talk of the rise of the 'new tourist' – an individual who shuns the homogenised, mass-market tourism products and destinations in favour of a more adventurous, active and individualised approach to holiday-taking. The 'new tourist' is well-educated, discerning, demanding, environmentally aware and prepared to pay a premium for high-quality products and services. As international tourism expands, the number of these 'new tourists' will undoubtedly grow, but their numbers will always be overshadowed by the bulk of tourists who will continue to buy packaged holiday products, visit popular destinations and make their holiday choices primarily on the basis of price.

Sustainable tourism – the way ahead?

One possible solution to the environmental and socio-cultural problems associated with tourism is to adopt sustainable development principles. Sustainable tourism is an emerging concept that has grown out of increased concern about the negative environmental and socio-cultural impacts of unplanned tourism development. An extension of 'green tourism', which focuses on environmental concerns, sustainable tourism is part of a much wider global debate on sustainable development, highlighted by the Brundtland Report in 1987 and the Earth Summits in 1992 and 2002. The sustainable approach to tourism development implies that the natural and cultural resources of tourism are conserved for continuous use in the future, while still bringing benefits to the present society. Although gaining favour with academics and researchers, there remains the problem of converting principles of sustainability into practical measures to protect environments and cultures. It is likely that the range and variety of tourism products based on the principles of sustainability will increase in the future, but the incorporation of such principles into mass-market products will remain a big challenge.

Activity 26.2

Make a detailed presentation of a general, current issue that affects the travel and tourism industry, explaining in detail the nature of the issue and how it impacts on the industry.

This activity is designed to provide evidence for P1 and P5.

Sector-specific travel and tourism industry issues

As well as the general issues discussed in the previous sections of this unit, specific sectors of the travel and tourism industry each have their own matters to consider. As you have learned from

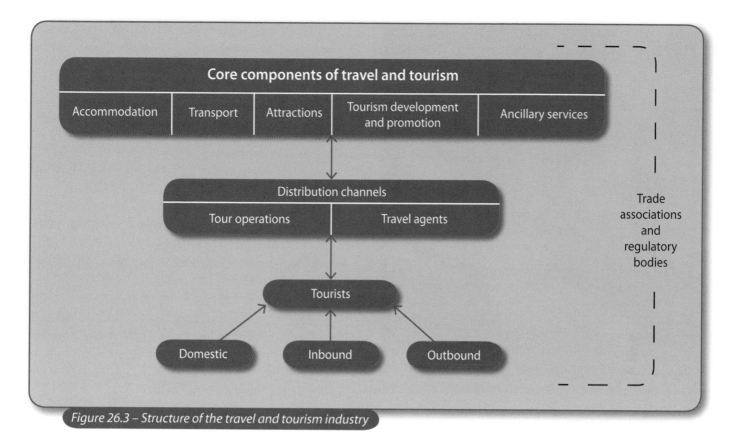

Figure 26.3 – Structure of the travel and tourism industry

other units on your course, the travel and tourism industry consists of a variety of sectors that work together to provide tourists with a range of products and services, as shown in Figure 26.3.

The accommodation sector

There are many issues that affect the demand for, and supply of, tourist accommodation, including:

- Greater concern for product quality – operating in a highly competitive environment, providers need to provide high quality accommodation for an increasingly demanding and discerning travelling public;

- Customer service – increased investment in staff training by hotels and other accommodation providers will help improve profitability;

- Value for money – all guests, whether on business or leisure travel, expect good value for money, regardless of the price paid for the accommodation;

- Changes in demographics and family structures – issues such as the ageing of the population and more single parent households will affect product development and marketing strategies;

- Changing work patterns – more women in the workforce, growth in home working and the move towards more contract and part-time employment will influence the demand for tourist accommodation;

- Health and fitness – accommodation providers can capitalise on the trend towards healthy lifestyles by providing suitable facilities for guests, such as fitness suites and leisure facilities;

- New technology – changes in technology will affect booking methods and could be used by accommodation providers to control many of the mundane operations associated with the sector, thereby freeing staff to concentrate on delivering enhanced levels of customer service.

Successful providers of hotels and other types of accommodation need to offer products that are targeted at particular market segments. The trend

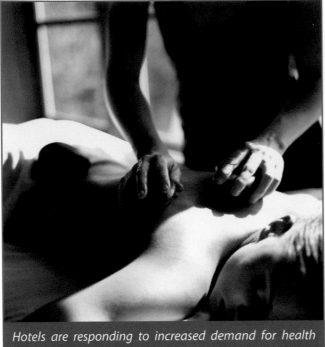
Hotels are responding to increased demand for health facilities (courtesy of Best Western Hotels/Travmedia)

towards branding accommodation products, so cleverly exploited by the Accor Group in its European hotels, will be further refined in order to match these market segments with readily identifiable accommodation types.

The transport sector

Transport for tourism consists of a wide variety of air, land and water-based services. Current issues affecting the transport sector include:

- Growth of low-cost airlines – companies such as esyJet, Ryanair, bmibaby and flybe are transforming the way we travel today, by offering cheap flights to increasing numbers of destinations across Europe. The low-cost airline model, originally developed in the USA, is now being introduced in China, India and other Far East countries;
- The availability and cost of fuel – at the time of writing, oil is trading at more than $100 a barrel, thereby increasing costs for airlines, train operators, taxi firms and coach companies;
- Impact on the environment – the aviation industry,

criticised for its carbon emissions, is working on new fuel developments and is introducing more fuel-efficient aircraft to reduce its impact on the environment;
- Airport expansion – as travel by air grows in popularity, airports are having to expand their facilities and services to cope with increasing passenger numbers. There is often opposition to any new airport expansion, particularly from people living nearby;
- High-speed rail services – travel by train is considered a more environmentally-friendly form of transport and high-speed rail services are being developed in the UK and on the continent;
- New technology – faster, more comfortable and more fuel-efficient types of transport are the result of developments in technology. The internet is quickly becoming the preferred method for booking transport services for tourism, while technology is changing the ways that airports and train stations operate.

The attractions sector

The attractions sector plays a crucial role in the UK and international tourism industry. Given that it is a highly competitive and dynamic industry sector, there are many issues that the operators of attractions, and those responsible for their planning and development, will need to consider in the future. Of particular concern are:

- Visitor management – by their very nature, attractions are a 'magnet' for people and their vehicles to what is often a small, closely-defined area. This can lead to congestion, physical erosion, pollution and a general spoiling of the visitor experience. Planners and managers in cities, country areas and in coastal resorts must implement policies that minimise the negative environmental and social impacts of tourist attractions;
- Authenticity – attractions and events are sometimes criticised for conveying images that fail to appreciate and value the true cultural identity of destination areas, resulting in a loss of authenticity. This can be reduced by

sensitive management of attractions and the early involvement of local communities in their development;

- Advances in technology – tourists who are exposed to new technologies in their work and everyday lives are looking to attractions to provide a similarly stimulating environment while they are at leisure. Developments such as virtual reality, animatronics, mobile and internet technologies will increasingly influence the attractions sector;
- Nature of the visitor experience – as well as appreciating technological improvements in tourist attractions, today's increasingly discerning tourists will be looking for the highest quality in both product presentation and customer service.

Travel agents and tour operators – the travel intermediaries

Travel agents are the retailers of the industry, selling holidays and other travel products. Tour operators, on the other hand, actually assemble the component parts of a holiday – accommodation, travel options, transfer services, car hire, etc. The distinction between the two is becoming less clear, especially since the growth in online retailers, such as Travelocity and Expedia, which have both agent and tour operator functions. The fiercely competitive nature of these sectors of the travel and tourism industry will mean that the profit margins of agents and operators will continue to be squeezed. Successful travel agents and tour operators must respond to a variety of

Attractions are developing new experiences for visitors (courtesy of the National Space Centre, Leicester/Travmedia)

issues that are likely to shape the demand for their services, for example:

- Continued growth in the long-haul market – helped by new aircraft technology and cheaper flight costs, destinations such as the USA, Australia, the Caribbean and the Far East, continue to be popular with both package and independent tourists;
- Growth in independent travel – the trend away from package tours towards more independent travel is likely to continue. In order to retain market share, tour operators will need to offer more flexibility in the design of their holidays, while some travel agents will seize the opportunity and offer a more customised service to their clients;
- Growth in short holidays and breaks – both domestic and outbound operators continue to provide short breaks to meet growing demand. Developments in transport, such as the growth of high-speed rail services and the deregulation of European air fares, will stimulate increases in this sector;
- Demand for activity and health-related holidays – growing interest in health and fitness offers an opportunity for travel organisers to develop greater variety in their activity programmes;

- Continuation of the trend towards last-minute bookings – changes in lifestyle and work patterns, plus growth of online booking, will mean a shorter lead time for travel purchases;
- Greater concern for quality – concern over indifferent standards of package holidays have dogged tour operators in recent years, making it crucial for holiday companies to put quality at the top of their agenda when planning new products;
- Increased concern for the environment – customers expect their travel intermediaries to operate in a manner that is respectful of the long term well-being of the environment when assembling their packages.

Activity 26.3

Make a detailed presentation of a sector-specific, current issue that affects the travel and tourism industry, explaining in detail the nature of the issue and how it impacts on the industry.

This activity is designed to provide evidence for P1 and P5.

Travel agencies face increasing competition

Be able to conduct research into a current issue affecting the travel and tourism industry, using appropriate resources

For students intending to go on to higher education (HE), knowing how to plan and conduct a research project will be useful skills to have when stepping up to a higher level of learning. Students who are planning to follow a career in the industry without going to HE will also find the process of carrying out research a useful exercise to prepare them for the world of work. All companies and organisations in travel and tourism need to gather and analyse market research data and feedback to help their businesses grow – the more objective this process, the better are likely to be the outcomes.

Research plan

To be truly effective, any research activity needs to follow a carefully planned process, as shown in Figure 26.4.

In addition to the stages shown in Figure 26.4, researchers need to be aware of ethical issues when carrying out their work. These are any issues that could lead to embarrassment, discrimination, harassment or exploitation of any people who may be contacted as part of the research. For example, respondents who choose not to take part in a questionnaire survey must have their wishes respected. Furthermore, all material that is collected through primary research must be gained with the consent of the people concerned and all findings must be kept anonymous and confidential at all times.

Hypothesis and terms of reference

Establishing a hypothesis is at the core of the research process in travel and tourism. Research is about answering questions and a hypothesis is a statement that a researcher proposes to be tested by further

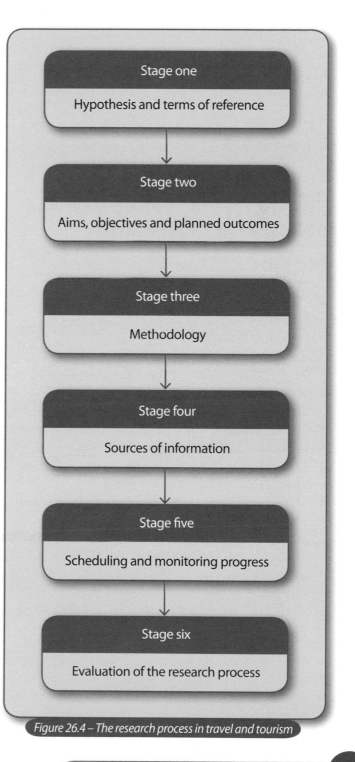

Figure 26.4 – The research process in travel and tourism

research. For example, a research question may be 'what is the relationship between scuba diving and the damage to coral reefs?' A hypothesis on the same topic could be expressed as 'the increase in scuba diving in an area leads to an increase in the damage to coral reefs', i.e. there is a positive relationship between the two. Research is then carried out to test whether there is indeed a positive relationship or not.

The 'terms of reference' for a research project are the parameters (or limits) within which the researcher must operate. These could be financial, linked to a particular timescale or a statement of the geographical area that must be covered by the research.

Aims, objectives and planned outcomes of the research

An aim is a general statement of intent, whereas objectives are more specific outcomes that are expected from a research study. For example, the aim of a piece of travel and tourism research could be 'to investigate the impacts of tourism in Cyprus'. From this, the following specific objectives of the research could be:

1. To establish the positive economic benefits of tourism to the island;
2. To investigate any negative environmental impacts of tourism in Cyprus;
3. To explore negative and positive socio-cultural impacts of tourism on the island;
4. To discover how the positive impacts of tourism are currently being developed;
5. To investigate how the negative impacts of tourism are being minimised on the island at the present time.

Whatever the agreed objectives of a research project, they must be SMART, in other words:

- **S**pecific – it's no use having 'woolly' ideas that are not well thought through or clearly defined;
- **M**easurable – objectives must be capable of being measured so that you know if you have achieved your targets;

- **A**chievable – setting objectives that are wildly optimistic wastes everybody's time;
- **R**ealistic – objectives must fit in with the overall aims of the research study;
- **T**imed – it is important to set time deadlines to review progress.

Remember also that setting objectives is not a 'one off' activity – they must be constantly monitored and updated in the light of changing circumstances as the research project develops.

Activity 26.4

Devise the aim and objectives for a research project that investigates a current issue affecting the travel and tourism industry.

This activity is designed to provide evidence for P2.

Methodology

This part of the research plan is all about the methods that will be used to achieve the research objectives. These could be purely primary research methods, only secondary research methods of a combination of the two. The plan will need to include information that answers the following types of questions:

- What methods will be used to collect the data?
- How much data needs to be collected?
- What type of data is needed?
- Who will collect the data?
- How many people will be interviewed?
- Where and when will interviews be carried out?
- How will the data be analysed?

The research plan must give full details of how these issues will be addressed.

Sources of information

Sources available to travel and tourism researchers are covered in detail from page 259 onwards, with examples and limitations of a range of primary and secondary sources. Resources that researchers need to consider when planning a research project include:

- Finance – e.g. cost of printing questionnaires, travel to sites, etc;
- Staffing – e.g. who will carry out the primary research and who will be responsible for their training;
- Equipment – e.g. computer software for data analysis, flashcards for visitor surveys, etc.

Scheduling and monitoring progress

Your research plan should have in-built dates for specific tasks, plus dates when progress should be reviewed to make sure that the research process is achieving its objectives. Key tasks to be built into a work plan or schedule could be:

- Establishing aims, objectives and choice of topic;
- Deciding research methods;
- Starting data collection;
- Completing data collection;
- Analysing data;
- Completing the research report.

The research plan should identify contingencies at each stage of the process. Contingencies are alternative strategies that can be used in the event that part of the research process does not go according to plan. For example, if somebody who volunteered to carry our some visitor surveys fails to turn up or is ill, you could appoint another person as a reserve.

Evaluation of the research process

The research plan should indicate how the research is to be evaluated once the whole process is completed. Evaluation is likely to focus on a number of issues, such as:

1. Whether the aims, objectives and terms of reference were realistic;
2. To what extent the chosen research methods

were successful in achieving the objectives of the research;
3. Whether the correct sample was chosen;
4. How you would change the research process if you were to carry out the same project again.

Sources of information

As we saw in the first section of this unit, researchers can access both primary and secondary sources when gathering qualitative and quantitative data for their projects. We will now investigate a range of sources in greater detail, highlighting specific examples that could be of use when carrying out a research project in travel and tourism, while at the same time explaining the limitations of each source.

Books

The number of textbooks concerned with travel and tourism has grown steadily in recent years as the subject has grown in popularity in schools, colleges and universities. It is now possible to find a variety of books that focus on:

- The history and development of tourism;
- The structure of tourism;
- Tourism economics;
- Marketing in travel and tourism;
- Tourism policy and planning;
- Impacts of tourism;
- Tourism destinations;
- The management of tourism.

Even 'niche' topics, such as wine tourism, e-tourism, rural tourism, tourism crises and Olympic tourism, have textbooks devoted to them. Books are a useful starting point when trying to decide on a research topic and for gathering general travel and tourism information. Many have bibliographies (see page 263) with suggestions for further reading. The references contained in these will help you to delve further into a particular subject area. Make sure that any books you use are relatively up to date – travel and tourism textbooks published more than five years ago may not give the current position on topics and issues, but there are, of course, exceptions to this rule.

Remember also that travel and tourism textbooks are written to cater for different levels of understanding, from pupils in schools to researchers studying for PhDs at university. Using a book that is clearly at the wrong level for the qualification you are taking will not help you achieve your aim.

Journals

There are two types of journals that you may come across when carrying out a travel and tourism research project. Academic journals, such as the Journal of Sustainable Tourism, Tourism Management or Annals of Tourism Research, contain research papers that have been written by lecturers and researchers. These are very specialist pieces of work and are used mainly by students in universities taking degrees in tourism. They are unlikely to be of use to you when completing the assignment for this unit, but you may still stumble on them when carrying out secondary research on your topic. The other type of journals are likely to be of more use to you. These are travel and tourism industry journals and periodicals, such as Travel Trade Gazette, Travel Weekly and Business Traveller, which have up-to-date articles on current issues affecting the industry.

Newspapers

Newspapers provide topical stories on a very wide range of issues of concern to the general public. Most have a travel section, containing articles and advertisements for holidays, flights and destinations. Newspapers are good for giving you ideas about topics to consider for a travel and tourism research project – recent articles in The Independent, The Times and The Guardian have covered the growth of cruising, mergers and acquisitions in the travel and tourism industry, tourism's contribution to global warming and the growth of low-cost airlines. Most newspapers have very good companion websites that allow readers to search for articles on specific subjects.

Websites

It would be easy to think that you can find everything you need for a travel and tourism research project with the click of a mouse, but this just isn't the case. Relying too much on the internet can result in a project that is, at best, poorly-researched, and at worst, a bad case of plagiarism (copying), something that is treated very seriously by awarding bodies. Clearly, websites have an important role to play in research, but the problem is that the internet often provides too much information and it is difficult to sift the useful material from the rest. The secret to using the internet as a research tool is to make your searches as refined as possible. Reliability of the information found on the internet can also be a problem for travel and tourism researchers. Make sure that the web pages you are using come from a reputable source, such as a government department, national tourist office or respected newspaper. Check also that the information is current – some web pages have been on the internet for a long time and are of dubious value for the serious researcher.

Travel Trade Gazette

The companion website to this textbook www. tandtonline.co.uk) provides registered users with free access to the latest news from the travel and tourism industry, and is a useful starting point when trying to decide on a topic for a research project.

Television

TV has a variety of programmes that feature travel and tourism – from documentaries on the impacts of tourism and 'docusoaps' that look behind the scenes in airlines and airports, to whole channels devoted to selling holidays, flights and cruises. TV programmes give a flavour of an destination or topic, but are limited as a serious research tool. You may find it useful to look at some TV programmes on travel and tourism when thinking of an idea for your research project for this unit.

Activity 26.5

Using the issue that you selected for Activity 26.4, make a list of the sources of information you would use when researching the issue, e.g. books, journals, articles, newspapers, websites, etc. Present your sources as a bibliography that follows the Harvard System of referencing.

This activity is designed to provide evidence for P2.

Statistical sources

Statistics are a useful way of justifying points that are made in research projects, by providing sound evidence related to a point in time or showing trends, e.g. the growth in the number of tourists to a destination, the number of passengers using a particular airport or comparisons of the types of transport used by visitors to a visitor attraction. Statistics add credibility to a research project, provided that they are presented and interpreted correctly, up-to-date and from a reliable source. Travel and tourism statistics are available from a variety of international, national, regional and local sources, including:

- The World Tourism Organisation;
- The World Travel and Tourism Council;
- Office for National Statistics;
- VisitBritain;
- Visit Wales;
- Visit Scotland;
- Northern Ireland Tourist Board;
- Regional Development Agencies (RDAs);
- Local authorities;
- Trade associations, e.g. ABTA;
- Professional bodies.

www.tandtonline.co.uk contains a bulletin on travel and tourism statistics that can be downloaded from the website.

Activity 26.6

Visit the Office for National Statistics website www. statistics.gov.uk and gather information on the range of travel and tourism statistics provided on the site.

This activity is designed to provide evidence for P2.

Results from primary research

So far in this section we have examined the details of secondary sources of information – newspapers, journals, the internet, statistics, etc. However, the results that you generate as part of a research project are themselves an important data source. Any results that you have collected from surveys, observation or focus group meetings, may well be the most important part of your research project. This sort of information must be presented logically in a research project, with appropriate explanation, analysis and discussion of the data. The results must relate directly to the aims and objectives of your research that were agreed at the beginning of your project.

Referencing

When writing a research project, essay, dissertation

or any other piece of academic writing, it is important that you reference (or cite) any material that you use from another source, whether it is taken from a book, journal, newspaper or the internet. Correct referencing is a good habit to get into, since it:

1. Gives credibility to a piece of research;
2. Avoids the charge of plagiarism (copying somebody else's work);
3. Allows the reader to trace and check material;
4. Provides the opportunity for the reader to investigate a topic in greater detail.

Referencing is a two-part process – the first is making reference to other sources in the main body of an essay or report, while the second is including a list of all sources consulted at the end of the essay or research report (this is known as a bibliography).

There are a number of styles of referencing in use, but one of the most popular and readily accepted by the majority of the academic community is the Harvard System.

The Harvard System

The Harvard System, also known as the author-date method, is named after the university of the same name in the USA. It is used for both parts of the referencing process in academic reports and essays, i.e. referencing in the main body of the piece of work and when compiling the bibliography at the end.

The following are the rules for using the Harvard System when referencing in the main body of the work.

1. If the author's name occurs naturally in the sentence, the year is given in brackets, for example:

   In the chapter on airlines, Youell (2008) suggested that globalisation would ……..

2. If a direct quotation is used, the name, date and page number should be used, for example:

   As Youell (2008, p.356) said, "tourism has the ability to help developing nations.."

3. If the author's name does not occur naturally in the sentence, both name and year are given in brackets, for example:

   A more recent study (Rickerby 2008) has shown that travel and tourism is a ……

4. When an author has published more than one cited document in the same year, these are distinguished by adding lower case letters (a,b,c, etc.) after the year and within the brackets, for example:

   Youell (2008a) discussed the role of travel agencies in …………….

5. If there are two authors, the surnames of both should be given, for example:

   Holland and Youell (2008) have proposed that tourism could be ……..

6. If there are more than two authors, the surname of the first author only should be given, followed by et al., for example:

   Tourism contributes more than 50 per cent of the total economic output of the country (James et al. 2006).

7. If the work is anonymous, then "Anon." should be used, for example:

   In a recent article (Anon. 2003) it was suggested that tourism could …….

8. If it is a reference to a newspaper article with no author, the name of the paper can be used in place of "Anon.", for example:

   More people than ever seem to be booking their holidays online (The Guardian 2007).

9. If it is a reference to a web page, the following format should be followed:

   Department for Culture, Media and Sport 2008. About us [online]. http://www.culture.gov.uk/about_us/ [Accessed 29 March 2008].

Bibliography

A bibliography is a listing, in alphabetical order of author/organisation names, of all the sources used to complete a research project or other piece of academic work. The following are the rules for using the Harvard System when compiling a bibliography.

Books

1. Author's surname, followed by their initials;
2. Year of publication (in brackets);
3. Title of the publication (in italics);
4. Place of publication;
5. Name of publisher.

For example:
Rickerby, S (2008) *Travel and Tourism Case Studies*, Aberystwyth, Travel and Tourism Publishing.

Articles in journals, newspapers and magazines

1. Author's surname, followed by their initials;
2. Year of publication (in brackets);
3. Title of article (in quotation marks);
4. Name of the journal, newspaper or magazine (in italics);
5. Day and month of publication;
6. Page number(s).

For example:
Harris, S (2008) 'Are travel agents facing extinction?' *The Independent on Sunday*, 25 July, p.33.

Internet sites

1. Author's surname, followed by their initials (or use name of the organisation);
2. Year of publication (in brackets) or use 'no date' if none is given;
3. Title (in italics), followed by [online] in square brackets;
4. URL address;
5. Date accessed [in square brackets].

For example:
Department for Culture, Media and Sport 2008. *About us* [online].
http://www.culture.gov.uk/about_us/ [Accessed 29 March 2008]

Figure 26.5 shows how a bibliography should be presented using the Harvard System.

British Tourist Authority/English Tourist Board (1996) *Tourism Intelligence Quarterly* Vol. 17 No. 4, London, BTA/ETB.

Burns, P and Holden, A (1995) *Tourism: A New Perspective*, UK, Prentice Hall.

Department for Culture, Media and Sport 2008. About us [online].
URL http://www.culture.gov.uk/about_us/ [Accessed 29 March 2008].

Department of National Heritage (1997) *Success through Partnership: A Strategy for Tourism*, London, DNH.

Gunn, C (1994) *Tourism Planning*, New York, Taylor & Francis.

Hall, C M (1994) *Tourism and Politics*, Chichester, Wiley.

Holloway, J C (1994) *The Business of Tourism*, 4th edition, Harlow, Longman.

Inskeep, E (1991) *Tourism Planning: An Integrated and Sustainable Development Approach*, New York, Van Nostrand Reinhold.

Pearce, D (1989) *Tourist Development*, Harlow, Longman.

Rickerby, S (2008) *Travel and Tourism Case Studies*, Aberystwyth, Travel and Tourism Publishing.

Thomas Cook Group (2007) *Annual Report and Accounts*, Peterborough, Thomas Cook.

United Nations (1987) *World Commission on Environment and Development, Our Common Future* (the Brundtland Report), Oxford, Oxford University Press.

World Tourism Organisation (1994) *National and Regional Tourism Planning: Methodologies and Case Studies*, London, Routledge.

World Tourism Organisation (1996) *International Tourism Overview 1995*, Madrid, WTO.

World Travel and Tourism Council (1995) *Agenda 21 for the Travel and Tourism Industry*, London, WTTC.

Youell, R (2007) *Travel and Tourism for BTEC National Book 1*, Aberystwyth, Travel and Tourism Publishing.

Figure 26.5 – An example of a bibliography

Activity 26.7

Propose a research plan to investigate the current issue that you chose for Activities 26.4 and 26.5. Explain how the proposed plan enables exploration of the current issue.

This activity is designed to provide evidence for P2 and M1.

Activity 26.8

Using a range of appropriate sources of information, carry out research on the current issue that you chose for Activities 26.4 and 26.5. Evaluate the research undertaken and recommend improvements to your own research skills for future projects.

This activity is designed to provide evidence for P3, M2 and D1.

SECTION 3 # Be able to communicate findings on a travel and tourism issue using appropriate media and conventions

Having planned your research, and collected and analysed your data in line with your agreed plan, you are now in a position to communicate the findings (results) of your research.

Communicate findings

Regardless of the medium that you use to do this – extended document, group discussion, presentation or written report – there are certain procedures and processes that you will need to consider, for example:

- Presenting your own and others' arguments – any points that you make must be based on factual information and ideas that you have gathered during your research study. Your own arguments should be concise, evidence-related, logical and coherent. Other peoples' arguments will have been summarised from the sources that you consulted during your research, e.g. books, articles, newspapers, the internet, interviews, etc. You should go beyond simply repeating any

survey results that you have collected, but rather explain how your research adds to the sum of knowledge about the issue in question;

- Drawing conclusions from your findings – this part of the research process focuses on drawing conclusions from your own primary research and secondary sources that you have investigated. No new material should be used at this stage – you should make your conclusions based purely on what you have discovered up to this point in the research study;

- Summarising data – this could be qualitative or quantitative data, depending on the nature of your research study. Charts and graphs could be used to summarise complicated figures, as appropriate;

- Engaging an audience – if you are communicating your findings by way of a presentation, you will have an audience in front of you to engage with, and you should be prepared to answer questions on your research project. Most research findings are communicated using a written report, although this is often followed by a presentation to clarify points and issues. The style of writing and presentation of any report or essay should present information in a clear and concise manner, with jargon kept to a minimum.

Using appropriate media to communicate findings

When completing the assignment for this unit, you are likely to be told by your tutor which medium to use to communicate your findings – extended document, group discussion, presentation or

Title page – title/sub-title, author(s), date of completion

Summary – a brief overview of the whole report

List of contents

Acknowledgements – the chance to thank key individuals who have helped with the research, e.g. tutors, family members, friends, interviewees, etc.

Introduction – aims, objectives and expected outcomes of the research, plus an overview of the structure of the report

Review of secondary research sources

Research methodology – choice of methods, justification, sampling, survey piloting, ethical issues, etc.

Presentation and analysis of results

Discussion of results

Conclusion – summary of key findings, research limitations, suggestions for further research, etc.

Appendices

Bibliography

Figure 26.6 – Structure of a research report

written report. Each medium has its advantages and disadvantages, for example:

- Extended document – this could be an essay or a short report. A researcher would be able to outline the research process in such a document, but it would not allow the type of in-depth analysis and discussion possible in a full, written research report;

- Group discussion – this has the benefit of allowing the researcher to go beyond what is actually written in a report and explain complex issues to the members of the group;

- Presentation – as with a group discussion, making a presentation gives members of the audience the opportunity to ask questions of the researcher to clarify any points they may not fully understand;

- Written report – this is the most common method for presenting the results of a research study. It gives the reader the chance to dwell on issues contained in the report and use the references to delve further into a subject area or topic.

The structure of a typical research report is given in Figure 26.6.

Using appropriate conventions to communicate findings

You learned earlier in this unit that it is important to reference (or cite) any material that you use from another source, whether it is taken from a book, journal, newspaper or the internet, using an appropriate referencing system, such as the Harvard System (see page 262). We have also discussed the conventions concerning what should be included in a research plan (see page 257) and the structure of a research report (see Figure 26.6).

Using appropriate vocabulary is another convention to be considered when reporting on a research study. For example, it is acceptable to use words and phrases that are commonly used in relation to the issue that you are researching, but you must avoid using jargon or over-complicated language. Also, you should not use discriminatory language or use phrases that are likely to offend. Another convention is to avoid writing in the first person (I think that …… etc.) as this doesn't present a scholarly approach to research. At all times, consider the 'audience' that will be reading your report or attending your presentation and use appropriate terminology.

You should keep within any stated word limits when writing a research report and make sure that it is presented as a professional piece of work, with no spelling mistakes and correct grammar at all times. Always allow plenty of time to read through the report before it is finally presented.

SECTION 4 — Understand the impacts of a current issue on the travel and tourism industry

In the first section of this unit, we discussed many issues that currently affect the travel and tourism industry – some general and some specific to particular sectors of the industry. Part of the assessment for this unit asks you to explain how a current issue impacts on the travel and tourism industry. Clearly, any impacts will be specific that the particular issue that you choose, but it is possible to group them under a number of headings, for example:

- Loss of customers;
- Development of new markets;
- Loss of revenue;
- Changing demands;
- Additional costs;
- Changes to products and services.

It is also important to remember that certain issues will not only have impacts on the travel and tourism industry, but also society in general, for example issues to do with global warming, loss of wildlife habitats to tourism development and the impact of tourism on culture in destination areas.

Loss of customers

The great majority of travel and tourism organisations are private sector enterprises, whose primary aim is to make a profit – for the owners and any shareholders they may have. Losing customers is not something that any organisation wants, especially those which are keen to maximise their revenue – fewer customers equals less sales opportunities.

The types of issues that could result in a travel and tourism company losing customers are those concerned with:

- Poor customer service standards;
- Integration – e.g. a company being taken over by a competitor;

- Inadequate market research – i.e. failure to understand its customers;
- Products not matched to the market served by the company;
- A sudden natural disaster;
- A safety or security issue affecting customers, e.g. an accident at a theme park or terrorist threat.

Development of new markets

Developing new markets for travel and tourism products and services means attracting new customers to a company. The ageing of the population is an issue that offers an excellent business opportunity for travel and tourism customers to cater for this growing market. Generally, people are remaining much more active until later in life, thereby giving companies the chance to capitalise on new business. The growing numbers of travellers who are concerned about the environment also present the chance for a company to adapt its holiday products to attract these customers. In the same way, the rise in single-parent households could be targeted by travel and tourism companies, by perhaps offering more 3-person rooms in hotels and other accommodation establishments. Changing work patterns could also be an opportunity for a travel and tourism company to offer products that fit in with a different way of working, e.g. more short breaks outside peak holiday seasons.

Loss of revenue

Loss of revenue usually goes hand-in-hand with losing customers (see above). Issues such as poor customer service, failure to update products in line with customer expectations and outdated work practices, are all likely to result in revenue losses.

Changing demands

One of the issues we discussed earlier in this unit were changes in consumer demand, brought about by higher education standards, more disposable income, better access to technology and a desire to take part in new experiences while on holiday. One of the impacts of this issue is the development of new holidays and travel products that go far beyond traditional 'sun, sand and sea' holidays. These include more types of adventure tourism, trips that focus on health and 'wellbeing', more long-haul holidays to developing nations and an increase in independent travel. Customers are also demanding higher product and service standards – while travelling to their destinations, in their accommodation, during visits to attractions and when dealing with travel agents and tour operators.

Adventure tourism (courtesy of Dragoman Overland)

Additional costs

Issues that could lead to an organisation incurring extra costs include:

- Extra PR (public relations) work to counteract bad publicity, e.g. the poor media coverage that British Airways received when Terminal 5 at Heathrow opened for business in March 2008;
- Poor customer service leading to staff training;
- Investment in IT equipment to keep up with advances in technology, e.g. self-serve ticket machines at airports and railway stations;
- Employing extra staff after a natural disaster to help a business get back on its feet;
- Borrowing more money to attract a new market.

Changes to products and services

Issues such as demographic changes, a greater concern for the environment, changes in consumer demand, technological developments, emerging economies, globalisation and integration in travel and tourism, could all trigger changes to travel and tourism products and services. Examples include more cruising holidays, an increase in demand for ecotourism holidays, more long-haul travel and the development of new tourist destinations.

Activity 26.10

Choose one current issue affecting the travel and tourism industry, and write a short report that explains how it impacts on the industry. Use the findings from your research into a current issue to recommend actions for the travel and tourism industry.

This activity is designed to provide evidence for P5 and D2.

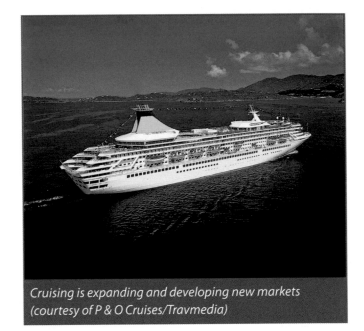

Cruising is expanding and developing new markets (courtesy of P & O Cruises/Travmedia)

Unit summary

This unit has focused on a range of current issues affecting the travel and tourism industry, plus the techniques used to research an issue in greater depth. You have examined the various methods that can be used to carry out a research project and investigated primary and secondary research sources, and the difference between qualitative and quantitative data. You have found that current issues affecting travel and tourism can be divided into those that affect society in general, such as global warming, and those that are specific to particular sectors of the industry, for example the use of technology and changes in consumer demand for travel products. The unit has shown you how to present a research plan and has given you the opportunity of comparing different sources of information, including books, journals, newspapers and the internet. You have looked in detail at the Harvard System of referencing and compared different ways of communicating research findings. Finally, you have examined some of the impacts of current issues on the travel and tourism industry. Throughout the unit you have been shown many industry examples to help illustrate points in the text.

If you have worked methodically, by the end of this unit you should:

- Understand methods that can be used to research a current issue affecting the travel and tourism industry;
- Be able to conduct research into a current issue affecting the travel and tourism industry, using appropriate resources;
- Be able to communicate findings on a travel and tourism issue using appropriate media and conventions;
- Understand the impacts of a current issue on the travel and tourism industry.

You are now in a position to complete the assignment for the unit, under the direction of your tutor. Before you tackle the assignment you may like to have a go at the following questions to help build your knowledge of current issues in travel and tourism.

Test your knowledge

1. Name three types of primary research.
2. What are 'research methods'?
3. What are 'ethical issues' in research and why are they important?
4. What is the difference between an aim and an objective?
5. Name two general, current issues that affect the travel and tourism industry.
6. What are 'contingencies' in research?
7. What is the difference between qualitative and quantitative data?
8. Name two current issues that affect the accommodation sector of travel and tourism.
9. Where can you find statistics on world tourism trends?
10. What should be included in a research plan?
11. Name two current issues that affect the attractions sector of travel and tourism.
12. Why is it important to reference your sources in a research report?
13. Name four types of media that could be used to communicate research findings.
14. Name two current issues that affect the travel agency sector of travel and tourism.
15. Name two current issues that affect the transport sector of travel and tourism.

Answers to these questions can be found on the Book 2 Tutor's CD-ROM that accompanies this book (ISBN 9780955019050). Full details can be found at www.tandtpublishing.co.uk

Unit 26 Assignment

Current Issues in Travel and Tourism

Introduction

This assignment is made up of a number of tasks which, when successfully completed, are designed to give you sufficient evidence to meet the Pass (P), Merit (M) and Distinction (D) grading criteria for the unit. If you have carried out the activities throughout this unit, you will already have done a lot of work towards completing the tasks for this assignment.

Scenario

This assignment is based around you completing a research study on a significant, current issue affecting the travel and tourism industry. Your tutor will help you to choose a suitable issue from the range of topics discussed earlier in this unit. The assignment asks you to:

1. Explain the methods that could be used to research a current issue affecting the travel and tourism industry;

2. Propose a detailed research plan for your study;

3. Carry out your research in accordance with your plan

4. Present the findings of your research;

5. Explain how the issue you have researched impacts on the travel and tourism industry.

TASK 1

For this task you must make a presentation to the rest of your group in which you must:

(a) **Explain** the different methods that could be used to research a current issue affecting the travel and tourism industry. Having described a variety of general and sector-specific issues affecting the industry, you should present the advantages and disadvantages of each research method, explaining the differences between primary and secondary sources, and qualitative and quantitative data.

This task is designed to provide evidence for P1.

TASK 2

Having described a range of current issues affecting the travel and tourism industry in Task 1, you must now choose one significant, current issue that will be the focus of your own research. For this task, you must:

(a) **Propose** a research plan that explains how you will research a current issue affecting the travel and tourism industry. Your plan should include information on your hypothesis, terms of reference, aims, objectives and planned outcomes; sources of information and resources; task and review dates; the monitoring process and contingencies; ethical issues and evaluation.

This task is designed to provide evidence for P2.

To be considered for a Merit grade for this task, you must also:

(b) **Explain** how your proposed research plan enables exploration of the current issue you have chosen.

This task is designed to provide evidence for M1.

TASK 3

This task focuses on you carrying out research into the current issue you have selected for your research study. You must:

(a) **Use** appropriate sources of information to research a current issue affecting the travel and tourism industry, using a standard referencing system such as the Harvard System.

This task is designed to produce evidence for P3.

To be considered for a Merit grade for this task, you must also:

(b) **Conduct** independent research into a current issue affecting the travel and tourism industry, using at least four different types of sources of information, showing awareness of the limitations of the sources. Your four different types of sources could be websites, books, journals and interviews.

This task is designed to produce evidence for M2.

To be considered for a Distinction grade for this task, you must:

(c) **Evaluate** the research undertaken and recommend improvements to your own research skills for future projects. You should highlight strengths and weaknesses in your own research methodology.

This task is designed to produce evidence for D1.

TASK 4

Having carried out your research, you now need to communicate your findings. For this task you must:

(a) **Communicate** a current issue affecting the travel and tourism industry, using appropriate conventions to convey your findings.

This task is designed to produce evidence for P4.

To be considered for a Merit grade for this task, you must:

(b) **Communicate** information about a current issue clearly, concisely and coherently, using specialist vocabulary, making connections and synthesising arguments.

This task is designed to produce evidence for M3.

TASK 5

For this task you must make a presentation to the rest of your group in which you must:

(a) **Explain** how the current issue you have researched impacts on the travel and tourism industry.

This task is designed to produce evidence for P5.

To be considered for a Merit grade for this task, your presentation must also:

(b) **Provide** a comprehensive analysis of the researched current issue, combining and recognising different points of view.

This task is designed to produce evidence for M4.

To be considered for a Distinction grade for this task, you must:

(c) **Use** the findings from your research into the current issue to recommend actions for the travel and tourism industry.

This task is designed to produce evidence for D2.

Index

Title: **Introducing Travel and Tourism**
Publication date:
30 June 2008
Author: **Bob Holland & Ray Youell**
Price: **£14.99**
Format: **Paperback, 140 pages**
ISBN: **9780955019074**

Brand new full-colour text book providing in-depth coverage of the travel and tourism industry. Written to cover Unit 1 of the new 4-unit WJEC A level in Travel & Tourism, this book is also suitable for AS and level 2/3 Travel & Tourism qualifications from other awarding bodies. Containing over 140 pages of information, as well as more than 150 images of tourism destinations around the world, this publication gives the appropriate level of detail and insight which candidates need to fully understand travel and tourism.

Title: **Travel and Tourism Case Studies**
Publication date:
31 March 2008
Author: **Stephen Rickerby**
Price: **£15.99**
Format: **Paperback, 175 pages**
ISBN: **9780955019067**

Up-to-date case studies of 15 real travel and tourism organisations, with discussion points and questions, suitable for GCE AS/A2, BTEC, OCR and C & G Nationals, plus Foundation Degree. Printed in full-colour, the cases include bmi, the Giant's Causeway, South West Tourism, Kuoni, Virgin Trains, Novotel, TUI and Legoland Windsor. Each of the case studies outlines the history and development of the organisation, examines its structure and operations, staffing, customer service, finance, funding and marketing.

Title: **Travel and Tourism for BTEC National Award, Certificate and Diploma Book 1** (2nd edition)
Publication date: **31 May 2007**
Author: **Ray Youell**
Price: **£22.99**
Format: **Paperback, 408 pages**
ISBN: **9780955019029**

Title: **Travel and Tourism for BTEC National Award, Certificate and Diploma Book 1** Tutor's CD-ROM
Publication date: **1 August 2007**
Author: **Ray Youell**
Price: **£59.99 + VAT (£70.49)**
Format: **CD-ROM, 302 pages**
ISBN: **9780955019043**

The complete package for the 2007 BTEC National specifications!

Two full-colour student textbooks with accompanying Tutor's CD-ROMs.

Extensive coverage of 20 units – with student activities, assignments, case studies, industry examples, PowerPoint© presentations, weblinks, etc. across the books and CDs. PLUS full access to extra resources on tandtONLine – our unique website for staff and students.

All you need to deliver the Award, Certificate and Diploma – from the most respected author in the field.

Title: **Travel and Tourism for BTEC National Award, Certificate and Diploma Book 2** (2nd edition)
Publication date: **31 March 2008**
Author: **Ray Youell**
Price: **£22.99**
Format: **Paperback, 300 pages**
ISBN: **9780955019036**

Title: **Travel and Tourism for BTEC National Award, Certificate and Diploma Book 2** Tutor's CD-ROM
Publication date: **30 April 2008**
Author: **Ray Youell**
Price: **£59.99 + VAT (£70.49)**
Format: **CD-ROM, 200 pages**
ISBN: **9780955019050**